Art & Class
How the middle classes hijacked the nation's galleries

David Kennedy

Fisher King Publishing

Art & Class
How the middle classes hijacked the nation's galleries

Copyright © David Kennedy 2024

All rights reserved

Print ISBN 978-1-914560-98-9
Ebook ISBN 978-1-916776-22-7

No part of this publication may be reproduced or distributed in any form or by any means, or stored in a database or electronic retrieval system without the prior written permission of Fisher King Publishing Ltd.

The right of David Kennedy to be identified as the author of this work has been asserted by him in accordance with the Copyright, Designs and Patents act, 1988.

Thank you for respecting the author of this work.

Published by Fisher King Publishing
fisherkingpublishing.co.uk

Dedication

In memory of Susan Kennedy
(aka Dr. King)

"As the director of a national museum based outside the M25, I wrestled with metropolitan bias and London-centric funders, philanthropists and Trustees. David Kennedy's brilliant book illustrates how back in Victorian times, things were different and argues powerfully for why, despite some change recently, we still need to see a fairer distribution of cultural spend around the country."

Colin Philpott
Former Director of the National Science and Media Museum

"Every future curator should read David Kennedy's inspiring but challenging story of the relationship between art and audiences since the 18th-century. Inspiring, as he shows that once upon a time - at Vauxhall Gardens in the 1740s, at the National Gallery in the 1850s and in the great new Museums of the industrial north - all classes crowded together in front of great art. Challenging, because Kennedy shows that in modern times many Museums and art institutions have become less democratic, not more; fewer working-class people visit the National Gallery than 150 years ago. A captivating, mischievous and genuinely radical new perspective."

Christopher Woodward
Director The Garden Museum

Aknowledgments

Many thanks to Rick Armstrong and all the team at Fisher King for their hard work and support and to the following people: Ian, my brother, who gave me excellent advice. Sophie and Charles Forgan, Colin Philpott, Christopher Woodward, Michael Belshaw and Janet Davidson who all read the manuscript and provided helpful comments and to Phil Williams who helped with the statistics.

From the very beginning and over many a long walk Geoff Downs has been a constant support.

I attended two very good Arvon Courses and I should like to thank the tutors: Laura Barton, Sathnam Sanghera, Catherine Merridale and Miranda France.

Also thanks to TLC and Suzanne Rennie, Dave Prost, Ross Jamieson and Paul Goodman for all their help.

Many friends have listened patiently to my ramblings over the years, namely Richard Wixey, Alan Mainwaring, Peter Rennie and Jane Glaister. Tom Garbutt, of Smallprint, has been a great help and Hannah Hunt, my tutor at the Open University, gave me the confidence to take up writing after doing my degree.

To my family for all their love and support and especially to the grandchildren, Oscar, Finlay, Isaac and Beau for their enthusiasm and energy when I was flagging. Finally to Isaac for the inspirational Quill which sits on my desk. The book has been a long time in the making so apologies to anyone whom I have missed.

Foreword

Art and Class tells the story of art gallery visiting which has been hidden from history for too long. When Victorian galleries were full of working-class visitors why are less than 8% of today's visitors from the working classes? When and why did the working classes stop visiting art galleries and why does this matter? The working classes are not only subsidising the middle-class gallery goers, but they are also being denied cultural capital which is a key requirement for entry to the elite universities and the elite professions.

I have known David for many years and when he was working at Bradford Council he promoted exhibitions which attracted people from all classes in record numbers. An exhibition on the history of The Independent Labour Party, which was founded in Bradford, brought in trade unionists while an exhibition of the pictures which people have in their homes attracted record numbers who had never visited a gallery.

In conclusion David argues that if the boards of the national galleries were more diverse and not dominated by a metropolitan elite then they would have policies which would attract people from all classes.

This is a timely challenge to the curators, the directors and the trustees of our national galleries.

Jane Glaister OBE
Past President of The Museums Association

Contents

Introduction	1
Chapter 1 - Art in the Park	9
Chapter 2 - London Gets Galleries	22
Chapter 3 - The National Gallery	32
Chapter 4 - Art Comes to the East End	68
Chapter 5 - Leisure	88
Chapter 6 - The Manchester Art Treasures Exhibition 1857	100
Chapter 7 - Regional Galleries	121
Chapter 8 - A New World	153
Chapter 9 - Conclusion	185
Bibliography	i
Endnotes	xix
Appendix Currency Conversion	xliii
Index	xlv

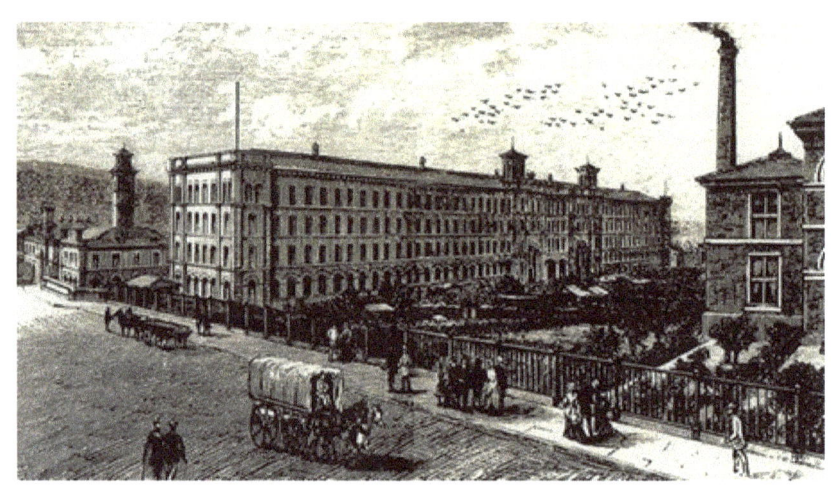

Salts Mill circa 1880

Introduction

On a bright autumn day in 1857, the workers from Salts Mill in Yorkshire were waiting for special trains to take them on a day trip. The mill bands were on the platform playing stirring Yorkshire tunes and the millhands were in a holiday mood. Titus Salt was taking his 2,500 strong workforce on an outing. But they were not going to Blackpool: they were going to Manchester to see the world's greatest display of art. Closer to home, the Manchester mill owners took their workers from the cotton mills while Thomas Cook turned a clear profit taking 46,000 people from Newcastle and the North East.

But it was not just the workers who flocked to see the paintings. The exhibition was truly classless: Prince Albert opened it, Queen Victoria visited it, Engels enjoyed it, Dickens took the train up from London and Napoleon III came all the way from Paris. The organisers employed a young Charles Hallé to provide music, and when the exhibition closed, the Hallé Orchestra was born. Between May and October, 1.3 million people from all classes visited the Manchester Art Treasures Exhibition.

Travel through time, and galleries are now the preserve of the upper and middle classes. Today fewer than 8% of visitors to our great galleries are from the working class.[1] Why and when did the working classes stop visiting art galleries? And why does this matter?

These questions and this book were prompted by an exhibition of John Martin's paintings at Tate Britain in 2011. John Martin was a master of Victorian narrative whose apocalyptic paintings drew enormous crowds. In 1855, his Last Judgement triptych was displayed at St. George's Hall in Bradford and was so popular with the millhands that opening hours had to be extended into the evening. Martin died in 1854, but his paintings continued to tour the world and by 1861 eight million people had seen his work.

But while the masses queued to see his paintings, the elite of the art world lined up to attack him. A review in the Edinburgh Literary Journal described his work as "humbug" while Ruskin stated that he did not regard him as a painter[2]. Charles Lamb disliked Belshazzar's Feast because of its popularity. [3]Martin was to join the long line of artists whom the public love but the critics loathe.

The debate about Martin's work throws a fascinating light on the world of high and low art. As Martin Myrone, curator of the Tate exhibition, states, "It is hard not to read the intensity of such criticisms as arising from some form of class prejudice." [4]But it was the popularity of Martin's work with the millhands that caught my imagination and led me to discover a forgotten world of art written out of history and far removed from today's rarefied galleries.

This book starts in 1740, when art became accessible to all classes through the paintings on display at London's Vauxhall Pleasure Gardens, and finishes in 2023. It describes the advent of public art in the 18th century, the development of the national galleries in London and the explosion of municipal galleries, all of which were crowded with working-class visitors.

The First World War and the Depression brought an end to the building of new galleries, but the late 1930s saw paintings taken to the masses by the Art for the People project, which toured the country until the end of the Second World War. But in the grey days after the War, when people most needed the joy of seeing fine art, their heritage was hijacked.

In the 18th century, the commercial imperative brought art to the working classes. In the 19th century, Members of Parliament fought to prevent the National Gallery from being moved to the middle-class suburbs of South Kensington. Elsewhere in London, aesthetic evangelists brought art to the most deprived neighbourhoods in the city. In the regions, mill-owners and manufacturers built new galleries and filled them with art which their workers enjoyed. Whether through commercial drive, political patronage or northern businessmen, the nation's galleries were providing art for the people, and the people flocked to see it.

All this came to a sudden halt in 1946. Keynes, the economist, seized control by establishing the Arts Council, slashed the Art for the People budget and poured money into opera and ballet.

At the same time, curators finally won a long-running battle against councillors and trustees. The 20th-century elite had decided that Victorian narrative was sentimental trash and that councillors and trustees were simply wrong. In the words of the prominent art critic, Clive Bell: "The normal man… cannot know whether a work of art is beautiful, [nor] can he know whether a thing is vulgar".[5]

As Robert Hewison, the cultural historian, states,

> whereas in other areas of the economy the effect of the post-war welfare state settlement had been to redistribute resources from the rich to the poor and uneducated, in the arts the flow has been in the opposite direction – general taxation was subsidising the recreations of the educated and the rich.[6]

Roy Strong, former Director of the Victoria and Albert Museum, (V & A), puts it more bluntly, stating that after the establishment of the Arts Council, "the winners… were the ever-burgeoning and aspiring middle-classes, who found to their delight arts activities for which in the past they would have had to pay dearly now came cheap."[7] The same thing happened in 2001 when the Labour Government re-introduced free opening of the national galleries with great fanfare, but for which they set aside £100 million to compensate the national galleries. [8]Visitor numbers increased dramatically, but it turned out that the middle classes were simply visiting more often and working-class numbers actually declined. [9]As many commentators have stated, what was once "art for the many not the few", has now become "from the many to the few".

Britain is becoming an increasingly unequal country. The key numbers focus on wealth, but inequalities in health, housing, education and leisure reveal a deeply divided society. I do not want to insult people living in poverty, poor health and poor housing by suggesting that visiting art galleries is high up their list of priorities, but that does not mean that they should be denied the opportunity. So why, if the working classes no longer visit art galleries, does this matter, and why should we care?

The working classes are not only paying for the cultural activities of the middle classes but they are also being denied access to art through membership and charging policies while taxation policies also favour the middle classes.

The national galleries all operate membership schemes which give free access to charging exhibitions if you can afford an annual subscription and while access to the galleries is free most of the major exhibitions carry an entrance charge.

On a different level taxation policies allow the wealthy to offset their paintings against tax. Since 1982, when the Arts Council's Acceptance in Lieu scheme was introduced, the Treasury has foregone over £1 billion which could have been spent on schools and hospitals.[10]

Art is a key aspect of cultural capital which is the knowledge and appreciation of the high arts which middle-class children absorb through visits to galleries and concerts which are beyond the reach of working-class parents. This precious commodity opens the door to the elite universities and then on to high paying jobs. Students at the elite universities score highly on cultural capital while working-class graduates getting jobs in the elite professions earn 16% less than their middle-class peers.[11]

In this book, I have not explored the more esoteric definitions of class. Class is always changing, and new centuries and new ways of working demand new categories. In the 1980s and 1990s, politicians shied away from the concept of class. They used euphemisms such as "hard-working families", which in turn was succeeded by "strivers". In 1997, John Prescott, Deputy Prime Minister in the Blair Government, famously said "We're all middle class now."

By 2016, following the European Referendum and the American presidential election, class was back on the political agenda, and the term 'working class' re-appeared. But as Richard Hoggart famously said, in his introduction to The Road to Wigan Pier, "Class distinctions do not die; they merely learn new ways of expressing themselves....Each decade we shiftily declare we have buried class; each decade the coffin stays empty."[12] In 2011, the BBC conducted the largest-ever survey of social class in Britain with 161,000 people answering a questionnaire. Academics, working with the BBC, came up with seven new categories: elite, established middle class, technical middle class, new affluent workers, traditional working class, emerging service workers and the precariat. In Victorian times, the precariat[13] would have been known as the 'residuum', people who were in and out of work and who for most of their lives were living in dire poverty. In order to cross the centuries, I have used the less accurate but well-known and easily understood categories of working, middle and upper class.

The academic literature on the definition of class would fill a small library, and government statistics can always be challenged. Nonetheless, the reality is that our art galleries are now the preserve of the middle and upper classes no matter how you define class or spin the statistics. If you want to challenge these assertions, stop now and read the literature referred to in the bibliography. If you are willing to accept broad definitions of class and government statistics, then read on.

The sociology of culture that explains why art galleries are the property of the middle classes is even more impenetrable than the literature on class. The journey from Veblen to Bourdieu, by way of Gramsci and Foucault, is the intellectual equivalent of climbing the north face of the Eiger in winter but without the views. We shall not attempt the ascent.

It is sometimes argued that the working class now have more activities on which to spend their leisure time and prefer television and the cinema to visiting art galleries. Hollywood narrative has replaced Victorian narrative. This is both patronising and misleading. Why do the middle classes continue to visit galleries: are they not interested in television and cinema? Certainly, there are more leisure activities available today, but in 1875 there were 375 music halls in London alone, packed full of working-class people enjoying themselves.[14] Today there are 500 brass bands in England: in 1887 there were 40,000.[15]

The boards of the national galleries are dominated by the same metropolitan elite who established the Arts Council in 1946 and the curators all come from the same middle-class, curatorial courses. London stills manages to appropriate by far the largest part of the nation's arts budget with £21.00 per head compared with £4.50 for the East Midlands.[16] The gap on capital spending is even larger. Between 2010 and 2022 London's galleries and museums have received £1 billion to spend on new buildings and refurbishments while between 2005 and 2014 173 regional galleries and museums closed due to financial cuts.[17]

If the metropolitan elite could be persuaded to widen their boards and the curators came from a more diverse background today's galleries would show paintings that attracted people from all classes and enable working-class children to compete on a level playing field with their middle-class peers.

The national galleries refuse to show contemporary, dramatic narrative, which was so loved by the Victorians, but when regional galleries show Jack Vettriano, Banksy and Beryl Cook visitor numbers break all records.

One of the difficulties in writing this history is the lack of evidence from the working-class people who visited the art galleries and exhibitions. Most of the evidence comes from upper- and middle-class observers, either acting as witnesses to parliamentary select committees or writing about the working classes. There are a small number of primary sources, but as an example, we cannot tell whether the workers whom Titus Salt took to the Manchester Art Treasures Exhibition went voluntarily or because the mill owner insisted. On balance, however, taking the evidence of the packed galleries and exhibitions and the tales from the East End and South London, it is clear that the visitors went gladly and enjoyed the experience.

To claim that the middle classes have hijacked art hints of conspiracy theory. As we shall discover, the answer is far more complex, but the outcome is the same. This book takes us from exhibitions full of kitchen maids and stable boys to galleries dominated by the middle classes.

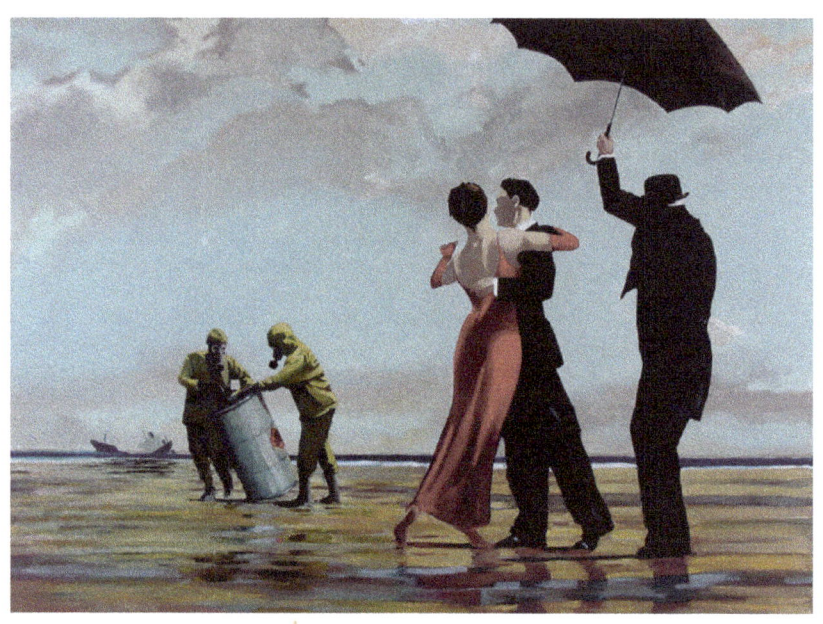

Toxic Beach - Banksy interpretation of a famous Jack Vettriano painting

Chapter 1

Art in the Park

It was the number of prostitutes that was surprising. The crowd had come to hear the latest work by the man who had given them the *Messiah*, the most glorious piece of sacred music ever written, and here he was rehearsing his new work in a London park throbbing with prostitutes.

High culture and low life: prostitution and art make unlikely bedfellows. But in addition to Handel's music, the masses, promenading through Vauxhall Gardens Pleasure Park, could enjoy a wide range of paintings over ten years before art exhibitions became a fixture of the London season.

On a beautiful summer day in June 1749, Vauxhall Gardens was at its height. There had been a three-hour traffic jam at London Bridge as crowds converged from all corners of the city to hear Handel's *Fireworks Music*. But it was a good-natured crowd, who were looking forwards to strolling in the park, enjoying the food, admiring the paintings and listening to the music.

Until the 18th century, art in Britain had been the prerogative of royalty and the aristocracy, whereas on the Continent, people could view great art in the churches and cathedrals, even if they could not visit the chateaux and palaces. Yet at a time when the public had no access to art, Europe's greatest paintings were flooding into the country as the British aristocracy indulged in a collecting mania.

On completion of their Grand Tour, they would come home with paintings for their country houses. In 1725, over 750 paintings and 6,000 prints were brought back from Italy alone.[18] Richard Boyle,

Third Earl of Burlington, returned with 800 trunks packed full of art and sculpture and then commissioned a purpose-built art gallery, in the popular Palladian style, to house his collection. Today there are more Canalettos in London than Venice.

With old wealth from agriculture and new wealth from coal, the English aristocracy were Europe's leading collectors throughout the 18th century. Just as the English Civil War led to the break-up of great English collections, so the French Revolution opened up a new market for the British connoisseur. The Duke of Orléans had amassed one of Europe's greatest collections of old masters, but he was a victim of the guillotine, and his collection was auctioned in 1798. The Duke of Bridgewater, the great canal builder, the Earl of Gower and the Earl of Carlisle formed a syndicate and beat the market by buying low and selling high. Bridgewater spent more time in France examining the canals rather than art, but a shrewd strategy enabled him and his colleagues to add to their collections at no cost. The great works of the Orléans collection ended up in England, and even today many of them are still in the same country houses.[19]

These collections enabled the aristocracy to show off their cultural taste, and though the collections were not open to the public, the landed gentry and the middle classes could visit the great houses and view the paintings. There was no charge, but you were expected to tip the housekeeper who, as a forerunner of the National Trust volunteer, would conduct a tour.

In *Pride and Prejudice*, Elizabeth Bennet travels by coach to Derbyshire with her aunt and uncle. There, ostensibly as tourists, they are shown round Pemberley by the housekeeper and see Mr. Darcy's collection of paintings. Although keen to see Darcy's estate and perhaps dissimilating, Elizabeth reflects many of today's exhausted gallery-goers when she states that, "she was tired of great houses; after going over so many, she really had no pleasure in fine carpets or satin curtains."[20]

By visiting the great houses, the middle classes could show off their sophisticated taste and differentiate themselves from the working classes. But the masses had not yet had the opportunity to tire of culture. Then, in 1729, a young entrepreneur brought art to the people when he took on the lease of the Vauxhall Gardens pleasure park and turned it into London's most popular cultural attraction, with a major emphasis on contemporary art.

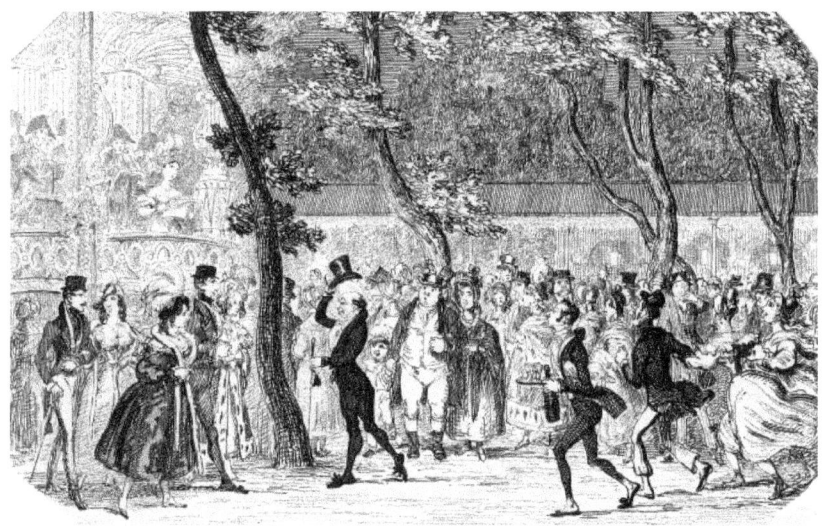

Vauxhall Gardens courtesy of Jane Austen's London janeaustenslondon.com

Art has returned to London's parks with the Serpentine Gallery in Hyde Park, the Frieze Art Fair in Regent's Park and the less exclusive Affordable Art Fair in Battersea Park. None of these events could claim a large working-class audience. Waldemar Januszczak, the Sunday Times art critic, writing about the Serpentine Gallery, declared that, "anyone below the rank of garden-party invitee is made to feel underdressed" but in 1740 over 100,000 people from all walks of life were visiting Vauxhall Gardens.[21] Every summer they saw new work by artists such as Hogarth, Hayman, Gravelot and Monamy, whose works now hang in major galleries around the world.

Today London's parks are full of people enjoying themselves, but the high point of parks as places of unbridled pleasure was the 18th and 19th centuries. Between 1661 and 1861, over 60 pleasure gardens were opened, and the most popular and successful was Vauxhall Gardens. You could see Hogarth's paintings, listen to Handel's music and watch Canaletto as he painted the appreciative audiences. The art was but a part of the great show, but in commissioning paintings and mounting major exhibitions, Vauxhall Gardens stayed ahead of its rivals. For the first time, contemporary art was available to people from all classes, and the public flocked to see it.

Vauxhall Gardens had developed from Spring Gardens, which was originally a series of walks covering several acres. Food and drink were available together with music and other entertainments, but Spring Gardens, like the other pleasure gardens, was also renowned for the availability of the ladies of the night.

In his diary, Pepys complained about the ladies plying their trade to the rowdy young men, while in *The Spectator*, Addison has Sir Roger de Coverley protest that the gardens would be better, "if there were more Nightingales and fewer Strumpets." William Byrd, who founded Richmond in Virginia, was a regular visitor. He wrote in his diary of having visited Spring Gardens in the summer of 1718, where on meeting a young woman he, "rogered [her] twice and slept pretty well, but neglected my prayers."[22]

But all this was to change when the gardens were leased to Jonathan Tyers in 1729. This ambitious and energetic twenty-seven-year-old entrepreneur had a strong moral streak, and he saw art and beauty as a means of improving the lower orders while also making money. He came from a well-off family who worked in the leather business and owned several buildings in Bermondsey, but he kept his commercial past a secret and was soon moving in cultured circles, befriending Hogarth, Handel and Fielding. He was socially ambitious, creating his own coat of arms and having a family portrait painted by Francis Hayman. By the age of thirty-two, he had bought a country house with eighty acres of land, where he established a significant collection of contemporary British art including Hogarth and Hayman, Gainsborough and Stubbs.

But despite his social ambitions, Tyers the businessman was an egalitarian. The gardens were open to all, with only one entrance and only one ticket price. Everyone from the Prince of Wales to the lowest orders mixed amicably in an amazingly classless setting.

Tyers quickly made Vauxhall more respectable by attracting families and people from all classes while trying to exclude prostitutes. In the first year, he ran up large losses and by 1730 was in despair. One day Hogarth met him roaming the streets looking grim. Asked why he was so preoccupied, Tyers replied that due to heavy losses he was accruing through the park, he was trying to work out the best way to commit suicide[23]. Hogarth persuaded him to delay his death and give him and his colleagues a chance to bring art to the park as a new attraction. Tyers agreed and never looked back.

It was a turning point for the park and a turning point for British art. Although Tyers did not know it, he established the first public gallery showing contemporary British art, and the public loved it. This appealed to Tyers' wish to bring beauty to the masses and enabled Hogarth to find an outlet for his work and that of his friends and students from the St Martin's Lane Academy. In particular,

Hogarth introduced Tyers to Francis Hayman, who at this time was a scenery painter at the Drury Lane Theatre but would become one of the country's leading artists and a key player in the formation of the Royal Academy. Tyers accepted Hogarth's ideas and not only commissioned paintings but new buildings, statues and music.

The many pleasure gardens in London ranged from small gardens attached to inns to the grand avenues and attractions of Vauxhall. They all provided food and drink with the larger ones putting on music, dancing, fireworks and vaudeville. By the mid-18th century, three gardens stood above the rest and were in fierce competition: Vauxhall, Marylebone and Ranelagh.

Marylebone was the most disreputable and focussed on the three Gs of the 1700s: gin, girls and gambling. It was located where the King Edward VII Hospital now stands near Harley Street, but it never attracted the families that went to Vauxhall and after a short life closed in 1778.

Ranelagh stood at the other end of the social spectrum and as a consequence attracted older and more conservative visitors. In an attempt to keep out the lower orders, it charged an admission fee of half a crown when Vauxhall was only charging a shilling. The entry fee and the high moral tone put off the younger generation, and while Ranelagh at one point provided stiff competition to Vauxhall, it eventually closed in 1803.

Vauxhall consequently saw off the competition and became London's major attraction. What distinguished it from its rivals was the cultural programme with the focus on art. Tyers the aesthete wanted to establish himself as a connoisseur of fine art, but Tyers the businessman wanted art which would attract customers from all classes.

Throughout the period when Tyers was developing Vauxhall Gardens, Britain was engaged in a series of wars with Spain and France running from 1739 to 1763. The War of Jenkins' Ear, the War of Austrian Succession and the Seven Years' War all took place over a period of almost 25 years, during which time Tyers was alert to the power of patriotic paintings to draw in the public.

A key feature of the Gardens was a series of supper boxes where people could enjoy their evening meal while watching the crowds promenading. Tyers originally had Hayman produce a range of theatrical and rural scenes which were on canvases that could be pulled up to form protective sides to the boxes as the evening drew on. Promenaders were able to admire the paintings while also taking in the beauty of the ladies enjoying their supper. But as Britain entered into war with Spain and France, Tyers recognised an opportunity to promote paintings that glorified British victories.

Britain and Spain had been at war intermittently for many years in the West Indies, but a Spanish coast guard cutting off the ear of Robert Jenkins, the captain of a merchant ship, sparked off the eponymous War of Jenkins' Ear. In July 1739, a fleet set sail for the Caribbean under the command of Admiral Vernon and captured the silver-exporting town of Porto Bello. This dashing venture made Vernon a national hero overnight, with both the *London Magazine* and the *London Evening Post* headlining his exploits. On his return, Vernon mania took hold of the country: he was made a Freeman of the City of London and offered various Parliamentary seats, while the now famous Portobello Road was named after the battle. Across the country beacons were lit, medals were struck, and the pottery industry went into overdrive producing commemorative plates and mugs. Tyers immediately responded by commissioning Peter Monamy, a prominent seascape painter, to provide four paintings for the supper boxes, the first of which would depict the taking of Porto

Bello and which was completed within months of the battle. Two of the three further paintings depicted ships at war while the fourth showed a young man saying goodbye to his lover against a backdrop of the fleet setting sail. The painting of Porto Bello was an immediate success and drew large crowds, helping to establish the Gardens as the nation's first public art gallery.

The popularity of the paintings led Tyers to erect a purpose-built art gallery named The Prince's Pavilion. At this time, a major revival of Shakespeare was taking place. In 1741, his memorial was unveiled in Westminster Abbey, and in the same year, David Garrick made his name with his interpretation of *Richard III*. Tyers, ever quick to catch the popular mood, commissioned Hayman to do a series of four major works based on scenes from Shakespeare's plays.

Hayman, who had recently illustrated a new edition of Shakespeare's works, drew on scenes from *King Lear*, *The Tempest*, *Hamlet* and *Henry V*. He played on both the popularity of Shakespeare and the wave of patriotism in the year when Bonnie Prince Charlie and his army reached Derby before being driven back to Scotland and eventual defeat at Culloden.

Building on the success of the Prince's Pavilion, Tyers' next development was to extend a building known as the Rotunda by adding the Pillared Saloon, which was originally designed to display portraits of the royal family. George III and Queen Charlotte, who were visitors to the gardens, sat for a portrait which was hung in the Saloon, but these were soon replaced with four paintings commissioned from Hayman illustrating scenes from the Seven Years' War, again capturing the mood of the moment and attracting large numbers. These paintings have not survived but, as large historical paintings, have a key place in the history of British art, pre-dating the great French artist Jacques-Louis David's historical paintings by almost fifty years. Hayman chose a fresh approach to the topic with two of the four paintings showing British generals magnanimous in victory. The paintings, for which Hayman was paid £2,000, were done over a period of four years while the war was still raging. The public waiting in expectation for each new painting were not disappointed. A monumental 12 by 15 feet each, the paintings were hung in the Pillared Saloon and were a massive draw. Many of the people who flocked to see the paintings would have had friends and relatives who had taken part in these great battles. At a time when 33% of men and 66% of women were illiterate, and before national newspapers had been established, the paintings were the precursor to Pathe News at the cinema and social media today.[24]

The first painting, which went on display in the summer of 1761, showed General Amherst giving out food to local people. The second, in 1762, commemorating the defeat of the French fleet at Quiberon in Brittany, was an allegory titled *The Triumph of Britannia*. The third painting, which was done in 1763, showed Clive receiving an Indian nawab after the Battle of Plessey, when a British victory over the French secured supremacy in India. The final painting, for the 1764 season, was of prominent British generals, done in the Roman style, complete with togas and was entitled *Britannia Distributing Laurels*.

None of these paintings have survived, but the combination of Tyers' showmanship, releasing a new painting each year, and Hayman's mastery brought in ever greater numbers.

These long-forgotten artists have paintings in all the great galleries of western art, from The Tate in London to the Metropolitan Museum of Art in New York. They may not be of the quality of David's paintings, which are so prominent in the Louvre, but their place in British art history should not be overlooked. Cork and Borg, in their history of Vauxhall Gardens, describe it as, "the first true public gallery of modern British art." They state that, "Contemporary British works of art were never just decorations at Tyers' Vauxhall, they played an absolutely fundamental role; and because they were seen by huge numbers of people as part of their everyday lives, a mass audience for contemporary art was born."[25] Tyers is described as, "one of the great patrons of contemporary British art", and Cork and Borg decry the fact that he does not feature in modern art histories.[26]

But, returning to our core focus: did the working classes go to see the art at Vauxhall Gardens in large numbers, or was it restricted to today's class of gallery visitor?

The figures speak for themselves: the park was open from May to August, and at its height in 1824 had 200,000 visitors. The annual average between 1740 and 1840 was over 100,000.[27] There were certainly many other attractions: the fireworks were magnificent, there was food and drink, and the music was a major feature with composers such as Handel and Thomas Arne, who composed *Rule Britannia*. But the art works were the key feature enabling Vauxhall to outsell its rivals. The partnership of Tyers as impresario and Hayman as artistic director was a winner.

Contemporary descriptions by visitors to the Gardens consistently emphasise the inclusion of all classes from the Prince of Wales to the lowest serving classes. Coke and Borg note that, "as a direct result of Tyers' policies Vauxhall attracted a wider cross section than any other comparable attraction."[28] *The Vauxhall Observer*, which as the house journal was somewhat biased, wrote of the importance of associating the two estates of the Aristocracy and the Commonality, adding that, "we know of no place so well calculated for it as Vauxhall."[29]

But less subjective reports attest to the mixing of the classes and the attendance of a wide range of visitors from the labouring classes. A poem from the *Gentleman's Magazine* describing Vauxhall in 1732 lists, "an oyster girl, a barber's apprentice, a lawyer, an army captain, a doctor, a vicar and a number of prostitutes."[30] We can assume that the prostitutes' primary reason for visiting was not a regard for art, but it is clear that Vauxhall attracted large numbers of the working classes, who for the first time were able to see and enjoy modern paintings. A Russian visitor, writing in 1790, noted that the Garden had, "men of fashion" and, "flunkeys" and, "the finest ladies" alongside, "women of the street."[31] Deborah Epstein Nord, in her book *The Pleasure Garden: From Vauxhall to Coney Island,* quotes a range of sources demonstrating the wide appeal of Vauxhall Gardens.[32] Historian James Southworth writes of, "Honest citizens with their wives, apprentices with their masters, women of easy virtue, their pimps.... pugilistic hoodlums and all other concomitants."[33]

Tyers had to make a profit, but in his mission to bring art to the masses, he tried to keep entry prices as low as possible. He pitched the price at 1s., which was between 6d. at the disreputable Marylebone Gardens and 2s.6d. at the upmarket Ranelagh. For special events, such as the rehearsal for the *Music for the Royal Fireworks*, he charged 2s.6d. As David Hunter notes, in his biography of Handel, when you add the cost of the toll of 4d. at London Bridge, 6d. for the turnpike or 6d. for the hire of a boat, such events excluded all but the most wealthy.[34] But in 1750, 1s., was less than a day's wage for an artisan when a loaf of bread cost 1d. Jonathan Conlin, Professor of History, suggests that employers would give their servants a day out at Vauxhall as an annual treat,[35] and many of the labouring classes would save up for a visit once a year so the admission charge of 1s. did not prevent people from the working classes attending. The price remained at one shilling until 1792, when Tyers' granddaughter doubled the cost to two shillings, leading Boswell to complain of the danger of making the gardens less inclusive.[36]

Vauxhall Gardens featured prominently in both contemporary drama and fiction. William Congreve and John Vanbrugh both include it in their plays while Fielding, Goldsmith and Thackeray all used the Gardens in their novels. Neither the plays nor the novels give us a true picture of the social status of the visitors, but in *Pendennis* Thackeray has Fanny, the daughter of a porteress, visit the Gardens. On a lighter note, in *Vanity Fair* he refers to the, "slices of almost invisible ham" for which the Garden was infamous. One wit commented that it was so thin that you could read a newspaper through it, while Dickens talked of, "carvers…exercised in the mystic art of cutting a moderate-sized ham into slices thin enough to pave the whole of the grounds."[37]

Tyers had created London's most successful pleasure garden by combining his business skills with his love of art, and in so doing, giving the masses access to art that was previously only available to the upper classes. He died in 1767 at the age of sixty-five when the gardens were at their height, and to commemorate his passing, Handel's *Dead March* was played every year on the date of his death.

Seventy years later, in the 1840s, the upper classes were still buying their food and drink from the park, the middle classes were bringing their own food and the working classes were still paying the entry fee even if they could not afford to dine.

Art can now be seen in a wide range of locations across London, from the popular Vauxhall Art Car Boot Sale in the East End to the exclusive Frieze Art Fair in Regent's Park, but none of them attract a large working-class turnout. Go back two hundred and fifty years to the Georgian era, and the lower orders were flooding in large numbers to see the pictures at Vauxhall Gardens. The scenes from Shakespeare were popular, but the great history paintings by Monamy and Hayman drew in football-size crowds with people from all classes. Art was accessible to the people and the people loved it.

In the next chapter, we shall see how Hogarth and Hayman, who were both men of prodigious energy, while promoting the Gardens at Vauxhall were also involved with the new Foundling Hospital in Bloomsbury. This became a key meeting place for artists, and in this unusual location, they established London's first exhibitions of art for sale.

Chapter 2

London Gets Galleries

Hogarth and Hayman had created a mass audience for contemporary art south of the river, but north of the river they were moving in very different circles. By a strange twist, this involved the extreme ends of society and led to London's first art gallery being established in a children's home where the only members of the lower orders to see the paintings were the children in care. But this was the first step to establishing public exhibitions, which were to become so popular with the masses that the artists complained that the events were overwhelmed by the working classes.

Just as today, London was a city of extreme wealth and poverty and of tremendous vitality in the arts and the sciences. The development of the art world took place alongside unprecedented growth in books, newspapers and magazines. In 1714, London had 12 newspapers, and by 1811 this figure had grown to 52.[38] *The Spectator* first appeared in 1711, and the influential *Gentleman's Magazine* in 1731. The young aristocrats went to the continent for the Grand Tour, but London was the cultural, literary and philosophical centre of Europe. Voltaire escaped to London in 1728 and over the next three years wrote some of his most influential works. Rousseau had a tempestuous stay with Hume in 1756 after which Hume wrote to a friend describing Rousseau as, "plainly mad after long being maddish."[39] Canaletto, having run out of patrons in Italy, came to London in 1746, stayed for nine years and left a legacy of great paintings.

Hogarth and Hayman were at the epicentre of London's cultural life. Hayman was friendly with David Garrick and took his advice when painting scenes from Shakespeare. They were all friends in turn with Henry Fielding, who published *Tom Jones* in 1749. Samuel Johnson, who was also part of the circle, published his dictionary in 1755. Together with Reynolds, he wrote the introduction to the catalogue of the Society of Artists exhibition in 1762 and apologised for the necessity of raising the entrance fee in order to keep out the masses.

London was a hive of creativity, and Covent Garden was full of theatres, coffee houses, bordellos and inns. Rich and poor were not separated as today but mixed together with fine streets and grim back alleys side by side. In his book *The First Bohemians,* Vic Gatrell lists 146 artists who lived in the Covent Garden area.[40] This was the London that gave rise to Johnson's famous statement, "Why, Sir, you find no man, at all intellectual, who is willing to leave London. No, Sir, when a man is tired of London he is tired of life."

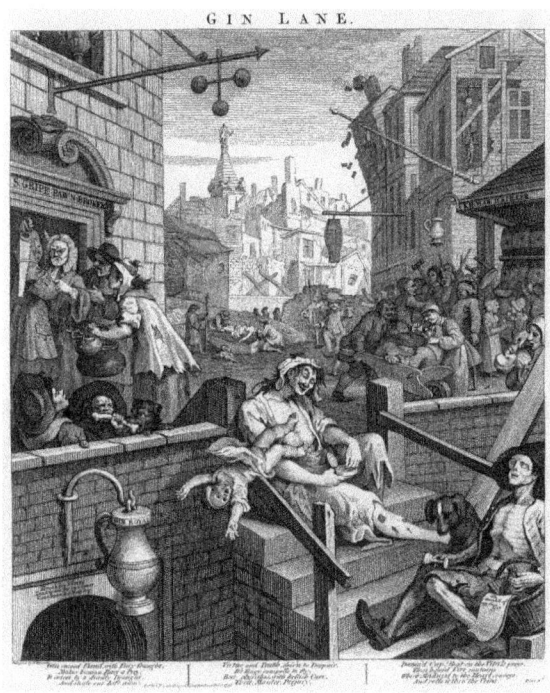

Gin Lane by William Hogarth 1751

Against the backdrop of the Jacobite Rebellion in 1745, the Seven Years' War and the American War of Independence, Britain was enjoying a period of unparalleled cultural and scientific growth. The art of the time reflected these great events, and the public, increasingly up to speed with the news, flocked in large numbers to see everything from grand portraits of Clive conquering India and Wolfe capturing Quebec to Hogarth's prints of Gin Lane. The world of science, which had not yet separated from the arts, was captured in oil with such famous paintings as *An Experiment on a Bird in the Air Pump* by Joseph Wright of Derby, known today for providing the backdrop to a key scene in the James Bond film *Skyfall*, when Bond meets Q in the National Gallery.

The reverse side of the coin was a city where the first influx of people from poverty-stricken rural areas was just beginning to occur. All too often, their dreams of wealth foundered in squalor and degradation. Large numbers from all classes flocked to see the art at Vauxhall Gardens, but in 1740, London was still a city blighted by mass poverty: 75% of all children died before the age of five,[41] one in five women were involved in a range of roles in the sex trade[42] and in 1743 gin consumption reached a record high as people tried to escape from the harsh reality of their everyday lives.[43] Hogarth was appalled at the filth and degradation surrounding his life. Only the very rich could avoid the smells and sights that assailed him as he walked around the city, and in 1751 he produced his famous print, *Gin Lane*, bringing to life the misery behind the grim statistics.

The horrors of life in London and the sight of dead children abandoned by their mothers so shocked Thomas Coram, a former sea captain, that he determined to open a home for foundlings. Originally spurned by the wealthy, who thought that such a home would merely encourage young women in their wayward ways, Coram persevered and came up with the idea of enlisting artists, musicians and writers in support of his Foundling Hospital.

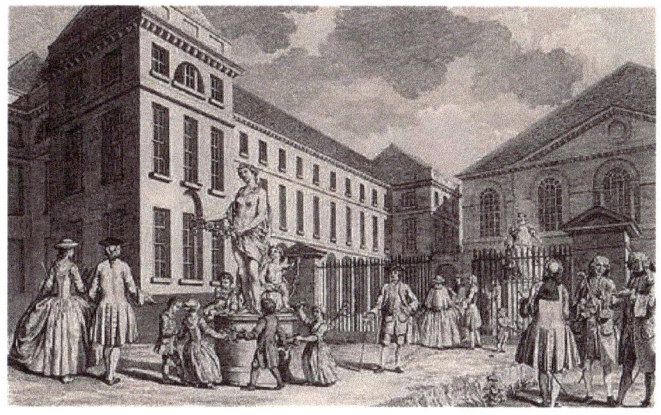

The Foundling Hospital in 1749 - Courtesy of The Foundling Museum

Just as Hogarth had helped Jonathan Tyers, so he helped Thomas Coram. He had seen how Handel's *Fireworks Music* had brought thousands to Vauxhall Gardens. Bringing to play his entrepreneurial skills, Hogarth saw that he could do the same thing for the Foundling Hospital while gaining publicity for his own work. Over two hundred years before Live Aid at Wembley, Hogarth promoted Live Aid at the Foundling Hospital with Handel conducting his *Messiah* to a full house of London society on 1 May 1750. Not one to miss an opportunity to promote his work, Hogarth had put his painting, *The March of the Guards to Finchley*, into a lottery to raise money for the hospital. People buying the print could pay an extra three shillings for a ticket to win the original, but Hogarth, sharp as ever, managed to ensure that the hospital had the winning ticket. The night before the sell-out *Messiah*, he presented the picture to the hospital. The *Messiah*, having had an uncertain start, was now a great success, and Handel would go on to conduct it every year at a fundraiser and also donated the manuscript to the Hospital.

In later years, Dickens lived next door and donated generously to the Hospital. It even features in *Little Dorrit* in the character of Tattycoram. The tradition continues to this day, and in 2012 Seamus Heaney and Carol Ann Duffy were among prominent poets who donated work to a collection entitled *Tokens for a Foundling*. Today the Coram Foundation helps disadvantaged children across the country. You can explore the history of the Foundling Hospital and see the manuscript of the *Messiah* at the Foundling Museum in Bloomsbury.

Despite the residents coming from the lowest end of society, visitors came from the top, and when the hospital was established in new buildings, it was stated that the paintings:

> ...being exhibited to the public, drew a daily crowd of spectators in their splendid equipages and a visit to the Foundling became the most fashionable morning lounge of the reign of King George II.[44]

The Hospital was now a home for foundlings, a salon for London society and a meeting place for artists. At one such meeting, London's first public exhibition was planned. Since few artists could earn a living from commissions, the purpose of the exhibition was to drum up sales. At a dinner in the Hospital in November 1759, chaired by the radical M.P. John Wilkes, the artists, led by Hayman, discussed a 'great museum of art'. The next step was to hold a meeting of, "all artists of the several branches of Painting, Sculpture, Architecture, Engraving, Chasing, Sealcutting and Medalling" at the Turk's Head Tavern in Soho.[45] The artists worked hard and played hard, and at their dinners and meetings vast quantities of food and drink were consumed to the accompaniment of music. Joseph Wright of Derby, who had a fine voice, often led the singing. In his diary, Academician Joseph Farington writes that:

> ...the meeting of the Academy did not break up till past twelve o'clock, when Hamilton, Smirke, and myself went to the Bedford Coffee House where we found Taylor, Rooker, Dance, Lawrence, Westall (all Royal Academicians). We staid till four in the morning.[46]

But despite the heavy drinking, there was serious work, and the outcome of the meeting at the Turk's Head was to be London's first major, public art exhibition that opened on 21 April 1760 and was an immediate triumph.

Some years earlier, William Shipley, originally a painter from Northampton, had established The Society for the Encouragement of the Arts, Manufacture and Commerce, today known as The Royal Society of Arts, and the exhibition was held at its premises near the Strand. The Society of Arts did not anticipate large numbers from the working classes visiting the exhibition and causing trouble, but they did anticipate trouble from the artists. The minutes of their meeting on March 1760 clearly state that, "said Committee have powers to reject such pieces as they may think unbecoming their Dignity to have exposed under their Permission." Then, expecting disputes between artists, the minutes go on to state that, "the Committee may appoint the places where all the Productions may be hung as exhibited in case any dispute shall arise among Artists about placing them."[47] They were well aware of the competition to be hung 'on the line' which was at eye level.

The show, at which there were paintings, drawings, engravings and statues was a great success. It only lasted for two weeks but attracted 20,000 visitors. Entrance was free, but 6,500 people bought catalogues at 6d. and the show made a profit of £165.[48] As Charles Saumarez Smith states in his history of the Royal Academy, the figures equalled those of today's summer show and demonstrated, "the astonishing public appetite for an opportunity to see paintings outside the realm of churches and private houses."[49]

Whereas visitors to the Foundling Hospital were confined to the upper classes, a contemporary description of attendance at the 1760 exhibition makes it clear that the working classes were present. John Gwynn, an early town planner, writes of the room being crowded:

> ...with menial servants and their acquaintances; this prostitution of the polite arts undoubtedly became extremely disagreeable to the professionals themselves, who heard alike with indignation, their work censured or approved by kitchen maids and stable boys.[50]

The paintings at Vauxhall Gardens had attracted an audience from all classes, and now the Society of Arts was to do the same. The kitchen maids and stable boys flocked to see the paintings, and given their long hours and limited time off, it is significant that they chose to use this valuable time to visit an art exhibition. The crowds queued to get in and at one point were so boisterous that the wonderfully named doorkeeper, Morgan Morgan, had a punch-up with the visitors. The minutes of the Society of Arts of 10 May 1760 are titled 'The Affair of the Porter' and tell us that Morgan Morgan, "being called in and examined declared that he did not strike the fist but pushed the Man gently with his hand to make way for some ladies and without any further provocation was struck upon which he made a blow at him." Windows were broken, requiring repairs costing 13s 6d. At an inquiry into these events, William Shipley spoke of, "irregularities committed by people coming to see the show." The Committee decided that there were insufficient grounds for prosecution, "but as they find there had been many irregularities committed by persons coming into the Society room to see the exhibition all persons coming to future exhibitions are expected to keep order."[51]

The large numbers from the lower orders dismayed the artists. They were worried that the tone would be lowered by the presence of kitchen maids and stable boys, who would certainly not be able to buy the paintings and would put off those with money whom the artists wanted to court. They complained to the Society of the, "intrusion of persons whose stations and educations disqualified them for judging of statuary and painting, and who were made idle and tumultuous by the opportunity of a show." In turn, the Society issued an order, "to exclude all persons whom [the officers] shall think improper to be admitted, such as livery servants, foot soldiers, porters, women with children etc., and to prevent disorders in the Room, such as smoking and drinking etc., by turning disorderly persons out."[52]

The following year, the artists asked the Society to restrict admission in order to keep out the lower orders. However, the Society was adamant that the show be open to all stating that, "the exhibition be free and open to the public at proper hours and under proper regulations" and that, "two Constables attend on the door on the Days of the Exhibition."[53] This led to a split among the artists, and a group calling themselves The Society of Artists of Great Britain, led by Reynolds, opened their own exhibition at Cock's Auction Rooms in Spring Gardens near Charing Cross. The catalogue was priced at 1s., and with sales of over 13,000, the show made a healthy profit. At the Strand, the Society of Arts show, albeit with fewer famous names, was still a success with reports that:

> ...the Crowd was so great ...by People pressing into the Exhibition room....that a deal of mischief was done; one of the Porters, who was employed by the Society to see Decorum observed, was knocked down, and otherwise greatly abused

and eventually eight constables were employed to keep order.[54] But even the restrictions at Spring Gardens did not prevent large numbers, which were, "productive of crowds and disorder."[55]

In 1762, the artists finally lost their patience. To keep out the labouring classes, the Society of Artists show charged 1s. per person. Reynolds and Samuel Johnson wrote a preface to the catalogue justifying the change, "when terms of admission were low, our room was thronged with such multitudes as made access dangerous and frightened away those whose approbation was most desired."[56]

Hogarth had now fallen out with both groups and in 1762 mounted a major exhibition of Signboards in a show designed to satirise the work of the other artists. The competition between the factions was intense, but in 1765 Reynolds and his colleagues succeeded in having the Society of Artists incorporated by royal charter. Three years later, they persuaded the King to give his approval to the Royal Academy, and on 10 December 1768, the Instrument of Foundation of the Royal Academy was signed by George III.

MORI and Gallup were not standing outside the exhibitions with their iPads in the 18th century, so we do not have sophisticated surveys analysing visitors by class and employment. Instead we have colourful descriptions of rowdy behaviour, instructions barring liveried servants, foot soldiers and porters and, in the case of the artists, straightforward outrage at the overwhelming number of working-class visitors putting off potential buyers.

In short, despite the lack of statistics, we have clear evidence that the kitchen maids and the stable boys were coming to exhibitions in numbers that the directors of the National Gallery and the Tate can only dream of, as they try to hit their equality targets. The lower orders of the 18th century equate closely to the precariat in the BBC Great British Class Survey of 2013. Today's cleaners and van drivers are almost completely absent from the great galleries in London and the many municipal galleries in the regions, whereas over 250 years ago those in charge were working hard to keep them out.

In the next chapter, we shall see that the working classes' love of art increased dramatically when the National Gallery opened in London.

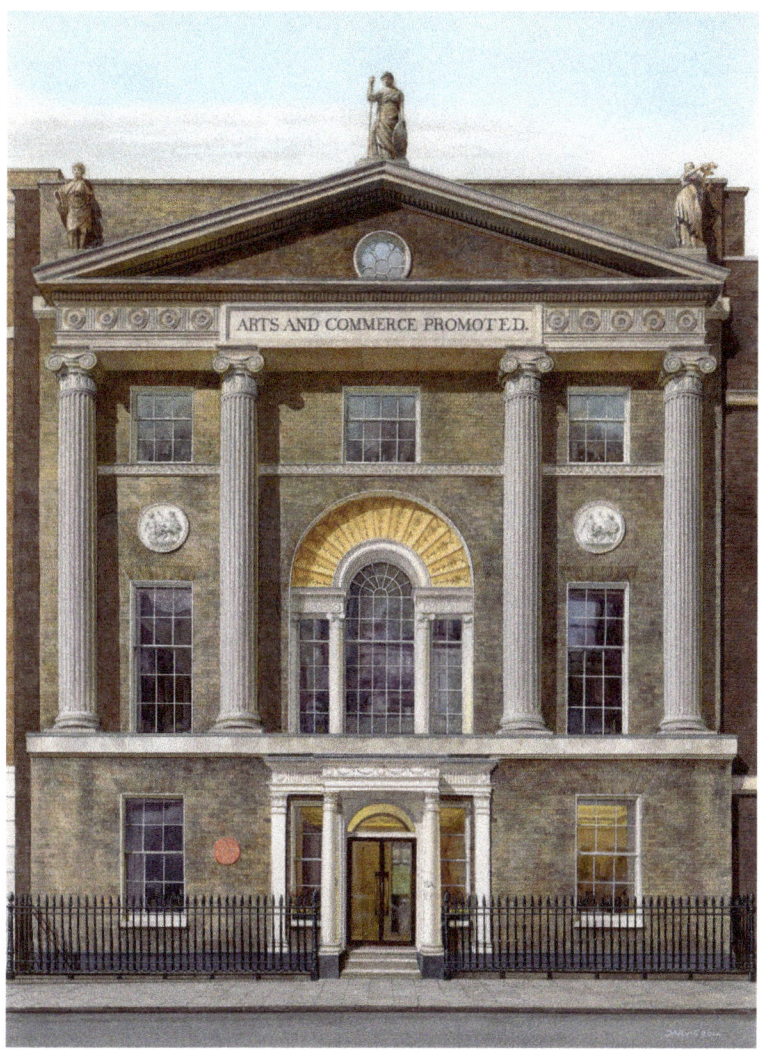

Royal Society of Arts - illustrated by Peter Jarvis: www.pjarvis.co.uk

Chapter 3

The National Gallery

By 1800, London was the cultural capital of Europe: the Society of Artists and the Royal Academy were showing art, the Society of Dilettanti was studying art, the auction houses were selling art and at the print shops people of all classes were queuing up to buy art.

The houses of the aristocracy and the newly rich were full of art brought over from Europe, and yet still there was no national gallery where the public could see the great masters. Despite emulating Europe's love of art, the British collectors did not emulate Europe's openness. Public galleries built on royal collections had begun to appear as early as 1760, with Dresden being the first major gallery. This was followed by the opening of the Bavarian royal collection in Munich in 1779, the Imperial collection in Vienna in 1792 and the Louvre in 1793. In Italy, a combination of the church and the commercial meant that art was on display everywhere from churches to galleries to street corners.

Only in England did the collectors keep their art hidden. John Winkelman, the great German art historian, berated the English, saying, "those barbarians, the English, buy up everything and in their own country nobody sees it but themselves."[57] Ulrich Gulbenkian, when asked to open his great collection to the public, famously replied, "Would I admit a stranger to my harem?"[58]

In England, Charles I had amassed a collection of over 1,300 paintings and nearly 400 sculptures and was described by Rubens as, "the most enthusiastic amateur of paintings in the world."[59] But Charles was also a man of many debts, and his collection was sold off under Cromwell to pay his dues. As a result, the royal plumber got a Titian while the royal glazier got a Correggio.[60] The collection was partly re-assembled when the monarchy was restored but it was not opened to the public. The combination of aristocratic aloofness and a private, albeit diminished, royal collection meant that England did not get a state-funded, purpose-built gallery till 1838 when the National Gallery was opened in Trafalgar Square. In later years, Prince Albert was generous in lending royal pictures to special exhibitions, though Queen Victoria would often refuse, unless it was connected with her beloved Prince, as when she donated twenty-two of her best paintings to the National Gallery in his memory.[61]

Although the public could not see the old masters locked away in great houses, they still had an insatiable appetite for art, and in London there was a growing commercial market for the display of contemporary paintings. While the politicians, led by the radical John Wilkes, were trying to persuade the government to open a national gallery, the world of commercial art and exotic exhibitions was booming. We shall return to the politicians and the reluctance of the government to fund a national gallery after exploring the art that drew large crowds from all classes in the late 18th and early 19th century

A mixture of exhibitions – sometimes attached to music halls, sometimes part of exotic shows and sometimes showing just one painting – brought in everyone from the working classes to the aristocracy. Just as foreign visitors had been surprised at the mixing of the classes at Vauxhall Gardens, so they noticed that these later shows were, "effective in the lowering, however brief, of the conventional barriers that kept class and class at a distance."[62]

The Royal Academy had held its first summer show in 1769 in rooms in Pall Mall and attracted 18,000 visitors. Like the Society of Artists, they charged a shilling in order to keep out the large numbers from the working classes wanting to attend, stating that:

> ...they have not been able to suggest any other Means than that of receiving Money for Admittance to prevent the room from being fill'd by improper Persons, to the entire exclusion of those for whom the Exhibition is apparently intended.[63]

In the same period many artists, such as Hogarth and Canaletto, held exhibitions in their homes. But the art that drew the large numbers were the sensational one-picture shows. One example was a painting showing the spectacle of Pitt the Elder having a stroke while speaking in the House of Lords. The artist, an entrepreneurial American named John Copley, drew 20,000 visitors, each paying one shilling in a period of six weeks in 1781. He showed *The Death of the Earl of Chatham* in a room near the Royal Academy and allegedly made £5,000 and 5,000 enemies by taking away crowds from the Royal Academy's summer show and reducing their take by £1,000.[64] Copley then mounted a picture entitled *The Floating Batteries at Gibraltar*, which was 25 feet by 18 feet. Playing on people's patriotism, he attracted 60,000 people to see the painting, which was so large that it had to be staged in a tent.

One place where the public could see fine art at no cost was the auction houses. They were open for several days before the sales, and while no one could accuse Sotheby's or Christie's of wanting to attract the working classes, the fact that they had to employ a constable to keep them out yet again shows the thirst for art among the labouring classes.[65]

There were many exotic exhibitions and shows in London at the turn of the century, but the most successful and dramatic was William Bullock's Egyptian Hall. The displays ranged from birds and animals to rocks and fossils and anything that would draw a crowd, and this included art. Bullock displayed paintings by a range of artists, of which the most famous was Gericault's *The Raft of the Medusa*. This was seen by 50,000 people and when Louis XVIII saw it he famously said, "Monsieur Gericault, your shipwreck is certainly no disaster."[66] At the same time, Benjamin Haydon's *Christ's Triumphal Entry into Jerusalem*, which included portraits of Keats, Wordsworth, Hazlitt and Lamb, was also drawing large crowds. Today Haydon is largely forgotten, but Gericault's 'icon of romanticism' has pride of place in the Louvre.[67]

Bullock was a shrewd commercial operator, and he showed these paintings in the sure knowledge that he could attract the public and make money. The success of *The Raft of the Medusa* led him to turn his largest rooms into galleries, and between 1823 and 1848 he mounted annual shows that included works by Murillo, Turner, Rubens and Titian. In showing the old masters, Bullock was not short-changing his audience.[68]

After Napoleon's defeat at Waterloo, London was subject to Napoleonic fever with exhibitions covering everything from his weapons to his Windsor soap. Bullock managed to obtain Napoleon's coach, complete with coachman and horses.[69] The show was visited by 200,000 people, but the craze also brought substantial art works to London. These included Lefèvre and David's famous portrait of Napoleon, for which admission was one shilling and which drew large crowds. Byron was so fascinated by the former emperor that when he fled London in 1816, he travelled in a coach that was a copy of the one used by Napoleon.

By 1820, the number of galleries, print shops, auction houses and artists' societies in London had created an art industry that was the envy of Europe. The Royal Academy was by now the leading venue and had already established its long tradition of internecine warfare among the academicians but a range of other institutions were also entering the art scene.

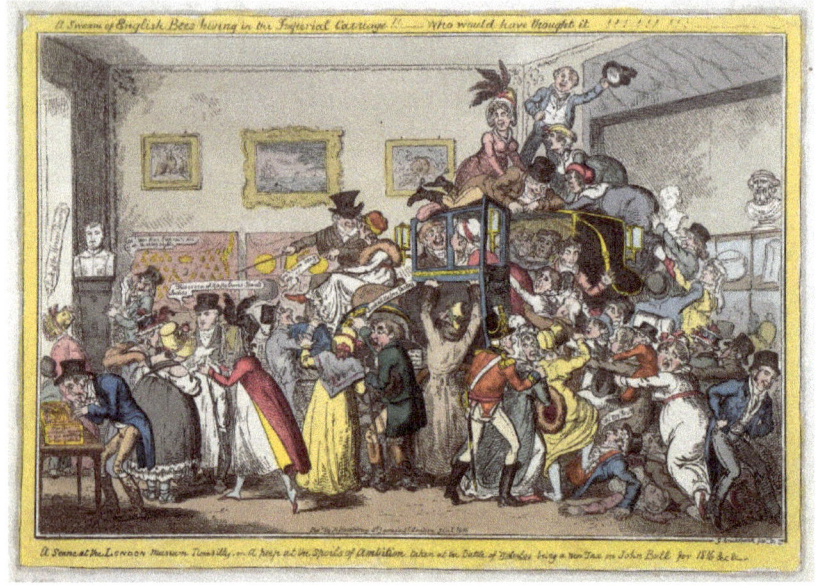

Napoleon's Coach at Bullock's Egyptian Hall 1816

The British Institution for Promoting the Fine Arts was founded in 1801 and was an elite gathering of people who had substantial private collections and who originally wanted to display and sell the works of British artists. The institution was initially very successful, raising £8,000 at a single meeting of subscribers in June 1805.[70] It then moved on to promote old masters, though its first one-man show was devoted to Reynolds. Just as sixty years earlier the Foundling Hospital had been the 'most fashionable morning lounge' in London, the smart set now went to the British Institution, which *The Times* described as, "the favourite lounge of the nobility and gentry."[71] Despite its exclusive membership, exhibitions were open to the public for only one shilling. Nonetheless, a picture of visitors admiring the paintings in 1815 shows the visitors dressed in the most fashionable clothes, and it seems safe to assume that they were not troubled by the lower orders.[72]

The British Institution may have managed to maintain exclusivity, but elsewhere the appetite for art among the working classes was undiminished. At the other end of the social scale were the growing number of music halls, which were anything but exclusive. In some halls the beer bottles were chained to the waiters' trays, and the orchestra pit was covered with wire mesh to protect the players from flying objects. Middle class they were not.

The Canterbury Music Hall, in London, was the first purpose-built hall and was opened in 1852 by Charles Morton, who was determined to provide a more refined experience. This was such a success that four years later he opened a new hall complete with art gallery. A ticket to the floor was sixpence and a further nine-pence to the gallery. A particular innovation was Ladies Evenings to which the men could bring their wives. But despite his efforts, much like Jonathan Tyers a hundred years earlier, Morton could not keep out the prostitutes who plied their trade between the tables.

The art gallery was however a great success, and Morton displayed paintings by Haydon, Maclise, Frith, Gainsborough and Ruysdael, many of which now hang in national galleries. It is unlikely that the dealers who provided the paintings would allow originals to hang in a music hall, but that did not take away from the public's enthusiasm. Just like Bullock, Morton did not display art for aesthetic reasons, but in order to bring in large numbers from the working classes and make a profit. One customer described the audience as, "artisans, soldiers, small tradesmen, and others in a similar walk of life", while another talks of, "respectable mechanics, or small tradesmen with their wives, daughters and sweethearts. Now and then you see a midshipman, or a few fast clerks with their mugs of beer."[73]

Evidence of the growing eagerness of the working classes to view art comes in two forms: disparaging reports of them attending exhibitions and, on a more positive note, actions taken to protect paintings from the large crowds of visitors.

Britain's first purpose-built public art gallery, the Dulwich Picture Gallery, was opened in 1817. Admission was by a ticket that could be obtained from print sellers in London which was apparently to prevent the gallery from being too congested. This does not seem likely given its location in an outer suburb and one contemporary quote is nearer the truth in stating that the need for a ticket ensured, "that none of an aspect decidedly plebeian came forward."[74]

The positive note is provided by descriptions of a show at the Royal Academy in 1822 when Wilkie's *Chelsea Pensioners Receiving the Gazette Announcing the Battle of Waterloo* was so popular that a fence was required to protect the painting. According to Wilkie's biographer, "Soldiers hurried from drill to see it, the pensioners came on crutches and brought with them their wives and children to have a look." One newspaper wrote that, "to judge by the crowds which poured in one might imagine that all Cockney-land was peopled with connoisseurs."

The evidence we have is qualitative, not quantitative. But the unfavourable remarks of the middle classes when they encountered the working classes in exhibitions, the reports of large numbers of common visitors necessitating the protection of paintings and finally the displays of high art in commercial enterprises all confirm that the labouring classes of the Georgian era were as keen to see art as their so-called superiors.

At one end of the social scale, the Society of Dilettanti, made up of young aristocrats back from their Grand Tour, and the British Institution with its wealthy connoisseurs were as far removed from the labouring classes as the art of the great houses. But at the other end of the scale, the public attracted by Bullock's exhibitions and Morton's music hall and art gallery was undoubtedly classless, with large numbers from the working classes. Entrepreneurs, such as Bullock and Morton, started out with enticing shows but added captivating art as they realised that this made money. Their exhibitions were high volume and low cost, and the labouring classes flocked to see them. Across all classes, the public now had a taste for art: all that was missing was a public gallery. This need was soon to be remedied.

Simon Heffer, in his history of the Victorians, describes the transformation of England in the first forty years of Victoria's reign from that of, "a wealthy country of widespread inhumanity, primitiveness and barbarism into one containing the germs, and in some measure, the evidence, of widespread civilisation and democracy."[75] As you drive through our cities today, the evidence of this change is there for all to see: magnificent town halls and railway stations, art galleries and libraries, churches of all denominations, universities and colleges. Many are no longer their former, glorious selves, but as Heffer notes, they are the visible legacy of the Victorian era.[76]

On the morning of 28 June 1838, the young Victoria was woken early by the noise of the crowds assembling for her coronation. It was a beautiful summer day, and heads of state from all over Europe created a colourful procession. At the other end of the social scale, 400,000 people lined the streets to watch the parade and see their new queen. The actual ceremony lasted five hours, and John Martin captured one of the key moments in his lavish painting, *The Coronation of Queen Victoria,* when the young queen entered the hearts of the nation by rising from the throne to help the elderly Lord Rolle as he stumbled and fell ascending the steps to give homage.

As Victoria began her long reign, one of the first of her many opening ceremonies took place when she opened the National Gallery in what was to become Trafalgar Square. The gallery had been a long time coming. The overwhelming view of politicians was that the state should not fund people's pleasures, but this was soon to be reversed. The first half of the 19th century saw the state slowly extend its role into areas that had previously been untouched. In addition to political change through the 1832 Reform Act, social change was evident in the Factory Act of the same year.

The first demand for a national gallery came from the radical M.P. John Wilkes, who in a speech to Parliament in 1770 asked the Government to buy Sir Robert Walpole's collection based at Houghton Hall. This was unsuccessful, and it was sold to Catherine the Great; she thought she had been overcharged and in her indignation refused to look at the paintings or even allow them to be unpacked.[77] On a happier note, the paintings were loaned by The Hermitage to Houghton Hall in 2013 and re-hung in their original locations.

There now followed a period when the government consistently refused to buy major collections that were put forward by their owners as the foundation of a national gallery. In 1798, Sir George Bourgeois and Noel Desenfans offered a collection with the stipulation that the government pay for a building. This was turned down, and the pictures became the core of the Dulwich Picture Gallery. The government then proceeded to reject further major collections, while at the same time, the Royal Academy refused an offer of Reynolds' works.

It seemed as if the country would never get a national gallery, but pressure was growing. When Sir John Leicester opened his collection to the public in 1818, an article in *The Examiner* called it:

...at once a satire on Government, and its example, that Government which unconscientiously creates sinecures of thousands a year for lazy, worthless courtiers and constitution-killers, but never expends a guinea in furtherance of British genius in Painting.[78]

Yet when Sir John offered his collection to the nation in 1823, he joined the lengthy list of the rejected.

When the Government finally capitulated and bought the Angerstein collection, it was not through a sudden change of heart, nor through a conversion to the aesthetic, but due to a financial windfall. In 1824, the year after Angerstein's death, his executors were still trying to sell his estate which included Titians, Rembrandts, a Velazquez and many other fine paintings, when the government received an unexpected repayment of a war loan from Austria allowing it to buy the collection, fund repairs to Windsor Castle and put £500,000 towards building new churches. Showing no hint of embarrassment, the Chancellor of the Exchequer, promoting himself as a lover of the arts, stated that:

> ...taking a more enlarged view of the subject, looking at the intimate connection of the arts, with all that adorns and ennobles man's nature, it appears to me to be consistent with the true dignity of a great nation, and with the liberal spirit of a free people, to give a munificent encouragement to the support and promotion of the Fine Arts.[79]

On 28 April 1824 the collection was opened to the public in Angerstein's house at 100 Pall Mall and at last the nation had a national collection, if not yet a purpose-built national gallery.

Agar Ellis, the M.P. who had persuaded Parliament to buy the collection, was adamant that it should be open to all and free of charge. This Tory, ahead of his time, would have been shocked to discover that if transported to London in 2023 he would have been obliged to buy a ticket for many of the major exhibitions in the national galleries. He insisted in 1824 that:

> ...there must be no sending for tickets – no asking permission – no shutting up half the days of the week; its doors must be always open, without fee or reward, to every decently dressed person; it must not be situated in an unfrequented street, nor in a distant quarter of the town. To be of any use it must be situated in the very gangway of London, where it is alike accessible, and conveniently accessible, to all ranks and degrees of men – to the merchant as he goes to his counting house – to the peers and commons on their way to their respective houses of Parliament – to the men of literature and science, on their way to their respective societies – to the King and the court, for it should always at least be supposed that the sovereign is fond of art – to the stranger and the foreigner who lodges in some of the numerous hotels with which St. James's Street, and the neighbouring streets (the *quartier* which may fairly be called the centre of London) abound – to the frequenters of clubs of all denominations – to the hunters of exhibitions (a numerous class in the metropolis) – to the indolent as well as the busy – to the idle as well as the industrious. In short, we consider the present abode of the National Gallery to be the very perfect situation.[80]

Unlike the British Museum, which had very restrictive admission policies, the National Gallery was accessible to all from the very start. A policeman on the door, "to see that no improper persons find their way into the galleries" was the only restriction.[81] By January 1825, over 70,000 visitors had admired the collection with the keeper, William Seguier, reporting to the Treasury that there was, "no injury of any description" to the paintings.[82]

The gallery was an instant success and, with the addition of two further collections, was soon short of space. The first was from the Rev. Holwell Carr, who funded his collection by somewhat dubious means. He returned from his Grand Tour enamoured of art and on hearing that a rich living was available immediately took holy orders and became vicar of Meinhot in Cornwall. He then proceeded to live in London, pay a curate to carry out his duties in Cornwall and use his income to amass a collection that included Titian, Canaletto and Rubens. The second collection was a bequest from Sir George Beaumont, who was a talented artist exhibiting regularly at the Royal Academy and a major collector. As he was a member of the aristocracy, his collection was funded through the more traditional route of straightforward land ownership.

As a result of this expansion, the gallery moved to larger rooms at 105 Pall Mall, but even these were totally inadequate and were described by Trollope as, "a dingy, dull, narrow house ill-adapted for the exhibiting of the treasures it holds."[83] But at last the governing classes had come round to the need for a proper, custom-built national gallery. The case for the gallery rested on the view that fine art had a beneficial effect on the lower orders, and that by seeing great art, the nation's workers might learn new skills in the field of design and enable our manufacturers to compete with France and Germany.

Peel expressed the first view in a debate in Parliament in 1832. Conscious of growing unrest on the Continent, he stated that:

> In the present times of political excitement, the exacerbation of angry and unsocial feelings might be much softened by the effects which the fine arts had ever produced on the mind of men... [a national gallery] was the most adequate to confer advantage on those classes which had but little leisure to enjoy the most refined species of pleasure. The rich might have their

own pictures, but those who had to obtain their bread by their labour, could not hope for such enjoyment.

A new National Gallery would, "not only contribute to the cultivation of the arts, but to the cementing of the bonds of union between the richest and the poorer orders of state …joined in mutual intercourse and understanding."[84] Some years later, Gladstone took a similar line, commenting that, "little has been done by national means for the fine arts" yet, "the higher instruments of human cultivation are also ultimate guarantees of public order."[85]

Putting the argument for the arts as a vehicle to improve the nation's manufacturing industries, Lord Ashley told the Commons that a Gallery would be, "extremely beneficial for artists and mechanics… he had reasons for believing that it would be frequented by the industrious classes instead of resorting to ale houses, as at present."[86]

The choice of what is now Trafalgar Square for the National Gallery was originally part of Nash's grand scheme for central London, but the government fell out with Nash. The competition to design the gallery was won by William Wilkins, who happened to be a friend of the trustees. Like many public projects, the Gallery finally cost three times the original estimate. In a creative attempt at what is today known as 'value re-engineering', Wilkins obtained a number of winged Victories originally intended for monuments to Nelson and Wellington. If you stand in Trafalgar Square and look up at the pediment, you can see the Victories with their swords replaced by paint brushes.[87] The site did however cater to all classes with Whitehall and its wealth to the south and many poor families living to the north, leading George Godwin, an architect and editor of *The Builder* magazine, to declare that art, "was a social bridge of no ordinary strength and size, helping to connect the 'two nations'."[88]

The National Gallery opened in 1838 and immediately attracted large numbers of visitors at a time when the country was entering the 'hungry forties'. It was at this time that the Condition of England novels, describing the lives of the working classes, first appeared. *Sybil* was published in 1845, and Disraeli famously wrote of the:

> Two Nations between whom there is no intercourse and no sympathy; who are as ignorant of each other's habits, thoughts *and* feelings, as if they were dwellers in different zones, or inhabitants of different planets; who are formed by a different food, are ordered by different manners and are not governed by the same laws.[89]

This was followed by Charlotte Bronte's *Shirley* and Mrs. Gaskell's *Mary Barton* with their vivid depictions of mill owners and mill workers. Dickens, unusually, set his story of industrial strife, *Hard Times*, outside London. Finally, Charles Kingsley's *Alton Locke* is located in the worlds of the clothing and agricultural industries and notably involves his characters in the Chartist movement talking of visits to the National Gallery.

Robert Putnam, the distinguished American sociologist, states in his work on inequality, *Our Kids: The American Dream in Crisis*, "Some of us learn from numbers, but more of us learn from stories."[90] More dramatically than any numbers, the Condition of England novels bring to life the appalling poverty of the early Victorian era; yet many people who were working a 60-hour week would spend their precious leisure time visiting art galleries.

When the Chartists held one of the largest-ever demonstrations in April 1848, the Government had a small army on standby headed by the elderly Duke of Wellington. The British Museum was defended by a militia of museum staff, regular troops and Chelsea pensioners ready to throw stones from the roof at any attackers.[91] The Chartists, not having read the works of Bourdieu, the French cultural sociologist, did not realise that the British Museum was a 'temple of symbolic violence' and made no attempt to attack it. Three months later, when the Chartists rioted in Trafalgar Square, the National Gallery was untouched.

Peel and Gladstone's high-flown rhetoric may have bypassed the common man, but he, his wife and his children flocked to the new National Gallery in numbers that compare well with today's figures. By 1851, annual visitor numbers exceeded 1 million. This was at a time when the population of Greater London was 2.2 million, and yet in 2013, with the population at 8.4 million, the number of visitors, excluding those from overseas, was only 2.3 million. As today, there will have been many repeat visits by middle-class gallery enthusiasts, but if we now move to descriptions of the visitors, the evidence clearly shows the gallery attracting large numbers from the working classes.

As the Condition of England novels give a far better picture of Victorian England than the bare statistics, so the evidence to the Parliamentary Select Committees from curators and attendants brings to life the visits of the labouring classes.

The Gallery was a key institution in the new world of museums and galleries. Following the Great Exhibition of 1851, Prince Albert wanted it relocated to his 'Albertopolis' in South Kensington, Gladstone, as Chancellor of the Exchequer chose paintings for it and Disraeli sat on Select Committees examining its operations. Unlike today, when politicians love to be seen at football matches but shun high culture, the Victorian politicians were deeply engaged with the world of art.

The first Committee to examine the arts was the 1836 Select

Committee on *Arts and their Connexion with Manufactures*. This committee was primarily concerned with the need to compete with France and Germany, where it was thought the design of their products was superior to those in England because their workers had access to art. The Committee bemoans that, "In nothing have foreign countries possessed a greater advantage over Great Britain than in their numerous public galleries devoted to the Arts and opened gratuitously to the people."[92]

At the same time, many witnesses attested that their workers, "had a great desire for such public exhibitions." One Mr. Nasmyth, who is described as 'intelligent', suggested that manufacturers would benefit greatly by encouraging the love of art in their workforce, and in order to achieve this, the Committee recommended that the forthcoming National Gallery:

> ...be opened in summer after the usual hours of labour. It is far better for the nation to pay a few additional attendants in the rooms, than to close the doors on the laborious classes, to whose recreation and refinement a national collection ought to be principally devoted.[93]

In response to a question from the Chair on whether his workers were impeded from seeing art, a Mr. C.H. Smith, who is described as an architectural sculptor, stated that:

> ...I have frequently heard them complain of that; and that the museums and exhibitions are not opened after their working hours, and that they have no opportunity of going to them, without not only having to pay for admission, but to lose their time, and of course it thus costs them much more than it does persons in easier circumstances.[94]

At this same committee, John Martin, the celebrated artist,

"complains of the want of correct design in the china trade", while Mr. Papworth, an eminent architect, "of its absence in the interior decorative architecture of our houses and in furniture."[95]

Following the opening of the National Gallery, the stage was then set for the 1841 *Select Committee on National Monuments and Works of Art*. This was the first committee to take evidence on the visitors to the National Gallery, and it is interesting to compare the testimony of Lt. Colonel Thwaites, the Assistant Keeper and Secretary, with that of John Wildsmith, who was an attendant.

In Thwaite's view, the visitors, although attending in large numbers, were very well behaved, leaving the policeman on the door with nothing to do but help the porters collect sticks and canes. But when asked if they showed much interest in the paintings, he states that:

> ...a considerable interest is shown by a few individuals, but I do not think that the mass of the people who attend, particularly on holidays, take any particular interest in them; they come and go without paying much attention to the pictures.[96]

In contrast, John Wildsmith, who spent his working hours on the floor of the gallery, states that interest in the paintings, "is increasing every day; I notice mechanics that come, and they appear to come in order to see the pictures, and not to see the company." He tells the Committee that he often hears remarks about the paintings and that, "Murillo is the greatest favourite with the public generally", while there is occasional criticism of Poussin, whom some people think, "a little too broad."[97]

The Committee praises the Gallery for its accessibility compared with the British Museum, which although free had very restricted access, stating that the National Gallery, "affords a still more gratifying instance of success from free admission." When the issue of Sunday opening is raised, neither the Assistant Keeper nor the Attendant has any objections.

Allan Cunningham, author of *Lives of British Artists,* declared to the Committee that:

> ...you see a great number of poor mechanics there, sitting wondering and marvelling over those fine works, and having no other feeling but that of pleasure or astonishment …men who are usually called the 'mob' cease to be a mob when they get taste…I saw a great deal of wonder and pleasure; there were what appeared to me to be shoemakers, masons and joiners…I have been three or four times lately and I have seen a great number of that class.[98]

Moving on to the 1850 Select Committee, which was Appointed to consider the present Accommodation afforded by the National Gallery, we now find the experts beginning to establish their position as guardians of the national collection and expressing concern at the effect on the pictures of large numbers of people. This Committee is more balanced, noting that while:

> It appears that the Gallery is frequently crowded by large masses of people, consisting not merely of those who come for the purpose of seeing the pictures but also of persons having obviously for their object the use of the rooms for wholly different purposes; either for shelter in bad weather, or as a place in which children of all ages may recreate and play, and not infrequently as one where food and refreshments may be conveniently taken.

They were also of the view that the central nature of the Gallery gave it, "the very great advantage of making the pictures accessible to the whole of the public."[99] While there are different views on the extent to which the labouring classes appreciate art, the evidence leaves no doubt that the Gallery drew large numbers from the working classes.

Dr. Waagen, the celebrated German art historian and Director of the Royal Picture Gallery in Berlin, stated that the average daily number visiting his gallery was 300 at a time when numbers visiting the much smaller National Gallery exceeded 3,000 a day.[100] He then expounds a view, which as we shall see was shared by Ruskin, that, "the lower classes are not capable of appreciating [works of art] but of enjoying them and I think the poor have great pleasure in contemplating them."[101]

The Keeper, Thomas Unwin, while shocked at the behaviour of some of the working classes, appeared to be very understanding. He stated that:

> I saw some people, who seemed to be country people, who had a basket of provisions and who drew their chairs round and sat down, and seemed to make themselves very comfortable; they had meat and drink; and when I suggested to them the impropriety of such a proceeding in such a place, they were very good humoured, and a lady offered me a glass of gin, and wished me to partake of what they had provided; I represented to them that such things could not be tolerated.[102]

He is especially concerned at the large numbers who came to the Gallery on Monday, which in Victorian times was known as Saint Monday due to the habit of workers taking the day off work. He tells the Committee that:

> Mondays, for instance, are days when a large number of the lower class of people assemble there, and men and women bring their families of children, children in arms and a train of children around them and following them, and they are subject

to all the little accidents that happen with children, and which are constantly visible upon the floors of the place.[103]

The number of visitors from the lower classes was so overwhelming that concern now arose over the damage that their 'exhalations' might do to the paintings. This reached such a pitch that Michael Faraday, the eminent scientist, was asked to investigate and advise the Committee on the best way to protect the paintings. When questioned, Faraday stated that, "the atmosphere is so charged with miasma and vapours from those crowds as to be liable to injure the pictures."[104] But when asked about, "numerous persons without apparent calling or occupation," being in the Gallery, he is more generous than Thomas Unwin when replying that, "I have seen persons there, women suckling their infants, and others sitting upon the forms but I could not say that they had not been looking at the pictures.'"[105] Faraday's solution was to put the pictures behind glass, though the Dean of St. Paul's is concerned that, "when ladies with very brilliant dresses look at pictures through glass, that reflection of the colour of their dresses is so strong as greatly to disturb the enjoyment and appreciation of the painting."[106] As Taylor states, "Either the gallery was ideally clean, and empty; or else the public would itself contaminate the very *mise en scène* of viewing."[107] The Gallery was now a runaway success, attracting both visitors and donations from wealthy collectors, and it soon became apparent that it was not fit for purpose, with Thackeray describing it as, "a little building like a gin shop."[108]

In true Victorian fashion, a new Select Committee set to work in 1853, followed by another one in 1857, with both of them debating whether to extend the current building or move to a new site. 'Gallery Wars' commenced with Prince Albert backing a move to Kensington while *The Times* set out to annoy the Queen by suggesting that there were at least three redundant royal palaces that could be converted. For once, Disraeli and Gladstone were in agreement, and when

Gladstone became Chancellor in 1853, he persuaded the Cabinet of the benefits of South Kensington and wrote to Prince Albert telling him of their decision. In the end, much to the Queen's annoyance, Parliament refused to back the move, and the Gallery remained in Trafalgar Square, but was radically extended.

The Select Committees were concerned about the effect of pollution on the paintings and public accessibility, and reading the minutes today, it is the focus on class which is most striking. Both Committees were concerned that any move from the centre of London would prevent the working classes from accessing art. Supporting the importance of accessibility, Ruskin explained his two-tier theory to the 1857 Committee:

> ...a collection, solely for the purpose of education, and for the purpose of interesting people who do not care much about art, should be provided in the very heart of the population, if possible, that pictures not of great value, but of sufficient value to interest the public of merit enough to form the basis of early education, and to give examples of all art, should be collected in the popular Gallery, but that all precious things should be removed and put into the great Gallery, where they would be safest, irrespectively altogether of accessibility.[109]

The Committee did not accept Ruskin's somewhat arrogant approach, and the collection was not divided as he would have wished. They were more impressed with statistics showing the numbers of workers from nearby companies who visited the Gallery with far more from the labouring classes than from the clerical trades.[110] William Coningham, a notable collector, told the Committee that he often saw working men in their 'fustian jackets' and expressed concern that if the Gallery was moved to South Kensington that many of them would be unable to make the journey.[111]

Art and Class

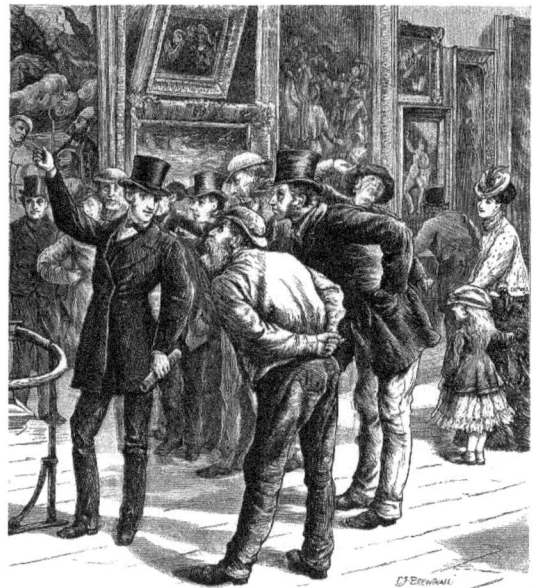
A party of working men at The National Gallery London

Similarly, when discussing the need to preserve the paintings from city centre pollution, the issue of accessibility held sway over that of preservation, "it was not the number of years that a masterpiece is preserved," that mattered, "but the number of eyes that see it."[112] On a lighter note, the Committee were deterred from considering Hyde Park when hearing evidence that the sheep in the park were covered in soot from the smoke.[113]

The Select Committees provide us with anecdotal rather than empirical evidence, though as noted, they did commission research into the numbers and types of workers who visited the gallery from nearby companies. They also put pressure on the Gallery to open in the evenings for the working man, and Saumarez Smith notes that by 1859, when the gallery was open three nights a week, visitors were being admitted at ten a minute.[114]

Moving on from the evidence of the Select Committees, contemporary accounts given by Taylor, in his book *Art for the Nation*, confirm the range of classes visiting the Gallery. He quotes a visitor in 1847 who noted that, "Nobility came in their coroneted carriages; gentry in their several vehicles; and tradespeople, country folk, young persons, and well-dressed domestics in their holiday clothes, on foot."[115]

On a more romantic note, Taylor also refers to Charles Kingsley's *Politics for the People,* where Kingsley, writing in somewhat lyrical tones, notes that:

> It is delightful to watch in a picture gallery some street boy enjoying himself; how first wonder creeps over his rough face, and a sweeter, more earnest, awestruck look, till his countenance seems to grow more handsome and nobler on the spot, and drink in and reflect unknowingly, the beauty of the picture he is studying. See how some labourer's face will light up before the painting which tells him a noble story of bygone days.[116]

On a final note, if you walk down river from the National Gallery to Tate Britain, you can see Turner's painting showing the House of Commons on fire in 1834. This led to the building of the present Palace of Westminster and, in a most democratic move, cartoons of the proposed frescoes for the new building were put on display in Westminster Hall in July 1843. Thousands of visitors flocked to see the exhibition, which had been curated by Charles Eastlake. He was then secretary of the Fine Arts Commission, and wrote that, "the daily throng is immense; the public takes great interest, and the strongest proof is thus given of the love of the lower orders for pictures, when they represent an event."[117]

We have now seen that without access policies and equality targets, the National Gallery was full of people from all classes. We shall next see how at South Kensington, Henry Cole implemented policies that would make the New Labour Social Exclusion Unit seem positively lethargic as he established the South Kensington Museum as a precursor to the Victoria & Albert Museum (V & A), implemented a loans scheme that covered the whole country and opened the Bethnal Green Museum in the East End, attracting nearly one million visitors in the first six months.

Henry Cole was every employer's nightmare. Bright and arrogant, he always knew best, and to his superior's chagrin, he was usually correct. To add to his employer's difficulties, he had impeccable contacts: Queen Victoria and Prince Albert. Today he would have been an award-winning tribunal litigant.

Cole left school at 15 and in 1823 went to work at the Records Office. He soon established a reputation as a difficult employee, writing letters, reports and pamphlets criticising the government's disorganised record keeping while at the same time demanding a pay rise. Eventually, Charles Cooper, Secretary to the Commissioners, could take no more, and Cole was dismissed. But Cooper had underestimated Cole's contacts. Within three months of being sacked, Cole had persuaded Charles Buller, a dynamic M.P., to establish a Select Committee to investigate the Records Commission. Cole sat alongside Buller at the hearings, helped select witnesses and essentially controlled the proceedings. The press were outraged at his behaviour, but the result was the reform of the Commission.

By August 1837, Cole was back at work on a higher salary as Senior Assistant Keeper. So began a long and distinguished career of battles with authority. Sir Henry Trueman Wood stated that:

> ...he liked his own way, and he generally got it, though his methods were not such as endeared him either to the superiors

whose orders he evaded or to the subordinates whose submission he compelled.[118]

In their biography, Bonython and Burton describe Cole as a, "rough, tough man to work with", but his outlandish behaviour was forgiven because he delivered extraordinary results.[119]

Primarily a civil servant, Cole's career combined official work with private ventures, lobbying and a wide range of side-lines. While still on the payroll of the Records Office, he went to work for Rowland Hill at the new Post Office. There he helped develop and promote the penny stamp while also inventing a set of patented letter scales. His next off-line venture was to write a column for the *Railway Gazette* campaigning against Brunel for the introduction of the standard gauge. Then came the creation of the first commercial Christmas card, which was followed by winning a prize at the Society of Arts 1846 Exhibition, for the design of a tea service which Minton put into production. Still employed by the Records Office, he now became involved in a campaign to build new docks in Grimsby, persuading Prince Albert to travel up from London to lay the foundation stone. His government salary in 1848 was £436 16s 8d, while his payment from the Manchester, Sheffield and Lincolnshire Railway Company for promoting the docks was £500.[120] At the same time, he was writing guides to London's historic buildings and children's books under the pen name of Felix Summerly. As Flanders states in her book on Victorian leisure, "Cole was one of those Victorian powerhouses who produced so much, in so many fields, that it is hard to know when he slept."[121]

Cole is a key player in our story because he had a mission to bring art and design to the working classes and not just in London but across the country. In common with many of his contemporaries, he believed that Britain lagged behind France and Germany in design, and if the country was to improve its exports, it must improve its design skills. Giles Waterfield, author of *The People's Galleries,* states that Cole redefined Fine Arts to mean, "beauty applied to mechanical production", classifying pictures and sculpture as the, "Polite Arts." In so doing, he raised the status of the craftsmen producing industrial art.[122] The Schools of Design, events such as the Great Exhibition and museums such as South Kensington would elevate and inspire the working man. In a paper entitled, 'The Functions of the Art and Science Department', delivered in 1857, Cole listed the various schools that now came under his control, stating that, "All these institutions had in view the promotion of scientific and artistic knowledge of an industrial tendency at the expense of the State."[123] The South Kensington Museum was to become a museum, a university and a home to scientific laboratories all in one. As Forgan and Gooday state in their paper, *A Fungoid Assemblage of Buildings,* "There was, therefore, still a period in mid-nineteenth century Britain when the museum rather than the laboratory, was the centre of scientific authority."[124]

Cole's breakthrough from Assistant Commissioner in the Records Office to becoming a national figure came in 1845 when he joined the council of the Society of Arts. Not satisfied with the Society's small-scale events, Cole began campaigning for a major exhibition, an effort which led to the Great Exhibition of 1851. He was seconded from the Records Office to a newly formed Executive Committee, and the success of the Exhibition was largely due to his energy and drive. Over six million people visited the Exhibition and as a result of the Victorians love of statistics, we know that they ate nearly one million bath-buns.[125]

Cole and Prince Albert were determined that the Exhibition would be open to all classes. In a campaigning speech to businessmen at the Mansion House, Cole told them that, "High and low, rich and poor, would have equally good access…those who rode down in omnibuses and those who went in private carriages would have equal facilities of approach."[126] Once the Exhibition opened, Cole and Prince Albert had a battle with the exhibitors. Just like the artists who wanted to keep the kitchen maids and stable boys out of their shows, so the exhibitors were worried that working-class visitors would deter the upper and middle classes from attending. For the first month of the Exhibition, the entrance charge was deliberately set high, but then Cole and Prince Albert insisted on days when the entrance would be only 1s or 6d. *The Times* thundered about the dangers of allowing access to, "the mob" while, as Flanders notes, *Punch* was unusually on the side of the workers.[127] In effect, the charge of 1s. would be beyond the very poor, but many artisans attended and there were railway outings from across the country from Mechanics Institutes and Benefit Clubs.[128]

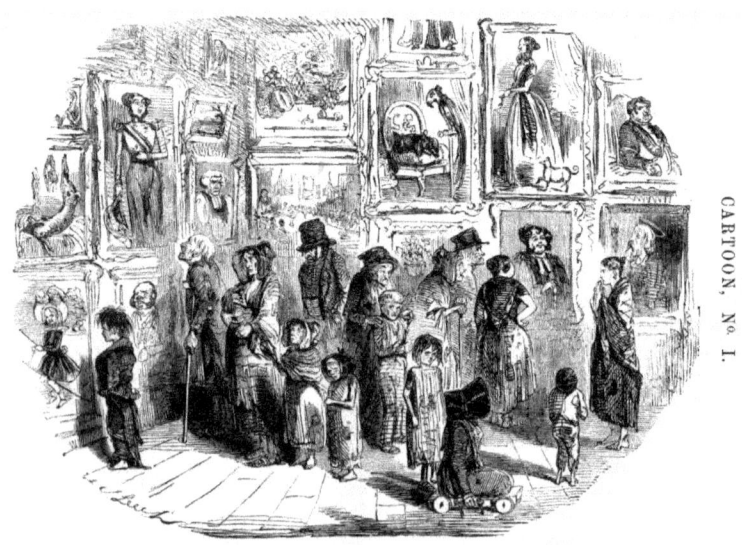

SUBSTANCE AND SHADOW.

Substance and Shadow Punch 1843

The Exhibition Commission even established a Working-Class Committee. Only two years after the massive Chartist demonstrations, the Committee included two Chartists who were joined by Cole, Dickens, Thackeray and the Bishop of Oxford. Sadly, the Committee did not work well and after only a few meetings was disbanded.

As in all Cole's ventures, he fell out with his superiors, and in February 1850 he resigned but diplomatic manoeuvres ensued and he was persuaded to return. After the Exhibition, he was made a Companion of the Order of the Bath and received a payment of £1,500.

The Great Exhibition was a major stepping stone in Cole's career, and in 1852, he finally left the Records Office and became head of the London School of Design with responsibility for all the schools across the country. A letter from Herbert Minton, of the china company, gives an insight into Cole's character:

> I am glad to hear that you have taken office in the management of the School of Design. You may be *very useful* if you will only be more mild & gentle than you usually are – not so obstinate & dictatorial – and believe that *you* may sometimes be *wrong and others right*. I hope this plain sailing may not prove unpalatable.[129]

Cole now set about persuading the Exhibition Commissioners to let him select items from the Exhibition and mount a display to promote design. Prince Albert allowed him to use Marlborough House, and this was in effect the birth of the Victoria & Albert Museum. Prince Albert and the Commissioners were determined that the Exhibition should leave a legacy, and with a combination of the Exhibition profits, private funds and Government grants, they began to buy land in South Kensington to build a new museum. The first buildings were temporary and, despite housing the School of Design, were attacked for their shabby appearance and they soon became known as the Brompton Boilers. *The Builder* stated that, "Its ugliness is unmitigated" while *The Civil Engineer* was even more critical, calling it, "a huge, lugubrious hospital for decayed railway carriages."[130]

Cole was not put off, and in his determination to attract all classes, he had a set of timber refreshment rooms built. Here he showed his flair for creative management. The hastily constructed buildings failed to pass the Office of Public Works specifications, so Cole transferred them to the Government, at which point they became exempt from the regulations. The final construction in the first phase was an elegant building to house the Sheepshanks collection.

Sheepshanks had inherited a successful Leeds textile company from his father and was able to retire at forty and pursue art collecting and gardening. He was socially conscious, insisting that his collection should not bear his name and presenting it to the new South Kensington Museum rather than the National Gallery. A key condition of his bequest was that, "the public, and especially the working classes, shall have the advantage of seeing the collection on Sunday afternoons."[131]

The South Kensington Museum opened to the public in June 1857. It was the first museum in the world to have gas lighting, which was installed by Cole so that the working classes could visit the museum in the evenings when it was open till 10.00 p.m. three nights a week.[132] *Lloyds* newspaper, in a column entitled 'A Light in the Dark', praised Cole's initiative, "Hitherto all our public buildings have been rigidly closed at dusk. As the sun went down, so the officials went out." Museums would now lure the working man from the public house, and there will be:

> No more evenings amid beer and tobacco. The anxious wife

will no longer have to visit the different taprooms of the neighbourhood to drag her poor besotted husband home. She will seek for him at the nearest museum where she will have to exercise all the persuasion of her affection to tear him away from the rapt contemplation of Raphael!

Lloyds concluded, "Is it Mr. Henry Cole or Prince Albert who has been the beater down of the dark prejudice that all intelligent pleasures should be closed for public enjoyment at nightfall?"[133]

Sheepshank's largely narrative collection was very popular with the working classes, and Richard Redgrove, who worked for Cole, reported that the working-class crowds were so large that it was necessary to protect the paintings with glass.

Cole had taken part in the battle over the siting of the National Gallery and was determined that South Kensington's location would not be an obstacle to attendance. In addition to the extended opening hours to attract the working classes, he staged a series of lectures where 350 seats were reserved for working men, and he negotiated with the General Omnibus Company for there to be a half-hourly service from the city to the Museum. Finally, Cole provided both labels and a simply written, cheap catalogue.

In 'The Functions of the Science and Art Department', he attacks the National Gallery, alleging that it failed to attract the working classes, while giving a somewhat subjective view of his own gallery:

> An observation of the evening visitors clearly proves, that a large proportion of them are not of a class who can frequent public museums in the daytime, excepting at Christmas and Easter holidays. On Monday nights especially, great numbers are strictly of the working classes.

He then continues with a typically Victorian description of the hard-working poor:

> In the evening, the working man comes to this Museum from his one or two dimly lighted, cheerless dwelling rooms, in his fustian jacket, with his shirt collars a little trimmed up, accompanied by his threes, and fours, and fives of little fustian jackets, a wife, in her best bonnet, and a baby, of course, under her shawl. The looks of surprise and pleasure of the whole party when they first observe the brilliant lighting inside the Museum show what a new, acceptable and wholesome excitement this evening entertainment affords to all of them. Perhaps the evening opening of Public Museums may furnish a powerful antidote to the gin palace.[134]

Cole was a fanatic for figures, and when he retired, he claimed that over 12 million people had visited South Kensington in the previous fifteen years – a claim that seems likely to be true as there were turnstiles on the door to record visitor numbers. Cole even claimed that between 1851 and 1862, "the value of the export of manufactures likely to be influenced by art-instruction has increased from £29,244,779l. to £43,799,501l."[135] The reports in the press confirmed Cole's view that there was a very large working-class contingent. *The Times*, not always a supporter, noted that, "The evening visitors exceed the diurnal in the ratio of 5 to 1 and the working classes abound."[136]

But Cole's vision extended beyond London. He oversaw a growth in the schools of design, but one of his most significant and lasting legacies was the South Kensington Circulating Loans scheme. Cole took the view that the art and the objects in Marlborough House, and later South Kensington Museum, belonged to the nation and not just London. This was a bold move. As we shall see in the chapter on the Art Treasures Exhibition, the National Gallery was firmly opposed to lending out its pictures and in 1857 refused to let any go to Manchester. Cole drew up a Department of Science and Art note whereby, "selections should be made of articles from each of the divisions of the Central Museum comprising glass, lace, works in metal, ivory carvings, pottery, woven fabrics & c.; and that they should be sent in rotation to local schools." Students were to be given free admission to see the items on loan, and, "to enable artizans, and others employed in the daytime, to share in the benefits to be derived from the collection, the fee on three evenings in the week should not exceed one penny each person."[137]

The original loans collection comprised 430 specimens and 150 drawings and photographs, and Birmingham was the first city to benefit. The scheme quickly developed and soon required trains with specially designed carriages, accompanied by a keeper from South Kensington who held the key to the collection. In March 1860, Cole with his love of statistics reported that the collection:

> ...has been visited by 359,125 persons and that it has realized in fees, which have been received by the local authorities, upwards of 8,352l. 18s. 1d. Although the most fragile articles, such as Sevrés porcelain and glass, have been transmitted at least 3,690 miles by railway, &c., and been packed and unpacked more than 60 times, no specimens have been broken or damaged.[138]

A report on the loans scheme presented in 1881 concluded that:

> ...from what has been said it will be seen that the South Kensington Museum exists, not wholly, nor even chiefly, as an institution for the exclusive advantage of the dwellers in, and visitors to London, but is in truth also a great National Collection or storehouse, formed and administered for the benefit of the

whole kingdom.[139]

In 1976, the loans scheme was suspended due to financial cuts. However, Cole would have been delighted when the V&A won the Museum of the Year Award in 2016, and the Director immediately announced that they would use the prize money to revive the scheme.

Local councils across the country were now beginning to build their own museums, and one of Cole's few unrealised dreams was the creation of satellite museums in the London boroughs but sadly the only one to be built was the Bethnal Green Museum. As South Kensington expanded, the infamous Brompton Boilers became redundant and were offered to the London Local Authorities. Gladstone had suggested a museum in Bethnal Green as early as 1851, and although money had been secured to buy land, there were no funds to build a museum. When the offer of the Brompton Boilers was made, Bethnal Green responded immediately, and a new museum was eventually opened in June 1872. The streets were crowded, and banners hung from every building as a procession of the great and the good, including Henry Cole in court dress, was led through the borough by the Prince and Princess of Wales, who were to perform the opening ceremony. On the day of opening, 25,500 people flocked to see their new museum. Sir Richard Wallace had generously lent his unrivalled collection of over 700 Old Masters, and the museum was an immediate success with 901,464 visitors in the first six months and a subsequent annual average of 400,000.

The Wallace Collection was originally intended to be on display for one year but remained for three and was followed by collections from the National Portrait Gallery, the Chantry Bequest and the Dulwich Gallery. There were also exhibitions of scientific objects from South Kensington, but for the first 25 years, Bethnal Green displayed some of the nation's best fine art and achieved higher visitor figures than the new Tate Gallery. Cole never replicated the success of Bethnal Green, but like South Kensington, it drew visitors till ten o'clock at night. Its impact on the East End demonstrated the working classes' thirst for great art.

It is no surprise that Cole had his detractors. W. Stanley Jevons, a prominent Victorian economist, did not believe Cole's claims about working-class visitors:

> At the South Kensington Art Museum, they make a great point of setting up turnstiles to record the precise number of visitors, and they can tell you to a unit the exact amount of civilising effect produced in any day, week, month, or year. But these turnstiles hardly take account of the fact that the neighbouring wealthy residents are in the habit, on a wet day, of packing their children off in a cab to the so-called Brompton Boilers, in order that they may have a good run through the galleries. To the far greater part of the people a large brilliantly lighted Museum is little or nothing more than a promenade, a bright kind of lounge, not nearly so instructive as the shops of Regents Street or Holborn.[140]

Cole was also attacked by the regional Schools of Design, who used his statistics to counter his statement that he served the whole country and not just London. A letter to the *Manchester Guardian* pointed out that the regional schools received only £11,859 7s. 7d. from a total budget of £68,401, 16s. 2d., asking, "Is it not monstrous that more than five–sixths of the entire grant should be consumed in London?"[141]

On a lighter note, Cole's friend, Charles Dickens, wrote that, "there is reason and good intention in much that he does... but that he over does it" and went on to use Cole as the inspiration for the doctrinaire school inspector in *Hard Times.*[142]

But his impact on the Victorian world of art museums and his legacy is incalculable. As Waterfield states, "The experiment of extended opening hours at South Kensington, made possible by the innovative introduction of gas lighting, was justified by the huge evening crowds that were satisfyingly identifiable as working class."[143] He also credits Cole, as a result of the loans scheme, "as the most influential individual in Victorian England for the creation of regional galleries."[144]

In their biography, Boynthon and Burton state that Cole, "was one of the most successful art museum curators of all time."[145] But perhaps it is best to conclude with Cole's autobiography where, quoting a speech he gave in 1873, he notes that:

> Since the year 1852, I have witnessed the conversion of twenty limp Schools of Design into one hundred and twenty flourishing Schools of Art in all parts of the United Kingdom, and other schools like them, in the Colonies and the United States. Five hundred night classes for drawing have been established for artisans. One hundred and eighty thousand boys and girls are now learning elementary drawing. Twelve hundred and fifty Schools and classes for Science instruction have spontaneously sprung up…whilst this Museum itself has been visited by more than twelve millions of visitors, it has circulated objects to one hundred and ninety-five localities holding exhibitions, to which more than four million of local visitors have contributed above ninety-three thousand pounds.[146]

All targets met.

At the start of the 19th century, art was put on display by commercial operators. Sometimes it was a single painting, such as *The Raft of the Medusa*; sometimes it was as an adjunct to exotic artefacts in a rowdy music hall. By the end of the century, the National Gallery, the

V&A and the Tate Gallery were providing free access to fine art. It is unlikely that the working-class visitors knew of the politicians' hopes that this would elevate their moral status, improve their design skills or simply keep them out of the drinking dens, but the radical shift from private to public laid the foundations of the nation's national and regional galleries.

In the next chapter, we shall see how the working classes in the East End not only flocked to Bethnal Green but to a whole range of galleries and exhibitions that displayed everything from Old Masters to Pre-Raphaelites.

Chapter 4

Art Comes to the East End

Henry Cole retired in July 1873, and far removed from the glories of South Kensington, a young vicar and his wife were about to usher in an extraordinary episode in British art history. When Samuel Barnett became vicar of St Jude's in Whitechapel, he could not have foreseen that his legacy would lead to Picasso and Warhol, Rothko and Twombly starring in his gallery. What he would have made of their paintings is best left unexplored, though we can be sure that he would not have approved of Allen Jones and his erotic paintings. Barnett was not the first to bring art to the East End, but he was the most successful and we shall visit the other pioneering galleries after exploring his work.

In his previous parish, Barnett had worked with Octavia Hill, and they were both visionary Victorian reformers. Hill laid the foundations for public social work and social housing and was a founder of the National Trust. Barnett established the first university settlement when he opened Toynbee Hall, and the model was not only replicated elsewhere in London but in Chicago and New York. But while they recognised that a lack of money, poor housing and poor education were major problems and devoted their lives to helping the poor, they believed that the real cause of poverty lay with the poor themselves. If only they could be uplifted, they could change their lives for the better.

Despite all their pioneering work, Hill and Barnett were merely following the long tradition of blaming the victim. Hill wrote that:

> ...people's homes are bad, partly because they are badly built and arranged; they are tenfold worse because their habits and

lives are what they are. Transplant them tomorrow to healthy and commodious homes and they would pollute and destroy them.[147]

Barnett took a similar view, saying that, "the want of clothes does not so loudly call for remedy as the want of interest and culture."[148]

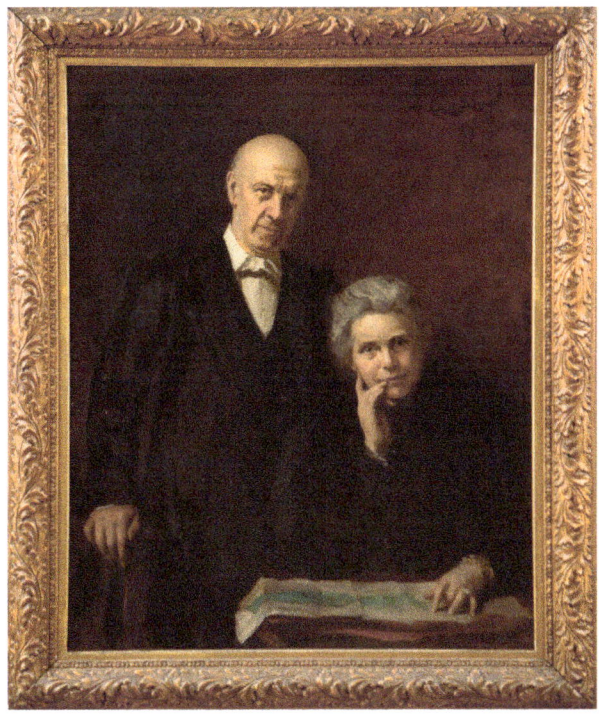

Rev and Mrs. Barnett

On arriving at St Jude's, Barnett estimated that only 5% of his parish actually attended church, and he and his wife came up with the idea of, "paintings that preach." Recognising that the people of his parish would not attend church, and even if they did, "they are weary of hearing sermons and do not care to pray",[149] Barnett became convinced that pictures that preach would bring his people to God. In his words, "the best pictures are those which speak most directly to people whose lives are spent amid harsh and often ugly surroundings."[150]

The Barnetts both came from wealthy backgrounds and had a wide circle of rich collectors and artists from whom they borrowed paintings for their first exhibition. They opened during the Easter holiday of 1881, and the three schoolrooms attached to the church became a gallery of all that was best in contemporary art.

The catalogue was written by the Barnetts and would have horrified today's curators, though it did have the advantage of being written in plain English. Mrs. Barnett, conscious that her husband was colour-blind and a convinced optimist, would often edit his descriptions, but she was not above laughing at her own words. Describing the death of a gladiator in a Roman amphitheatre, she wrote, "God kissed him and he slept," but was then amused to hear a visitor say, "The tiger clawed him and he died."[151]

A formidable figure, Mrs. Barnett tells of how when visiting the home of a wealthy collector to borrow some paintings, she felt obliged to tell Mrs. Young that she could not take those on offer, "because they are not your best. I cannot take your second-rate. The best must be lent for the service of the poor." A somewhat astonished Mrs. Young, when asking what was wanted, had the best pointed out to her and responded, "But you have chosen all the gems. How do you from Whitechapel know so much about art?" Mrs. Barnett apologised for her 'inconvenient knowledge' and was amazed some days later to find Mrs. Young in the schoolrooms measuring up with a view to lending her best paintings.[152]

The Barnetts used their redoubtable networking skills to bring to

Whitechapel some of the best art in London. In the biography of her husband, Mrs. Barnett lists some of the artists who lent paintings: Holman Hunt, G.F. Watts, Lady Butler, Alma-Tadema, Millais, Burne-Jones, Herkomer, Leighton and Rossetti. In addition they borrowed from the National Gallery and the British Museum showing Rubens, Rembrandt and other old masters. Only the best was good enough for the people of Whitechapel.

Their first exhibition ran for eight days and attracted 10,000 visitors. There was a charge of 3d. but two days were free, including Sundays. The following year, there was no charge, and in thirteen days they had 26,492 visitors and sold 4,600 catalogues at 1d.each.[153]

Open seven days a week, twelve hours a day from 10.00 a.m. till 10.00 p.m., the exhibition drew the wrath of the Lord's Day Observance Society. They demonstrated outside the building, but having failed to stop people going in, wrote to the Bishop of London asking him to ban Sunday opening. But Barnett was an enthusiastic member of the Sunday Society, believing that, "the cause of Christ has nothing to fear from the reasonable and careful extension of the principle of Sunday opening."[154]

The Bishop backed the objectors, but both he and Barnett were shrewd political operators. Barnett wrote to the Bishop saying that as someone who has lived, "as a neighbour amid people of the lowest type I think I have a right possessed by few to say what means will hasten that knowledge of God to which we clergy have devoted our lives." In a clever move, he did not ask the Bishop to give authority for Sunday opening but merely to, "suspend your judgement and give me time, by means of pictures and worship, to bring the people to God." The Bishop held his hand, and Sunday opening continued.[155]

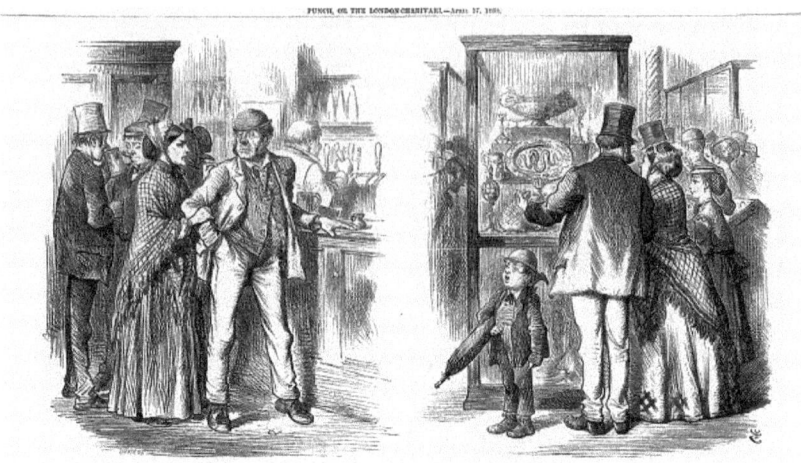

The Sunday Question, Punch 1869

The battle over Sunday opening raged on with great force. In 1895, Barnett used his inaugural address as President of the Sunday Society to declare that even the Trades Unions and Trades Councils were now in favour. Finally, in 1897, the Government amended the Lord's Day Act of 1781 to allow Sunday opening, and the Chancellor found funds to pay for extra staff in art galleries and museums. After his death, Mrs. Barnett wondered what Samuel would have made of cinema on Sundays, but concluded that if the films showed the wonders of nature, "they would help man to keep holy the Sabbath day."[156]

Not a group to give up the battle, the Lord's Day Observance Society continued the fight. In a fascinating pamphlet published in 1908, they made their case using page after page of statistics drawn from across the country. Their figures showed that large numbers of the labouring classes went to art galleries and museums:

> It cannot be truthfully said that the masses have no interest in the institutions concerned; for on Bank Holidays, in spite of numerous competing places of amusement, the National

Museums draw far larger crowds of visitors.[157]

But they argued that people preferred to go on Bank Holidays, using their statistics to show a decline in Sunday visiting. "It can hardly be pretended that these figures, when compared with the population of London, represent a widespread desire for Sunday opening," though noting that, "some of those most largely attended, admit the presence of a considerable portion of children and young people. They would make better Christians and better citizens if gathered into Sunday schools and Bible classes."[158]

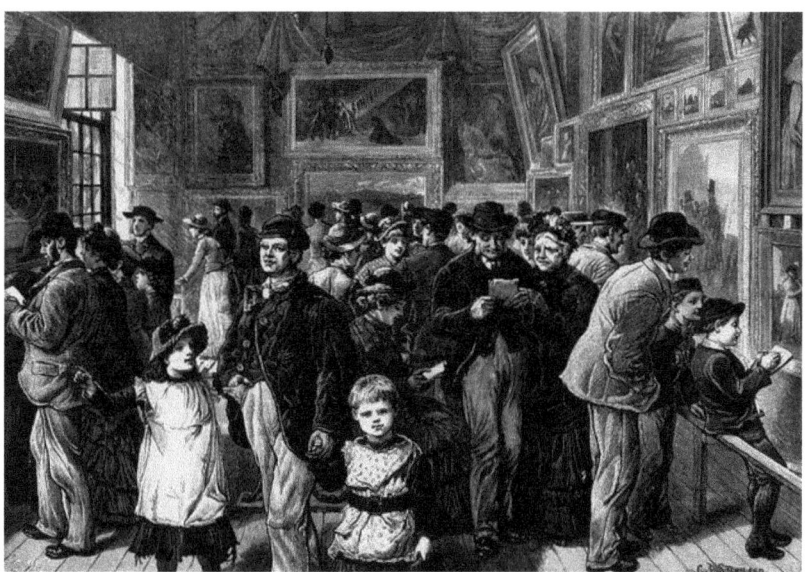

Voting at the Whitechapel Gallery 1884

The Barnetts' networking skills not only enabled them to display an extraordinary array of paintings, but to build up a strong group of influential supporters. When deciding not to take on the Barnetts, the Bishop would undoubtedly have been aware of the heavy guns that they could deploy. Just as Thomas Coram drew support from Georgian society, so the Barnetts built a network of wealthy collectors, artists, writers and politicians. Lord Rosebery, the former Prime Minister, opened the first exhibition in 1881, and in 1910 Winston Churchill, Arthur Pinero and Bernard Shaw sat on a committee to select paintings for an exhibition on Shakespeare. The historian George Trevelyan, the writer Kenneth Grahame, the critic Roger Fry and the pre-eminent Victorian intellectual, Matthew Arnold, were all regular visitors. On the artistic side, William Morris provided material to cover the walls of the classrooms, the Pre-Raphaelites lent paintings and gave lectures and even Queen Victoria was persuaded to provide pictures from the royal collection.

One of the strongest supporters was the artist G.F. Watts, who lent paintings but also gave generously, and even Punch acknowledged his contribution in a positive tone:

> Oh! East is East and West is West as
> Rudyard Kipling says
> When the poor East enjoys the art for
> Which the rich West pays,
> See East and West linked in their best!
> With the Art-wants of Whitechapel
> Good Canon Barnett is just the man who
> Best knows how to grapple
>
> So charge this Canon, load to the muzzle,
> All ye great Jubilee guns.
> Pictures as good as sermons? Aye, much
> Better than some poor ones.
> Where Whitechapel's darkness the weary
> Eyes of the dreary worker dims,
> It may be found that Watts's pictures do
> Better than Watts's hymns.[159]

Watt's influence extends through time and across the Atlantic. In 1990 Barack Obama was at a church service in Chicago where the Rev. Jeremiah Wright was preaching, and the title of his sermon was, 'The Audacity of Hope'. Using Barnett's practice of drawing on 'pictures that preach', the Rev. Wright's sermon was based on a painting by Watts entitled *Hope*. Wright described the scene:

> The painting depicts a harpist, a woman who at first glance appears to be sitting atop a great mountain. Until you take a closer look and see that the woman is bruised and bloodied, dressed in tattered rags, the harp reduced to a single frayed string. Your eye is drawn down to the scene below, down to the valley below, where everywhere are the ravages of famine, the drumbeat of war, a world groaning under strife and deprivation… and yet consider once again the picture before us. Hope![160]

This sermon was a key moment for Obama, who found tears streaming down his face. Fourteen years later, at the Democratic Convention, *The Audacity of Hope* was the title of the speech that was to catapult Obama to fame and the White House, and which would become the title of his bestselling book setting out his vision and values.

Every year, Barnett's visitors were asked to select their favourite painting. In 1889 they chose Holman Hunt's *The Triumph of the Innocents*, a glorious piece of Victorian narrative crowded with the spirits of the children massacred by Herod, and then in 1892 *The Annunciation* by Burne-Jones. Barnett despaired of the failure of his flock to appreciate landscapes, which he felt countered the grim East End environment, but the public loved his paintings that preach. Unfortunately, this annual event came to an end when it transpired that people thought they were entering a raffle for a painting and began choosing the one they thought would be the most valuable.

The visitor figures were increasing every year: in 1886, the Barnetts showed 300 pictures attracting 46,763 visitors, and by 1890, the figure was 50,000 visitors in three weeks, with sales of 17,738 catalogues.[161] The numbers trying to get into the exhibition were such that volunteers known as 'chuckers in' controlled the people waiting. Mrs. Barnett noted that:

> ...after four years we realised that there were serious dangers attending the picture shows to which the people came in such numbers that, at intervals, the iron gate at the end of the street passage had to be closed, to enable some of the crowd to leave the building before others were admitted.[162]

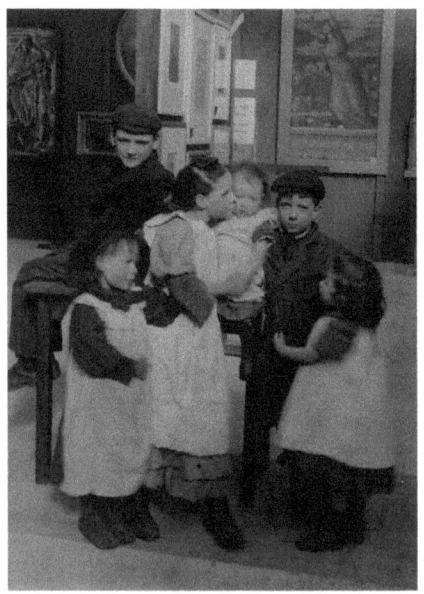

Children in Whitechapel Gallery 1901

By the late 1890s, the exhibitions had outgrown the classrooms despite them having been expanded, and the Barnetts embarked on a campaign to raise funds for a purpose-built gallery. This was a success, and in March 1901, Lord Rosebery opened the new Whitechapel

Gallery twenty years after he had opened the first exhibition in three dingy classrooms. Tragically, the Barnetts were unable to attend the opening, as they were at the funeral of their daughter.

The Gallery was an immediate success, attracting 206,000 people to the first exhibition, which lasted for six weeks. In the next ten years, there were over 3 million visitors with as many as 16,000 a day, and the Barnetts' legacy was firmly established.[163] The Whitechapel quickly became an established gallery of contemporary art and featured in early editions of Baedeker's guide to London, but the statistics and the descriptions of visitors to St. Jude's, and later Whitechapel, provide graphic evidence of the working-class demographic flocking to see the paintings.

The majority of visitors were in work and not the very poorest. In an article in the *Daily Chronicle* in December 1898, Barnett wrote of local people going:

> ...round the gallery methodically and intelligently, crowding it on Sundays and in the evenings between seven and nine-thirty at which hour they hasten away with a Cinderella-like rapidity, so that they may be ready for early morning work.[164]

In a similar tone, Barnett wrote that:

> ...it is sometimes amusing to hear the dogmas of those who, living amid the rich, settle what the poor do and what the poor like. They are so sure that what the poor like is common or even vulgar, and also that they might afford the time or money to visit South Kensington. As a fact our neighbours like what is ideal better than what is commonplace, and they certainly cannot afford time after work to clean themselves and travel to the west, spend an hour in a gallery, return, and get enough sleep before next morning's early rising.[165]

Mrs. Barnett provides evidence of the class of their visitors when describing how her husband had to stand on a chair when explaining the pictures, as, "many hot breaths and unclean clothes were not helpful."[166] At the 1890 exhibition, she writes of two girls who were, "hatless and sharing a shawl who might not be living the worst life, but if not they were low down enough to be familiar with it." In another comment, she remarks that, "the majority of visitors is drawn from the large body of what may be called home loving artisans."[167] Despite steadily growing literacy rates, Mrs. Barnett tells of many visitors hiding their illiteracy when offered a catalogue by pretending to have forgotten their spectacles.[168]

And not content with encouraging local people to visit their exhibitions, Mrs. Barnett took them on trips to artists' homes. Alfred Leighton and George Watts both opened their homes to visitors from the East End. After a visit to Watts' house, one visitor commented, "Well, I should not have believed I could have enjoyed myself so much, and yet been so quiet… where now can we see such things often?"[169]

If we overlay the visitor statistics of the Barnetts' exhibitions and the descriptions of these visitors with the work of Charles Booth in *Life and Labour of the People,* showing that 35% of those living in the East End in 1889 were in abject poverty, it is all the more extraordinary that people who were working long hours and living in poverty chose to spend their limited free time viewing art.

The opening of the new gallery heralded a new era with the appointment of the first Art Director, Charles Aitken, who in 1911 went on to become Director of the Tate. The Gallery now evolved in several directions, maintaining the commitment to fine art, but also developing ever stronger links with the local community through a range of different exhibitions and events. Specialist exhibitions, such as *Design and Workmanship in Printing* in 1906, were aimed at local craftsmen, while early shows built links with the Jewish community. The display *Jewish Arts and Antiquities* was mounted in both 1906 and again in 1927, while in 1923 an exhibition was devoted to Jewish artists including Pissarro. Another connection with the community was through children. In 1909 the Gallery hosted the *Stepney Children's Pageant* with music commissioned from Holst, and there were regular displays of children's work. The Gallery also initiated an open exhibition, known as the East End Academy, with both local people's work and that of professional artists. By 1938, its fame had spread to Glasgow, where the local newspaper wrote that:

> We are hearing a lot about art and the Academy these days, but how many of you know that in London there is an art gallery outside of which butchers and bakers leave their vans while they go in for a peep at the pictures?[170]

One of the Gallery's highlights was the display of Picasso's *Guernica* in 1939. Clement Attlee opened the exhibition, which was not staged by the Gallery but by the East London Aid Spain Committee. It lasted for two weeks, with Picasso declaring that there be no entrance charge, but asking people to bring a pair of boots for those fighting in Spain.

The Gallery continues to have strong links with the local community with a wide range of activities for both children and adults. Every year they invite an artist to work with local children, and in 2012, Eva Rothschild made a film showing what happens when young boys are let loose in a gallery. 2010 saw the Chapman brothers fill the galleries with drawings from their book *Bedtime Tales and Sleepless Nights,* and children could buy the *Jake and Dinos Colouring Book.*

Today, Whitechapel is one of many galleries displaying contemporary art, and for many years it has been a beacon of leading-edge art and design. The Barnetts, with their ability to laugh at themselves, would have appreciated Ian Breakwell's story in the *Whitechapel Centenary Review*. He tells of a local family who came into the gallery complete with shopping, but on seeing Robert Ryman's white-on-white paintings concluded that the next exhibition had not yet opened.[171] The Barnetts would not only have enjoyed the story, but would have been delighted that one hundred years on their vision was still alive, with local people going to the gallery and many children's activities. This was their legacy, and not only are they remembered through the Gallery, but they both feature in the Church of England Liturgical Calendar every year on 17 June.

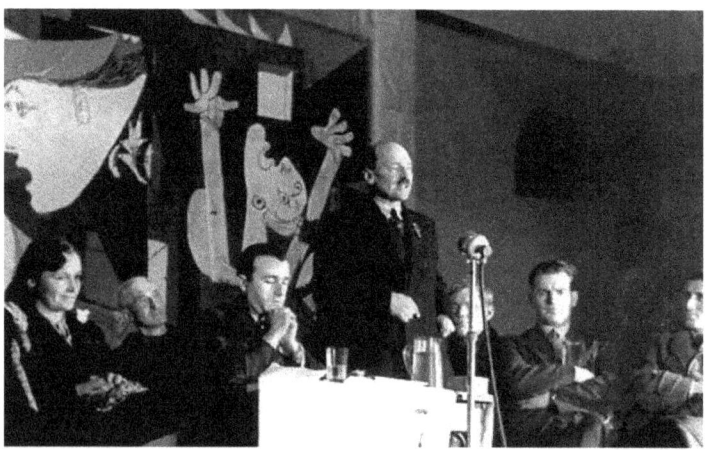

Clement Attlee and Guernica at Whitechapel Gallery, 1939.

But if we go back to 1881, art was also thriving south of the river. A young man named William Rossiter had set out on a mission to bring art and education to the people, albeit without the religious element. Rossiter was himself an artisan who originally worked for his father making luggage, but he took himself to a working men's college and became a teacher and a prolific author of textbooks. In 1868, he became manager of the South London Working Men's College in what is now Southwark, but in 1878 moved to a building in Kennington, not many miles from where we started in Vauxhall Gardens. A man in a hurry, he raised funds to add a free library and in no time had added paintings to the walls, turning it into the South London Fine Art Gallery.

Rossiter and his wife were committed to the people of South London, and when the Council took on the role of providing libraries, they moved to Battersea and then to Camberwell. Driving his project into ever more deprived areas, Rossiter talks of having cabbage stumps thrown at him by local youths. He describes the development of each gallery as three months of dread, six months of suffering and three months of gradual recovery.[172] In 1884, he appointed a formidable assistant who knew how to increase her visitor figures:

> If a poor little ragged monkey, seven or eight years of age, dressed in a pair of tattered trousers, part of a shirt and one brace, looks in at the door, he is asked to come in; he looks curiously and is again invited, and then Miss Oliver goes and pulls him in.[173]

The visitor figures showed that her methods worked. Before she arrived, the number for 1881 was 27,000, and by 1887 they had achieved 86,500, albeit in different premises.[174] Directors of today's galleries might learn from Miss Oliver.

Rossiter realised that his vision demanded a permanent, purpose-built gallery. He brought into play such prominent figures as Alfred Leighton, Burne-Jones and G.F. Watts, and although there were many difficulties on the way, a new gallery was opened in May 1891. Unfortunately for Rossiter, the gallery was only completed with help from Camberwell Council and a very long-suffering builder. After an interminable saga, Leighton, who was the chairman, showed considerable skill in human resource management by pensioning off Rossiter and Miss Oliver, who had both become impossible to manage. The building's debts were paid, and the South London Art Gallery was taken over by what is now Lambeth Council.

The work of the Barnetts and the Rossiters led to an explosion of art in the East End and South London. At a time when the economy was entering the depression of the 1880s, and with the East End losing industries and jobs, middle-class philanthropists were treating the area as an anthropological experiment. Toynbee Hall, which was opened in 1883, attracted young men from Oxford, while the Woman's University Settlement in Blackfriars brought Cambridge students from Girton and Newnham. The Victorian precursors to today's students were spending their gap year in the East End. They did not need to travel far to see Third World poverty.

Both South Kensington and the National Gallery were attracting people from all classes, but for nearly twenty years, the East End and South London were the centre of contemporary art. Baedeker stated, in 1892, that the Whitechapel show, "generally contains some of the best works of modern English artists, and now ranks among the artistic 'events' of the year." The Bethnal Green museum had opened in 1872, attracting over 900,000 people in the first six months. The Southwark and Lambeth Free Loan Exhibition drew 32,000 visitors in 1894, while a year later Mansfield House in East Ham had 100,000 in only four weeks. In 1886, the Bermondsey Settlement had 12,000 visitors.[175] Given the location of these exhibitions the great majority of visitors will have been from the working classes.

But the most popular attraction was the result of a novelist's imagination. Walter Besant, whose career included a chair in mathematics and the presidency of the Rabelais Society, was a keen walker whose outings took him to the East End. Walking through Hackney, Whitechapel and Bethnal Green, he, "understood that one of the things very much wanted in this great place was a centre of organised recreation, orderly amusements, and intellectual and artistic culture."[176] He then set about writing *All Sorts and Conditions of Men,* in which a rich heiress goes to live in a boarding house in Stepney, incidentally changing her name to Kennedy as part of her disguise. Here she meets a young man who had been born in Stepney, was adopted by the aristocrat Lord Jocelyn Le Breton and is now intent on devoting his life to the poor. Between them, they come up with the idea of a Palace of Delight that would provide a concert hall, a picture gallery, a library, a skating rink and lecture halls.

The novel was published in 1882, and Queen Victoria, cheered on by a crowd of 5,000 East Enders, opened the People's Palace in June 1887 – an extraordinary example of a novel leading to action as it had encouraged a number of people to raise funds in order to realise Besant's dream. The People's Palace was an enormous building. With lecture rooms, a swimming pool, a gymnasium and exhibition space, it only lacked the Palace of Delight's skating rink. Yet again the East End featured in Baedeker when he recommended the People's Palace as one of London's key buildings.

The temporary art shows drew large crowds, with 310,000 attending the six-week show in 1890.[177] But Besant had no illusions about solving poverty:

> Let me say a few words as to what this Palace may or may not do. In the first place, it can do nothing, absolutely nothing, to relieve the great fringe of starvation and misery which lies all about London, but more especially at the East End. People who are out of work and starving do not want amusement, not even

of the highest kind; still less do they want University extension. Therefore, as regards the Palace, let us forget for a while the miserable condition of the very poor who live in East London; we are concerned only with the well fed; those who are in steady work, the respectable artisans and the petits commis, the artists in the hundred little industries which are carried on in the East-end.[178]

But a report in *The Echo* in 1891 describes the efforts to open the Palace to the poor by giving away tickets:

Every evening some 1,500 had free entrance, and of these 1,400 were chronic sufferers from the most abject poverty. In fact more poor people have visited the Palace during the past three weeks than in any previous months. Even the children came. Numbers of youngsters from the poorest slums trooped in to such an extent that it was on some evenings necessary to place a limit on the inflow…Children-like they wanted to see the pictures.[179]

Besant had a clear vision that put recreation above education. When it was proposed that there should be no drinks in the Palace, his response was, "we might as well resolve that drink shall not be sold to the members of the House of Commons, and expect them to instantly close their cellars."[180] In later years, he regretted that, "unfortunately a polytechnic was tacked on to it; the original idea of a place of recreation was mixed up with a place of education."[181]

The People's Palace survived a major fire in 1931, but a replacement People's Palace eventually closed in 1956 and the remaining buildings were sold to Queen Mary College, which at that time was part of the University of London. By 1918, *All Sorts of Conditions of Men* had sold a quarter of a million copies. Besant had been accused by critics of creating an unrealistic novel, but he happily confessed to being, "a profound optimist." The realistic pessimism of George Gissing and Thomas Hardy may have ensured their place in the canon of English literature, but Besant's incurable optimism delivered healthy sales and the People's Palace.[182]

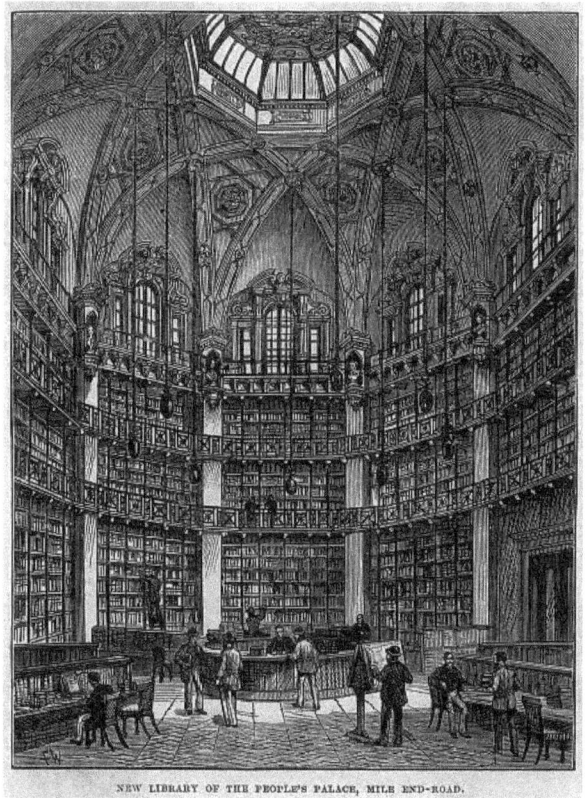

The Library of the Peoples Palace 1888

The final exhibition that warrants attention was the annual show staged at the Guildhall Gallery. Located in the City, the Gallery held a series of free exhibitions starting in 1890. These stayed open till seven in the evening and were open on Sundays. Although attracting 3 million visitors up until 1907, the location of the gallery was unlikely to attract a working-class audience. Borzello comments that despite their best efforts, the audience were, "art lovers and the educated."[183] Across the East End and South London, men, women and children were going in large numbers to see contemporary art. We have two strong primary sources showing the class of these gallery-goers. Firstly, the location of the galleries in the most deprived districts of London would put off all but the most determined middle-class visitor, despite Baedeker's praise for Whitechapel. If we take Charles Booth's estimate of 35% of those living in the East End in 1889 being in abject poverty, plus the impact of the Great Depression from 1873 to 1896, we have appalling deprivation.

The second primary source is the contemporary descriptions of the visitors to the galleries, though Borzello correctly cautions that the portraits of the poor visiting the galleries, "have been filtered through upper-class eyes. The poor themselves have left no reports."[184] The descriptions of visitors indicate that the great majority were in work, and the opening of the galleries till 10.00 in the evenings and on Sundays provides evidence of this demographic. There are occasional portraits of the very poor, such as those who were given free entry to the People's Palace or the children being pulled off the street in South London by the formidable Miss Oliver, but they were a minority. Newspaper pictures of crowded galleries show working men and their families in their best clothes perusing the paintings.

Mrs. Barnett's description of two girls who were, "hatless and sharing a shawl and who might not be living the worst life but if not were low down enough to be familiar with it," and her statement that the majority of visitors were, "home loving artisans," provide an accurate picture of the gallery-goers. The evidence clearly shows that many people who were working long hours and living in dreadful conditions chose to spend their limited free time visiting exhibitions.

In the next chapter we shall explore the world of leisure and nail the lie that people in the past had little to do in their free time.

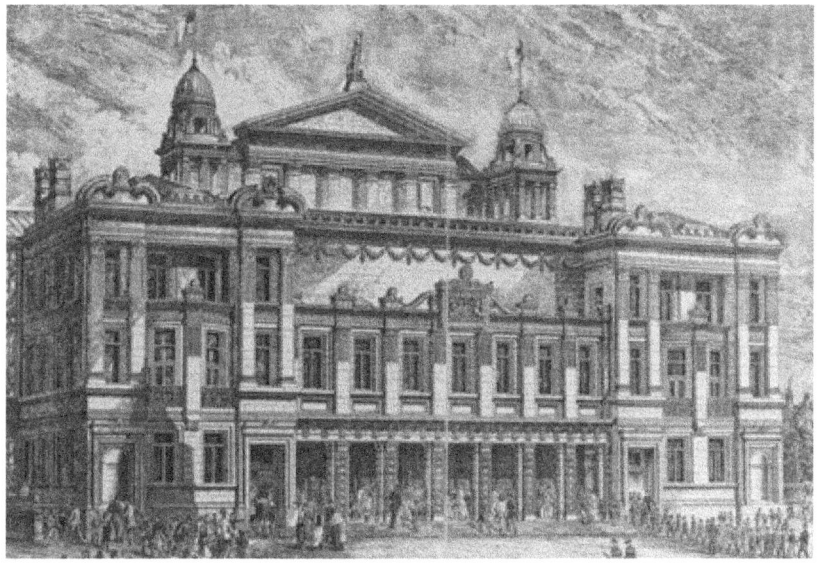

The People's Palace

Chapter 5

Leisure

We shall now take a break from art and lay to the rest the widespread belief that before cinema, radio and television people only went to art galleries because they had nothing to do in their leisure time. Not so. Outside the home, there was a rich range of leisure activities. With the decline of mining and the heavy industries in the 1980s, the number of working-class people taking part in activities outside work today is a fraction of those active in the 1880s. Today there are just over 500 brass bands in England: in 1887 there were 40,000.[185]

In the 18th century, work in the countryside was harsh and unremitting, but there were a significant number of holidays. The wakes, the fairs and the Christian holidays all added up to a surprising number of days off work. When workers moved off the land into the factories, they took with them the traditions of the wakes and fairs. In 1771, Josiah Wedgewood, deplored his inability to fulfil an order because of 'Stoke Wakes'. Five years later, he again complained, "Our men have been at play four days a week it being Burslem Wakes."[186]

Industrialisation eventually led to a reduction in the number of such holidays, but the tradition of St. Monday, when as we saw the National Gallery was full of families, lasted into the second half of the 19th century. St. Monday was an early version of work-life balance when workers would take time off if they had earned enough to keep their families and enjoy some leisure. At times of labour shortages and high wages, in 1864, a Birmingham factory inspector was writing that:

> ...an enormous amount of time is lost, not only by want of punctuality in coming to work in the morning and beginning

again after meals, but still more by the general observance of 'Saint Monday', which is shown in the late attendance or entire absence of large numbers on that day. One employer has on Monday only 40 or 50 out of 300 or 400.[187]

The leisure activities that had a rural history were often brutal and violent. Cock-fighting, bull running and bear baiting were all common. If you are a cricket fan, next time you go to a Test Match at Headingley, look out for the castellated entrance to the Leeds Bear Pit as you walk up from the station. The Society for the Prevention of Cruelty to Animals was founded in 1824, and after the 1835 Cruelty to Animals Act, these sports became illegal.

Cruel sports were not limited to animals. Bare-knuckle boxing and violent forms of football were also popular. The traditional Shrove Tuesday football match in Derby attracted up to one thousand players fighting for the ball, while workers often abandoned work to watch prize-fights on which vast sums were wagered. Boxing was especially popular with the literary set. In 1860, both Dickens and Thackeray watched one of the last bare-knuckle fights before the introduction of the Queensbury Rules, when the English champion, Tom Sayers, and the American champion, John Heenan, went to forty rounds before the match was declared a draw.

The rural fairs and wakes slowly declined, but four factors led to an increase in leisure activities across all classes. In 1851 the number of people living in towns and cities overtook those in rural areas, creating a large market for commercial leisure. At the same time, there was an increase in wages as the Hungry Forties receded and the great period of Victorian prosperity took off and per capita annual income was the highest in the world. In 1860, the average annual income in Britain was £32 6s. as against £21 1s. in France, and £13 3s. in Germany.[188] The commercial leisure market now had customers with money to spend and, with the reduction in the working week, free time to spend it. Textile workers were among the first to benefit from the introduction of half-day Saturdays when their week was reduced in 1850, but local disparities are illustrated by the fact that in the 1879–1880 football season, there were 811 matches played in Birmingham, but only 2 in Liverpool.[189]

Finally the advent of the railways opened up tremendous leisure opportunities. Just as the Lord's Day Observance Society campaigned to stop workers from visiting Canon Barnett's exhibitions on Sundays, so the wonderfully named Anti-Sunday Travelling Union managed to secure the closure of a surprisingly large number of railway services on Sundays in the 1860s.[190]

Urbanisation, increased wages, a shorter working week and the advent of the railways all added up to a leisure time boom.

As with Vauxhall Gardens in the 18th century, most of the new leisure industries in the 19th century were open to all classes. At the races, the middle classes sat in the stand, but the course and its surroundings were open to all. The railways had opened up race-going to the masses: in 1840, 25,000 spectators took the train to the races at Paisley, while in 1888, 100,000 went to watch the St. Leger in Doncaster. 'Criminals and low life types,' are highlighted in the Tate's description of William Frith's panoramic painting of *The Derby Day*, which was so popular that a barrier had to be erected to keep back the crowds when it was shown at the Royal Academy in 1858.[191]

Football, rowing and the now almost-forgotten pedestrianism all had both working-class participants and working-class spectators.

The Football Association was founded in 1863, and the first Cup Final was won by Wanderers in 1872. By 1888, 1,000 clubs were affiliated to the F.A. By 1909, 1 million people were spending Saturday afternoon watching football, and half a million were playing it.[192] The 'Beautiful Game' was here to stay.

Rowing was also a working-class sport in the Victorian era. Newcastle was a major centre for rowing, with many professional oarsmen coming from a mining background and their wages being raised in local public houses through an early form of crowdfunding. *The York Herald* of 23 February 1888 comments on the financial report to a meeting at the Joiner's Arms, "so far as monetary affairs were concerned everything passed satisfactorily plenty of money being forthcoming to support their scullers."[193] Thousands of fans lined the banks of the Tyne in May 1879, as the American champion, Edward Hanlon, defeated William Elliot of Blyth by five lengths and took home £400 in prize money.[194] Crowds of up to 130,000 paid homage to Harry Clasper, a former miner and famous oarsmen, whose funeral was held on a Sunday, "to meet the convenience of numerous bodies of working men."[195]

A popular sport that has all but vanished was pedestrianism, when walkers would try to beat the record for the number of miles walked in 24 hours. Large crowds would watch and wager vast sums as walkers, with such exotic names as the Gateshead Clipper or the Norwich Milkman, went round and round on wooden boards in large tents.[196] Road races were also popular and in 1844 were proving so dangerous that the magistrates in Northumberland ordered that a fine of 40 shillings be paid by anyone taking part in road races in Morpeth.[197]

Cricket defied the norm by being a working-class game in the south and originally middle-class in the north, but soon crossed all classes. Just as the Victorians saw art as the solution to class conflict, so cricket was viewed through a rose-coloured lens. The historian G.M

Trevelyan wrote that, "If the French noblesse had been capable of playing cricket with their peasants, their chateaux would never have been burnt."[198] Cricket has a long history, but the modern version perhaps began in 1787 with the opening of Lords Cricket Ground. The railways had a major impact, with 20,000 people attending when Nottingham played Sussex in 1835.[199]

But just as the working classes would vanish from art galleries, so a number of sports were subject to bids by the middle classes to exclude the lower orders. In 1886 the governing bodies of rowing and athletics banned professionals and anyone who was, "a mechanic, artisan or labourer."[200] In athletics, *The Times* declared that, "The outsiders, artisans, mechanics, and such like troublesome persons can have no place found for them. To keep them out is a thing desirable on every account."[201] In horse racing, a move to enclose courses and charge for entry in the 1870s at Sandown was soon followed by other courses. This inevitably led to the exclusion of the less well-off, but financial imperatives meant that even those from the working classes were granted admission if they could pay for their ticket.

For the labouring classes in the cities and towns, music hall and theatre were widespread and popular. By 1875, when the population of London was 4.2 million, there were 375 music halls.[202] In 2015, with a population of 9 million, there were only 94 grassroots live music venues.[203] As described in Chapter 3, the labouring classes flocked to the music halls. Theatre was also popular, and a description of a night at the theatre by a foreign visitor makes clear the nature of the audience:

> The most striking thing to a foreigner in English theatre is the unheard-of coarseness and brutality of the audience. The consequence of this is that the higher and more civilised classes go only to the Italian Opera and very rarely to their national

theatre…it is no rarity for someone to throw the fragments of his 'goute', which does not always consist of orange-peels alone.[204]

Cunningham quotes a piece of verse describing the antics of the audience in a Sheffield theatre:

> *To get reit into't gallera, whear we can rant an' roar,*
> *Throw flat-backs, stooans, an' sticks,*
> *Red herrins, booans, an' bricks.*
> *If they dooant play Nanca's fanca, or onna tune we fix,*
> *We'll do the best at e'er we can to braik sum o' ther necks.*[205]

In Glasgow, the audience were even more direct, throwing rivets from the shipyards to express their disapproval. As theatre became more popular in London, it spread to the poorer areas. In 1866, 63% of theatres were in the West End but 34% were in the East End.[206]

For those who could not afford the theatre, there were the Penny Gaffs. These were often no more than stand-up acts in the upstairs room of an inn with short shows based on famous crimes. At their height in the 1830s, there were 100 Penny Gaffs in London, often putting on nine shows a night. The largest held up to 2,000, and admission was 1p. or 3p. for the best seats.[207] They were especially popular with teenagers with, "a great part of the proceedings [being] indecent and disgusting, yet very satisfactory to the half-grown girls and boys present."[208]

In addition to the theatres and penny gaffs, circuses and menageries were very popular in Victorian times. Travelling circuses were originally relatively small, but by the 1840s, they had grown to include lions and elephants as well as the horses. Shrewd entrepreneurs saw an opportunity, and in the first half of the 19th century, permanent circuses were opened in London, Liverpool, Bristol and Bath, among other cities.

Menageries were originally the preserve of the aristocracy. Queen Charlotte kept elephants, zebras and one of the first kangaroos to come to Britain, but again sharp businessmen saw an opportunity. In London you could soon see every kind of exotic animal, including the rhinoceros that was immortalised by Stubbs in his famous painting of 1790. Travelling menageries also housed a wide range of specimens and toured the country attracting large crowds.

Listening to music was popular, but the number of people playing music reached its height in the Victorian era. By 1887, there were 40,000 brass bands, many of them linked to local mines and mills.[209] Similarly there were many choirs, again in the case of the Welsh Male Voice Choirs, linked to local mines. In 1895, the famous Treorchy Male Voice choir travelled to London to give a command performance for Queen Victoria.

At an individual level, many men, and it was mostly men, engaged in a range of pastimes from fishing to pigeon racing and billiards to bowls. In 1900, there were 20,000 registered anglers in Sheffield alone, and across the country, half a million pigeon fanciers.[210]

But it was the inns and alehouses where most men spent their leisure time. Every village had an inn, and in the towns and cities, there was no shortage of places to drink. In 1854, in one district in Newcastle, there was one public house for every 22 families, while Banbury was less thirsty with one for every hundred families. Charles Booth's estimated that by 1900, many working-class families were spending at least a quarter of their income on drink.[211] But the alehouses provided far more than just drink. Many provided newspapers and journals and were meeting places for football teams, Friendly Societies and even Literary and Philosophical Societies.

On a more active level, gardening grew dramatically, and for those with no land, there was the allotment. In 1845, allotments covered 2,200 acres, but by 1910 this had grown to 476,000.[212] One of the few leisure time activities to involve women, apart from visiting exhibitions, was gardening. As Margaret Willes states in her seminal book, *The Gardens of the British Working Class,* our image of working-class gardening is distorted by Helen Allingham's pictures showing idyllic cottage gardens.[213] Beyond this chocolate box image, there was an army of gardeners growing flowers and vegetables on every possible patch from allotments to window boxes.

Willes' book starts in the 16th century, but by the 18th century, gardening was well established among mill workers and miners, steelmen and shoemakers. In Paisley, the weavers favoured pinks as did the miners in Durham. In Lancashire and Yorkshire, auriculas were popular while in Nottingham, the lace workers grew roses. Tulips were grown in both the south and the north with Suffolk and London competing with Yorkshire and Lancashire. Today, the Wakefield Tulip Society, where the majority of the members were originally shoemakers, is the only one remaining and still holding its annual show with the tulips beautifully displayed in beer bottles. Even more exotic were the gooseberry shows, with entrants competing to grow the biggest and heaviest gooseberry. Two hundred years on, these only survive in Egton Bridge in Yorkshire and in a small number of villages in Cheshire.

The move from homeworking to industrialisation reduced the number of houses with gardens, and this, combined with the dreadful pollution of the Victorian city, led to a reduction in floral societies. But even in the grim alleys of the East End and among the back-to-backs of Bradford, the labouring classes still managed to grow produce that they proudly displayed. In the East End, the East Lea Amateur Horticultural Society, the East Tower Hamlets Society and the Tower Hamlets Society all met in different taverns and all competed fiercely at the annual show.

Bloomsbury, an area of great wealth and great poverty in the 1850s, was to become the centre of a new breed of gardener: the windowsill gardener. In an attempt to improve housing there was a large scale programme of redevelopment to create model housing for the working classes, but as a result the very poor, who could not afford the new rents, were driven into appalling conditions in overcrowded tenements. Little Coram Street, named after Thomas Coram of the Foundling Hospital, was a successor to the infamous Rookeries with families of ten living in a single room.

Into this deprived district came the Rev. Samuel Hadden Parkes who, like Canon Barnett, was on a mission to save the poor, but whereas Barnett favoured 'pictures which preach', Parkes promoted, "Flowers with a voice which speak of God and for God to the rudest and roughest amongst them."[214] This would not be gardening as we know it today, but 'Window Gardening.' Parkes stated that, "the condition of these people as a class is as distressed and as low as any in London" and liable to spread, "pestilential miasma" so feared by the curators at the National Gallery.[215]

He set about improving the lot of the poor and, having seen people cultivate plants on their windowsills, decided to promote flower growing across his parish. He established a flower show in 1860 which was held in the Little Coram Street Bible Mission Room and attracted 94 exhibits. Those showing were allowed free entry, but he drew over 200 visitors with adults paying 1p. and children a halfpenny.

Unlike most working-class leisure activities of the Victorian era flower growing involved the whole family and Parkes had categories for fathers, mothers and children, with the most common flowers on show being chrysanthemums, fuchsias and dahlias. By 1863, Parkes had persuaded the wealthy residents of Bloomsbury to allow his show to take place in Russell Square Gardens where, according to him, "it would be a boon to the poor, and would in a great measure ensure the success of these flower shows if they could be held in the larger squares of London."[216] The show was a triumph with over 3,000 visitors, and the Earl of Shaftesbury presented the prizes. Parkes records that:

> ...there were plants grown in areas by domestic servants; in the mews by the wives and children of stablemen; in the garrets by poor seamstresses, in kitchens by watercress girls; in first and second floors by costermongers; in any imaginable nook and corner by the children of National and Ragged Schools, and one even in the sick ward of the parish workhouse.[217]

The shows became famous and were replicated across London, with the Royal Horticultural Society planning an, "exhibition of plants grown by the working classes of London" at their summer show in Kensington.[218] Parkes went on to publish *Window Gardens for the Poor* and *How to Grow a Plant and Win a Prize* before moving to a new parish in Sussex, but he left a legacy of flower shows in some of the most deprived areas of London.

Today, when libraries are under threat of closure, it is useful to be reminded of their growth in the 19th century. There were several types of library, ranging from the subscription to circulating to the many libraries in miners' clubs and mechanics institutes. The subscription libraries – such as Mudie's in London, which by 1861 had a stock of 180,000 – had a largely middle-class membership, though the Liverpool Library records show a large proportion of skilled tradesmen as members.[219] Circulating libraries, where it cost only 1d. to borrow a book, had larger numbers of working-class borrowers.

The libraries that were clearly the domain of the working man were those in the miners' clubs and mechanics institutes. By 1850, there were 702 active mechanics institutes, though the jury is out on the proportion of members who were working class as in some areas they were taken over by the middle classes.[220] One where the membership would certainly have been working class was the Great Western Railway works at Swindon, which by 1900 had a library of 20,000 volumes. In Carlisle, which was largely a town of working-class weavers, in 1851 the Lord Street Working Men's Reading Room had to move to a new building, having outgrown the original premises only three years after it was founded.[221] By 1854 there were 24 reading rooms for a population of only 25,000. The Public Libraries Act of 1850 allowed Councils to fund libraries for the first time, but in a twist only Parliament could create, they were not allowed to use ratepayer's money to buy books. This was abolished by the 1855 Libraries Act, when many libraries then came under Council control.

With increased literacy, bookselling grew rapidly in the 18th century. In 1700, there were 200 booksellers in 50 large towns, but by 1790, the number had grown to 1,000 in 300 towns.[222] New books were far too expensive for the working-class reader, but there was also a growth in second-hand book shops and the sale of cheap tracts. The eponymous Cheap Tract Repository Society sold two million tracts for 1/2d. or 1d. as early as 1796.[223] In 1852, the librarian at Liverpool's first public library estimated that 110,000 books had been borrowed in the first year, and these had each been read by thirteen people.[224] Reading books, either borrowed or bought, was now a national habit.

This brief excursion into the world of Victorian leisure is an attempt to nail the lie that the only reason people went to exhibitions and art galleries was because there were no other leisure opportunities. In certain areas, such as brass bands, people were more active than today, and it is clear that before the advent of cinema and television people were using their limited leisure time to great effect. Though many activities were limited to men visitors to art galleries were often made up of women and families. Some activities cost more than others, and if you were unemployed, many of the activities would be beyond your reach. But the boom in commercial leisure was accompanied by a boom in personal leisure, and for most working-class families, and especially those living in towns and cities, there were many accessible attractions in addition to exhibitions and art galleries. It is demeaning and patronising to suggest that working-class people now prefer to sit at home and watch television while only the middle classes can appreciate the nation's art, and in the conclusion we shall explore this myth.

In the next chapter we shall leave leisure, leave London and travel to Manchester. In the summer of 1857, 1.3 million people from all classes visited the Manchester Art Treasures Exhibition, enabling the great and the good to declare their city a capital of culture.

Chapter 6

The Manchester Art Treasures Exhibition 1857

Two weeks after the Art Treasures Exhibition opened, Engels wrote to Marx, "Everyone up here is an art lover just now and the talk is all of pictures at the exhibition. S'il y a moyen, you and your wife ought to come up this summer and see the thing."[225]

Manchester, 'cottonopolis', city of a thousand slums, heart of the industrial revolution, was staging the world's largest ever display of art. The local businessmen were determined to show the London elite that they too could be cultured. In only fourteen months, they leased a site, built a station, erected a magnificent iron and glass palace and filled it with 16,000 pieces of fine art. Before anyone had invented project management, this was yet another example of the Victorian ability to deliver a vision on budget and on time.

Visitors came from all over the world, but at home they came from all classes. The exhibition was open for 142 days over the summer of 1857, and 1.3 million people came to see the art, listened to Charles Halle's music and ate in the magnificent refreshment rooms, which could serve 10,000 meals a day.[226] But what made the exhibition special was the large number of working-class visitors. Thomas Fairbairn, the driving force behind the exhibition, estimated that 700,000 visitors were from the labouring classes.[227]

Manchester was determined to repudiate its reputation as a city only concerned with making money. Engels had correctly portrayed it as, "Hell on Earth."[228] In 1807, Robert Southey described the city, "a place more destitute of all interesting objects than Manchester is not easy to conceive."[229] Alexis de Tocqueville wrote that, "A sort of black smoke covers the city. The sun seen through it is a disc without rays."[230]

In 1832, 1,000 people died of cholera while 2,000 lived in basement cellars. In 1841, life expectancy in Manchester was 26.6 years, and just over ten years later, when the New Chorlton Workhouse opened with a capacity of 2,500, it was always full.[231] The statistics are overwhelming, and the life of the working classes was always precarious. As Victorian England came out of the 'Hungry Forties', the year of the Exhibition saw the world enter the first Global Recession. Four years later, Lancashire and Manchester would be hit by the effects of the American Civil War and the 'Cotton Famine'.

The business community were conscious of their reputation. They knew that Matthew Arnold considered them to be philistines, but if Arnold had taken the trouble to look more deeply, he would have found the beginnings of a highly cultured city. The businessmen of Manchester were among the first in the country to establish a range of literary and scientific societies. Manchester's Literary and Philosophical Society was founded in 1781 and was followed by the Natural History Society, the Royal Manchester Institute (RMI), devoted to art, the Botanical Society, the Statistical Society, the Medical Society and finally the Geological Society in 1838.

In 1824, the first Mechanics' Institute outside London was opened, and by 1849, its annual exhibition was attracting 100,000 visitors when the city had a population of only 200,000. The admission charge was kept at two pence, and with the exhibition open on Saturday evenings, it attracted a large working-class audience. In 1856, the number of visits reached 250,000 giving an indication of the potential audience for the Art Treasures Exhibition.

And Manchester was not just a city of talking shops. With 156 professional painters, of which 40 were women, it had more artists than any other city apart from London and Liverpool.[232]

But despite this, Manchester knew that it was looked down upon by London and the aristocracy. When Sir John Leicester set up the R.M.I., he assumed that other titled collectors would support his initiative. Not so: he was spurned by the great majority of aristocrats. Even Sir Robert Peel, whose fortune came from cotton, refused support. Whether these rejections hardened the business community is not known, but when the idea of a great exhibition was put to them, they seized upon the proposal and put their undoubted ability behind planning, financing and delivering the world's largest exhibition of fine art.

On 26 March, 1856, a group of businessmen, Liberal in politics and Unitarian in faith, met in the Mayor's parlour. Within weeks, they had raised £74,000 to underwrite the exhibition. Determined to keep the credit for Manchester, the organisers turned down offers of money from people who were not Mancunians. Although they accepted his paintings for the exhibition, the committee rejected an offer of money from Sir John Boileau, who lived in Norfolk, writing to him that, "The Committee do not feel that there is any necessity for extending their guarantee fund and it has been hitherto almost exclusively confined to local residents."[233] Offers even came in from France and were similarly rejected. In a talk on the exhibition to the Historical Society of Lancashire and Cheshire, George Scharf tells of a French donation of £200 that was rejected on the grounds that they would only accept donations of £500 or more. "Telle est ici abundance de l'or; tel est l'orgeuil du riche," commented a friend of the potential donor (Such is the abundance of gold; such is the pride of the rich.)[234]

Learning from Sir John Leicester's experiences the committee went straight to the top. On 2 July, the Mayor led a delegation to

Buckingham Palace to seek support from Prince Albert. He not only gave his whole-hearted support but offered to lend pictures from both his and the Queen's collections. The very next day he wrote to Lord Ellesmere, President of the General Council of the Exhibition, putting his support in writing and emphasising his wish for the exhibition to be educational:

> The national usefulness might, however, be found in the educational direction which may be given to the whole scheme. No country invests a larger amount of capital in works of Art of all kinds than England, and in none, almost, is so little done for Art-education![235]

To add to the delight of the committee members, the Prince gave permission for them to use his letter when seeking support from others, and this time offers of paintings from private collections were overwhelming. Dickens went so far as to complain about, "an unwarranted sort of pressure," on private collectors. In *Household Words*, he wrote:

> Will you incur the odium of refusing your countenance, and your cherished valuables, to a glorious enterprise that is to awaken the million to a sense of the beautiful in Art? Will you refuse what Royalty itself has granted? Have you the courage to despise the noble example of His Grace of This or of My Lord That?[236]

George Scharf, who was in charge of the Old Masters and who would go on to be Director of the National Portrait Gallery, wrote that:

> ...my chief point of regret, however, as having impaired the tone of the gallery of ancient masters, was the rigid determination of the Committee to retain and hang whatever pictures had

actually arrived at the building. Had I been permitted to act upon my own judgement in this respect, I would at once, and unhesitatingly, had returned at least *three hundred pictures*.[237]

Although Scharf was overwhelmed by the offers of support, there were some conspicuous exceptions. Blenheim, Hamilton Palace, Bridgewater Gallery and several more notable collections were all absent. Even as early as 1857, the National Gallery found 'insuperable obstacles' preventing it from lending any paintings. Liverpool was apparently able to be most generous, and *The Art Journal* praised northern businessmen for their support of modern art, "The potentates of Lancashire live on in solid prose, and yet are magnificent in Art."[238]

In his guide to the Exhibition, Thomas Morris noted that:

> It is not pretended that the appeal was successful in every individual instance; we believe there was a single exception, but it was one at which Manchester can well afford to smile, being largely on the credit side of the account. Our fellow citizens, at a cost of about £6,000, last year erected a statue to the memory of the late Duke of Wellington, and it might, without any extraordinary flight of imagination, have been supposed that his successor would embrace this as a favourable opportunity for recognizing the compliment. However the writer has seen nothing announced from Apsley House.[239]

The original idea for the exhibition came from a Mr. Deane who had been Assistant Secretary to the Executive Committee of the 1853 Dublin Exhibition. He suggested the idea to Thomas Fairbairn who had been a commissioner of the 1851 Great Exhibition and who was a prominent Manchester businessman. Fairbairn became chair of the Executive Committee and was the driving force behind the success of the Exhibition. He worshipped at Mrs. Gaskell's Unitarian

Chapel but was a harsh employer and led engineering firms across the country in an attempt to break the newly formed Amalgamated Society of Engineers. In a long-running dispute, he wrote letters to *The Times,* under the pseudonym of Amicus, trying to show that supporting the union would harm both management and the workers. The employers eventually starved the workforce back to work after a four-month lock-out.

A man of contradictions, Fairbairn commissioned Holman Hunt to paint flattering portraits of himself and his family but rejected a knighthood for his work on the Exhibition. He also bought Hunt's *The Awakening Conscience,* showing a rich, young man with his mistress but brought Hunt back in 1856, and again in 1857, to re-paint her face to make her expression less painful.

One of the Committee's first tasks was to find a site. Today, if you are a Lancashire County cricket fan, you may not know that it was through the generosity of your predecessors that the Exhibition was sited on your cricket ground at Old Trafford. There was a long correspondence in the local press proposing competing sites that was only concluded with the publication of a satirical letter promoting Lower Broughton on the grounds that, "it was not flooded oftener than once a year, and then not much above the ancles [sic] and I live there."[240] The Committee were worried about air pollution and, when considering, "arial currents", decided that the solution was, "nine months in three in favour of the west."

The best site was Old Trafford, the home of Manchester Cricket Club, but the committee managed to persuade the Club to surrender their lease for two years for a sum of £1,000. Sir Humphrey de Trafford then leased the ground to the Committee on very generous terms.[241] The Committee next entered into discussions with the railway companies, who could see the opportunity to turn a clear profit. The companies offered free tickets for the Exhibition secretaries to travel round the country selecting paintings and then provided special carriages to transport the paintings to and from the Exhibition.

In a circular to potential lenders, the Committee assured, "Owners of works of Art that their contributions will be brought to the building without charge of carriage…and free of expense of any kind."[242] The Committee also praised the railways for their apparent generosity in setting their fares desiring:

> …publicly to acknowledge the very liberal spirit which has been evinced by the Railway Boards in framing a Tariff of Fares for the conveyance of Visitors to the Exhibition in 1857, and which when announced to the public, cannot fail to give entire satisfaction.[243]

Scharf took a somewhat more hard-headed approach to the Railway Companies noting that:

> …in the months of May and June the Art Treasures Exhibition at Manchester brought a clear profit to the Company of the North Western Railway of £20,000. What, therefore, must have been the profit on the whole period, if £10,000 for each of the first two months?[244]

Scharf was correct, and while the Exhibition made a surplus of £304.14s 4d, the London and North Western Railway made a profit of £50,000.[245]

A design for an iron and glass building, similar to that of the Great Exhibition, was quickly settled on. The Edinburgh company of C.D. Young, which had built the, 'Brompton Boilers', won the contract and delivered the building on time and on budget. Sadly, when the Exhibition closed, no use could be found for the building, and it was auctioned off for scrap.

The railway companies duly delivered the paintings, and when the Exhibition opened the French critic Théophile Thore stated that it was, "about on the level of the Louvre."[246] Praise indeed. The quantity and quality of the paintings was astonishing: 1,173 Old Master paintings, 689 Modern paintings, 386 British portraits, 969 watercolours, 260 Old Master drawings, 597 photographs, 1,475 engravings, 10,000 works of decorative arts, 500 miniatures, 160 sculptures and 63 architectural drawings.[247] The Exhibition contained pictures from the best private collections across the country.

In one case of creative accounting, the Committee – in league with Henry Cole – bought the entire Soulages Collection. This was a major collection of French and Italian renaissance art built up by the French lawyer Jules Soulages. When the Government refused to buy the collection for the South Kensington Museum, Henry Cole used an early form of crowdfunding to raise £11,000 from 73 contributors. The Committee of the Exhibition then agreed to buy and show the collection and then sell it to the government. Cole eventually got his money back and his paintings.[248] Sir Charles Eastlake, Keeper of the National Gallery, found himself in a similar position when his Trustees refused to let him buy Michelangelo's *The Virgin and Child with Saint John and Angels.* The painting was lent to the Exhibition by the Cabinet Minister, Henry Labouche, and as a result of its being shown, the Trustees finally relented and allowed Eastlake to buy. Since then, it has been known as *The Manchester Madonna.*[249]

The most popular paintings at the Exhibition were *The Three Maries* by Annibale Caracci, in the Old Masters section; *The Blue Boy* by Thomas Gainsborough, in the portrait gallery; and *Chatterton* by Henry Wallis, in the Modern Masters.

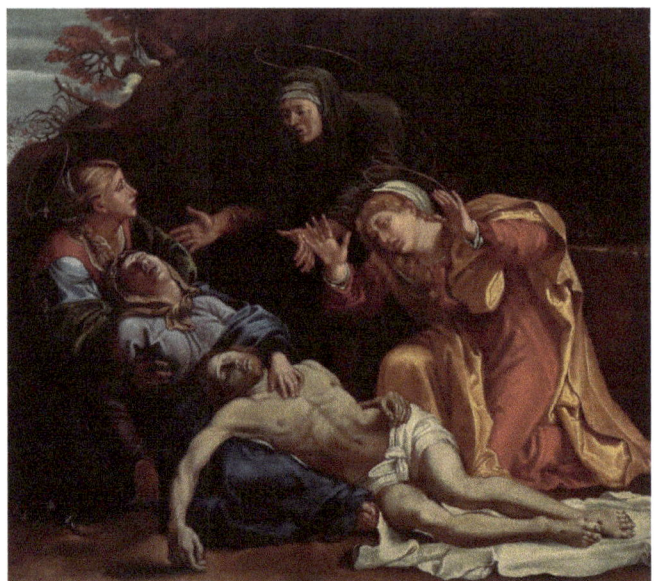

The Three Maries by Annibale Carracci

The Three Maries, was a classic piece of dramatic narrative so loved by the Victorians. It shows the three Marys, lamenting over the dead Christ following his crucifixion and at 4,000 guineas had the distinction of achieving the highest price at the Orléans sale. *The Illustrated London News* wrote that, "Crowds of people congregate round it the livelong day; and everybody goes away with the impression that it is one of the most marvellous representations of overwhelming, heart-rending affliction he ever beheld."[250] Scharf was less impressed with the learning of the crowds:

> This picture obtained from the first a most remarkable amount of popularity with the visitors to the exhibition, although I am afraid it is but a proof of the gregariousness of large assemblies and the readiness with which the general mass of people follow that which a few bold mouths praise.[251]

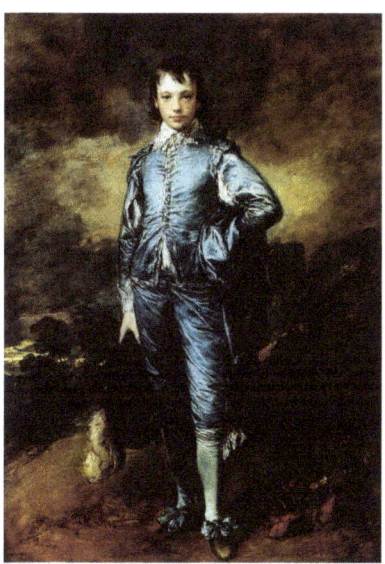

The Blue Boy by Thomas Gainsborough

The art world is always enlivened by artistic feuds: Ruskin v Whistler, when Ruskin attacked Whistler's *Nocturne in Black and Gold: The Falling Rocket* and accused him of, "flinging a pot of paint in the public's face." Turner v Constable, when they were hung side by side in the Royal Academy in 1832 and Turner outshone Constable by adding a bright red buoy to his seascape *Helvoetsluys* the day before the show opened. So at the Art Treasures Exhibition, Gainsborough's *The Blue Boy* gave the visitors the opportunity to see if his rejection of Reynolds' view that blue should never be dominant was successful. The portrait was given pride of place in the gallery, and as Scharf noted, "Gainsborough burst upon the world by means of this exhibition in quite a new phase."[252]

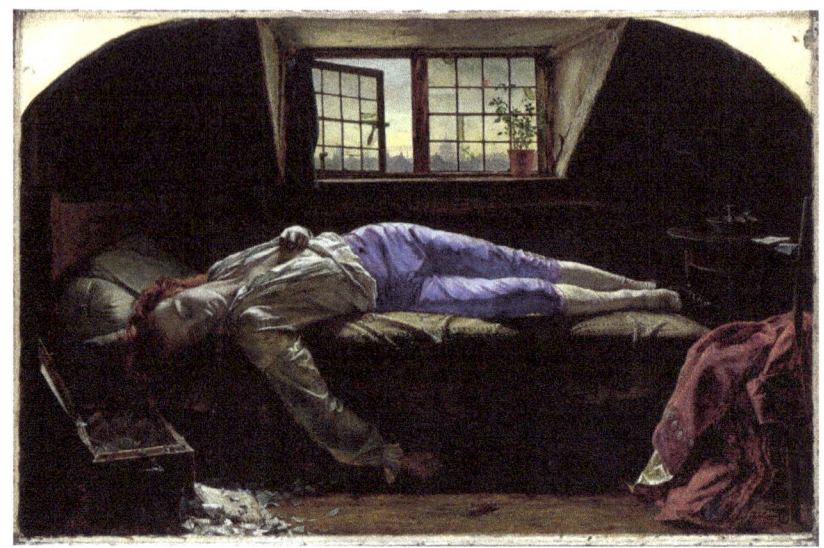

The Death of Chatterton by Henry Wallis

The most popular of all the paintings was *Chatterton*. Painted by Henry Wallis, it is a portrayal of the death of the poet Thomas Chatterton, who at the age of seventeen committed suicide by swallowing a phial of arsenic. To add to the drama, Wallis added a quote from Marlowe's *Dr. Faustus*, "Cut is the branch that might have grown full straight And burned is Apollo's laurel bough", and the painting was so popular that it had to be protected by two policemen. Although not a member of the Pre-Raphaelite Brotherhood, Wallis followed their overtly realistic style to the extent that Bobby Shuttle wrote in his pamphlet of his wife leaning across to straighten the covers on Chatterton's bed. The painting led to a correspondence in the *Manchester Guardian* in which it was stated that the painting was popular with the lower classes,[253] and for once, Ruskin agreed with the masses, describing it as, "faultless and wonderful; a most notable example of the great school."[254]

The Exhibition was not only the largest ever but had a major impact on the art world. George Scharf hung the Old Masters in chronological order which was a daring innovation. You could walk down the south gallery comparing works of the same period from France, Germany and the Netherlands.[255] The display of modern works also had a major impact. Sixty years later, Roger Fry, the most influential critic of his generation, wrote that the combined forces of the exhibition and Ruskin's address on *The Political Economy of Art,* which he gave in Manchester, "were the Mere Tekel [premonition of doom] of the orgy of Victorian Philistinism."[256]

Ruskin had been invited to visit the Exhibition and to give a talk at the Manchester Athenaeum. Expecting praise, the local businessmen who were not familiar with Ruskin's abrasive style must have regretted inviting him. He took the opportunity to berate the business community for the promotion of laissez-faire economics and more cruelly for mounting a temporary exhibition, decrying it as an ephemeral event – no more than a Victorian version of today's pop-up shows.[257] As Théophile Thore, the prominent French critic, presciently declared, "All this brought together yesterday, will be dispersed tomorrow."[258]

But apart from the size of the collection, what made the Art Treasures Exhibition exceptional was the spread of visitors from European royalty to English mill workers. The visitors covered all classes, but it was only the middle-class visitors who recorded their impressions. One of the most regular visitors was the novelist Mrs. Gaskell, who lived less than a mile from the Exhibition. Just as Engels had implored Marx to bring his wife, so Mrs. Gaskell wrote to her publisher, George Smith, "Hoping that you and Mrs. Smith will come and pay us a visit before our beautiful exhibition is closed. It is your bounden duty to come to see the Art Treasures."[259] The previous day she had visited the Exhibition for the first time with her friend Harriet Beecher Stowe and was entranced by the displays. Then in July, she is writing to Charles Norton, the first professor of art history at Harvard, telling him to come and see the Exhibition and hear Ruskin speak.

But eventually Mrs. Gaskell was worn out with taking friends round the Exhibition and turning her home into a guest house. As the summer drew on, she wrote, "we have two rooms and nineteen people coming to occupy them… we are worn out with hospitality." By September, she was telling Charles Norton, "I am very much tired… there comes a ring and there comes a caller. Our house has been fuller than full, day and night since you left… everyone will want to see the Exhibition before it closes."[260]

Gladstone and Disraeli both came, and Gladstone wrote:

> Off at 8. Reached Manchester at 11 and spent the day till 5 at the Exhibition: a wonderful sight materially, and not less remarkable morally, but bewildering to the mind & exhausting to the eye from vastness when viewed wholesale: it ought to be visited in compartments.[261]

Holman Hunt agreed with Gladstone's views and suggested to Ford Maddox Brown that he take a week to see the Exhibition.[262]

But it was the working classes who made up the majority of the visitors. As Thomas Fairbairn noted, more than half the 1.3 million visitors were from the working classes.

The Art Treasures Examiner, which was the official journal of the Exhibition, gives exhaustive lists of the numbers who came on factory outings. The largest of these was when Titus Salt brought his entire workforce from his mill at Saltaire plus the mill bands. The *Bradford Observer* reported that the party of 2,500 required three long trains and that, "The journey both ways was performed without accident or contretemps of any kind and all parties seem to have thoroughly enjoyed themselves."[263] *The Art Treasures Examiner* notes that the visitors, "all attired in their Sunday best…entered the Exhibition in an orderly manner with the bands playing *The Fine Old English Gentleman.*"[264] The workers were each given a copy of *A Peep at the Pictures*, and according to the *Bradford Observer*, "Mr. Salt was unceasing in his effort to direct the attention of the men to the more interesting pictures and works of art."[265] By chance Mrs. Gaskell and Miss Burdett Coutts, the wealthy philanthropist, were both there at the same time and, "expressed themselves delighted with the appearance and conduct of the workpeople."[266] On a different note, it would be interesting to know what the workers would have thought if they knew that 130 years later their mill would cease production and become a major art gallery devoted to David Hockney.

Nearer to home, Edward Potter – who was on the Executive Committee and who owned a calico printing works in Derbyshire – took his workforce of 800 employees. Potter, who was Beatrix Potter's uncle, wrote a letter to his employees which he gave them together with a ticket and a catalogue for the Exhibition. In his letter, Potter stated that:

> I am anxious that those of the working classes with whom I am most closely connected by the mutual tie of interest and respect, should be amongst the first to enjoy and benefit by what has been, and I hope will be for the next six months, a source of great delight and instruction to many.[267]

He then guides his workers through the Exhibition, "catalogue in hand." In the tradition of elevation and self-improvement Potter saw the Exhibition as a display of, "works which cannot prosper except amongst a free, industrious, educated, and therefore moral and religious people."[268]

The Art Treasures Examiner includes lists of outings from Thomas Fairbairn's engineering works, a glass factory in St. Helens, a sugar refinery in Liverpool on the same day as the King of Belgium and the Queen of the Netherlands, and many more excursions from mills and factories across the country. Never before or since have so many members of royalty and the working classes met and mingled under the same roof at the same time. In addition to the factory outings, *The Examiner* lists trips by working men's clubs, working men's colleges and temperance societies. Thomas Cook, whose first excursion was taking 500 people from Leicester to Loughborough for a temperance rally, put on trains from as far as Scotland to bring people to the Exhibition. On Wednesday 16 September, *The Examiner* describes how Mr. Cook, "the indefatigable manager of cheap excursions, who deserves great praise for his unwearied and successful excursions in catering for the public" brought 2,000 visitors from Scotland.[269] Perhaps Cook's most imaginative outings were his two, "Moonlight Outings" carrying over 3,000 visitors. The train would leave Newcastle at midnight, arrive in Manchester at 7.00 a.m., allow the visitors a full day at the Exhibition and then return to Newcastle at 6.00 p.m.

It is notoriously difficult to judge pricing and compare charges with today's prices. For many years, Tyers held the entrance fee to Vauxhall Gardens at 1s. to attract visitors from all classes. At the Society of Artists, they reluctantly imposed a charge of 1s. to keep out the kitchen maids and stable boys who were unlikely to buy their works. At the Art Treasures Exhibition, the standard charge was 1s. In 1857 the weekly wage of an unskilled mill worker was 10s., but skilled spinners could earn up to 25s.[270] For a period from 8 August to 12 September, the price of admission on Saturday afternoons was reduced to 6d. *The Art Treasures Examiner* notes that on 22 August, 20,610 visitors took advantage of the reduced price compared with an attendance of 10,362 on the previous Saturday, when the price had been 1s. The Executive Committee discontinued the reduced charge on the grounds that it, 'did not justify' being continued, presumably because they were getting enough visitors at the full price.[271] On the last week of the show, a record high of 29,160 was achieved on Tuesday 13 October, with people not wanting to miss the show before it closed on the final Saturday.

As with Vauxhall Gardens and the exhibitions in London, it is unlikely that the very poorest in society, or the residuum, were able to attend. However, given that the majority of train trips were from industrial towns and cities and that the Exhibition took place during a period of relatively high wages, it seems safe to assume that Thomas Fairbairn's estimate of 700,000 working-class visitors is correct.

That large numbers of working-class visitors came and saw the Exhibition is not in question. The key question is whether they would have come if their employers had not given them a day off work and paid for their tickets. One way of examining whether the working classes came to the Exhibition of their own accord is through the sale of catalogues and guides. At an early stage in planning the Exhibition, the Executive Committee made a controversial decision to have neither labels nor lectures in order to boost the sales of the official catalogue. Sales of the catalogue were indeed healthy, with 154,668 being sold at 1 shilling, but an unintended consequence of not having labels was a proliferation of unofficial guides.

These were written for every class of visitor, but many were specifically aimed at the working classes. The official catalogue, and a series of handbooks on each genre, reprinted from the *Manchester Guardian,* were written by experts such as George Scharf and gave full descriptions of the works of art. Next in the hierarchy of guides came Dr. Waagen's A *Walk through the Exhibition.*[272] Waagen was

Director of the Royal Picture Gallery in Berlin, but he had also catalogued the art in private collections throughout Britain in three magisterial volumes entitled *The Treasures of Art in Great Britain*. Waagen and others recognised the impossibility of taking in the whole Exhibition, and his guide was:

> ...not for the small number of connoisseurs, but for the larger proportion of lovers of art who seek both pleasure and instruction within the walls of the Exhibition...Moreover, [the visitor] will gain time by not being obliged to select for himself from this accumulation of objects what is most worth seeing.

Waagen's language was somewhat prolix and flowery, and the upmarket reviewer in the *Athenaeum* took him to task for using 'Wardour Street slang', the language of the antique dealers and art shops in Wardour Street.[273]

There were then a series of guides that were clearly aimed at the working classes. The most popular guide, *A Peep at the Pictures*, aimed, "to point out those pictures which from their subject, seem most likely to interest the working classes."[274] This guide highlighted such works as *The Three Maries*; told visitors not to miss *Chatterton*, despite the crowds surrounding it; and advised people to look carefully at *The Blue Boy* and judge for themselves whether Gainsborough, refuting Reynold's advice on the use of blue, "undertook to make it look well."[275] Recognising the enormity of the Exhibition, the anonymous author gives his readers a break from paintings, "You must by this time be tired of looking at pictures, so take a turn in the nave, and examine the sculpture."[276] *A Peep at the Pictures* was not an official guide, but copies were sent to Thomas Cook to give to his customers and the workers from Saltaire were each given a copy. It ran to three editions and sold at least 30,000 copies.[277]

Similar guides were Jerrold's *How to See the Art Treasures Exhibition,* which conducted the visitor through the Exhibition, "on a systematic plan."[278] More detailed but still only costing 2 pence was Thomas Morris's *The Painters and their Works with a biographical dictionary of 400 of the Painters.*[279] Finally, and for only one penny, *What To See And Where To See It or the Operatives Guide to the Art Treasures Exhibition* was, "Dedicated to the Working Classes of Lancashire and Yorkshire."[280] Recognising that, "the working man and his family appeared somewhat bewildered and dazzled by the immensity of the building and by the vastness of the number of paintings," the writer offers, "to the working class, and others, some brief hints as to the most interesting objects in the Exhibition and the place in which they may be found." In concluding, he, "hopes that should this unpretending *brochure* guide a few of the working classes to more enjoyment than they would have had without it, the writer will have gained his purpose."[281]

Finally there were guides written in local dialects, which were both instructive and amusing. *A Peep at t'Manchester Art Treasures Exhebishan by* Tom Treddlehoyle[282] and *Bobby Shuttle and his Woife Sayroh's Visit to Manchester un-th Greight Hert Treasures Palace Owd Traffort* were priced 4 pence and 6 pence, but unfortunately, we have no figure for sales.[283] Tom Treddlehoyle was the fictional creation of the local poet Charles Rogers. Using humour to guide the workers round the exhibition, Tom speaks of the effect of entering the magnificent buildings:

> It look az if ide gotten into an enchanted street, craaded wi goddesses an fairies, all white, ana't gold and silver ornamnets tho all pairtys a t'world wor browt together to decorate it we; an ta mack t'scene more grand t'sun shone thru t'crystal roof e dubble lustre while t'grand organ at t'far end glittered like a gate a gold on diamonds shewin t'way to sum still grander

plaice. Hev in cumpazed me astonishment a bit, ah moved on ta look at T' Sculpture.[284]

The publication of these guides by commercial printers indicates a market of working-class visitors who came to the Exhibition of their own volition. There were undoubtedly bulk sales of *A Peep at the Pictures* to employers bringing their workers, but they were a small number of the estimated total of 700,000 working-class visitors.

But once they arrived, after enjoying the train journey and buying their guides, did the workers admire the paintings and enjoy their visit? Were they educated and elevated? The evidence depends on whom you ask. Nathaniel Hawthorne, the American novelist, saw entranced workers; Dickens saw bored visitors.

Hawthorne's comments may be more reliable as he came and stayed with Mrs. Gaskell and made over ten visits whereas Dickens only came up from London for the day. Hawthorne, writing about a Saturday when the price was reduced, stated that, "The Exhibition was thronged with a class of people who do not usually come in such large numbers. It was both pleasant and touching to see how earnestly some of them sought to get instruction from what they beheld."[285]

Dickens decided to praise the Exhibition but deride the visitors. He states that even when the working men have been admitted free that as soon as they can, they go off to Knott Mill Fair or Belle Vue Gardens. He is especially hard on a group from a factory who apparently did not even stay for lunch, but he is equally dismissive of the middle classes, "the majority of the well-dressed crowd gossiped and grouped round the music, promenaded and looked and admired each other, did everything, in short, except examine the pictures."[286] In a letter to a friend, Dickens wrote somewhat patronisingly, "The care for the common people made for their comfort and refreshment, is also admirable and worthy of commendation. But they want more amusement, particularly (as it strikes me) *something in motion*, though it were only a twisting fountain. The thing is too still after their lives of machinery; the art flows over their heads in consequence."[287] It is hard to tell whether Dickens's article is based on hard evidence or the need for good copy.

'R.L.', writing in *Frasers Magazine,* took the view that on Saturday afternoons, "many of the poor, who would not otherwise have done so visited the Exhibition." While they enjoyed their afternoon, "R.L." did not think, "their knowledge would be much enlarged."[288] *The Art Journal* notes that on the occasions when they visited, the Exhibition, "was thronged with a company consisting principally of the labouring classes."[289] Scharf took the view that, "the lower and uneducated classes did not go to the Art Treasures willingly. Many went because they were told they ought to go." But when they were there, he was, "powerfully struck by the tone and manner of those among the lower classes who *did* stop to look at the paintings."[290] The *Art Treasures Examiner*, being the official journal of the Exhibition, took a very positive view, stating that, "By none we are assured, will the boon [of the Exhibition] be more highly prized than by working men."[291] In an article entitled, 'The Function of Art', the *Art Treasures Examiner* writes of, "thousands of our intelligent working people to whom the fine arts have a 'mission', which they will have first learned to recognise amid this beautiful collection, and which will continue to afford them 'a joy for ever.'"[292]

On the negative side, stories circulated that, "working people have looked in, and having walked about staring vacantly, have shrugged up their shoulders, and departed exclaiming, 'There's nowt but pictures here, let's off to Belle Vue.'" Or of, "a man sitting down gravely on one of the benches in the Grand Hall – and asking after having waited patiently for some time, 'When is the Exhibition going to start?'"²⁹³

Prince Albert's hopes of the education and elevation of the working classes may not have been achieved. The *Examiner* may have been overreaching itself in the column, 'Working Men at the Art Treasures Exhibition':

> ...a taste for the fine arts has an immediate bearing on the moral elevation of the working class. It throws an additional charm over the facilities of domestic life, and adds a silken cord to the ties that unite the family circle.²⁹⁴

Perhaps the *Art Journal* got it right when it stated:

> Still, from what we saw and heard as we mixed with them [many of the poor] in their rambles through the building, we do not think that their knowledge would be much enlarged by their visit: the majority of them would spend a pleasant afternoon, and there the benefit would end.²⁹⁵

The Victorians found it difficult to allow for enjoyment without education. In giving 1.3 million people of all classes access to the world of art, the businessmen of Manchester set the bar high, and in the next chapter, we shall see how cities and towns throughout the regions built on Manchester's success and created their own, "People's Galleries."²⁹⁶

Chapter 7

Regional Galleries

Today, self-made millionaires put their money into football clubs; in the late Victorian era, their money went into art galleries. Never before, nor indeed since, have art galleries in Britain been built and run by people with a working-class background, by people who did not go to university and by people who met and mixed with the working classes every day of their working life. The galleries were full of working-class people because the buildings and their collections were the creation of men, and it was predominantly men, from a working-class background. They had made their millions and transcended their working-class roots, but their work, their religion and their politics kept them in touch with the labouring classes.

Between 1850 and 1910, 68 new art galleries opened outside London, and this chapter tells the story of the businessmen who built the galleries, the people who visited them, the paintings they admired and the councillors and curators who ran them. As Giles Waterfield states, in his book *The People's Galleries*, the galleries, "were internationally unique in uniting the enthusiasms of civic leaders, wealthy individuals and the mass of the population to create galleries of popular art."[297]

As the Victorian era drew to a close, Birmingham and Bradford were two very different cities. One built on metal, one on wool; one with a multitude of small workshops, one with a mass of large mills. But both had working-class populations who flocked to their art galleries. In 1888 the population of Birmingham was nearly 500,000, yet there were over one million visits to the new Museum and Art Gallery.[298] In 1907, 800,000 visits were made to Cartwright Hall in Bradford when the population was less than 280,000.[299] By 1910, visitor figures were beginning to decline, but Birmingham was still achieving 800,000 visits and Bradford an astonishing 600,000. If he had lived as long as his wife, Prince Albert would have been delighted. In 2015, over one million people visited Birmingham's art gallery, but outside the big cities, galleries were closing and numbers were in decline. [300] In Bradford, with a population in 2014 of over 500,000, only 53,305 people visited Cartwright Hall, despite the sterling work to create one of the country's best cross-cultural galleries.[301]

The Businessmen

In London, the art world was still dominated by the aristocracy. Their great houses were full of works they had collected on their Grand Tours, and they consequently felt entitled to sit on the boards of the national galleries. Conlin summarises the situation, noting that, "Trustees were buying up Reynoldses and Gainsboroughs almost as quickly as aristocratic Trustees, like the 5th Marquis of Lansdowne, were selling them." To compensate for falling income on his estate, the Marquis had happily sold Rembrandt's *Mill* for a record-breaking £100,000.[302]

In her book *Stewards of the Nation's Art,* Andrea Geddes Poole examines the role of the aristocracy in controlling the National Gallery, The National Portrait Gallery, the Tate and the Wallace Collection, all of which were funded by the taxpayer. Between 1824 and 1939, the National Gallery had 70 trustees of whom 39 were aristocrats, while at the National Portrait Gallery 25 out of 67 trustees between 1890 and 1939 were of blue blood. At the Tate and the Wallace, it was a similar story.[303]

Outside London, the picture could not have been more different. Regional galleries, the great majority of which were municipal, were run by local councillors who were often local businessmen. Joseph Chamberlain – the driving force behind Birmingham's success and its art gallery and museum – despised the aristocracy, describing them as a parasitical class who, "toil not neither do they spin."[304] The grounded businessmen of the regions did not aspire to the House of Lords, and Thomas Ferens, who funded the Ferens Gallery in Hull, declined the offer of a title several times.[305] These men refused to succumb to the allure of London, and when they built galleries, they filled them with pictures that they and their workers could enjoy.

The difference between London and the regions was further emphasised by religion and politics. The businessmen were largely Nonconformists and Liberals while those dominating the London art scene were Church of England and Conservative. The Unitarian church, whose values encouraged members to work for the good of their communities, was dominated by Liberals who were a powerful force, building art galleries, museums, schools and hospitals and governing their cities with civic pride. Joseph Chamberlain was a prominent Liberal and Unitarian, and in the 1860s, the Unitarians in Birmingham provided 19 councillors and 6 mayors.[306] In Leeds, there were no Conservative mayors from 1835 till 1895, and such was the strength of the Liberals that the Unitarian Mill Hill Chapel was known as the 'Mayor's Nest'.[307]

In Manchester, the Unitarians and Liberals were equally powerful, dominating both the *Manchester Guardian* and the Council. The first museums act of 1845, with the wonderfully clear title *An Act for encouraging the Establishment of Museums in Large Towns*, was piloted through the House of Commons by two northern M.P.s: William Ewart, who represented Liverpool and then Wigan, and Joseph Brotherton, Salford's first M.P., thus enabling councils to raise money for art galleries and museums.

As we saw in the previous chapter, the London elite looked down on the northern businessmen refusing to support Sir John Leicester's initiative in establishing the Royal Manchester Institute, but they mistook their lack of education for a lack of learning. Their intellectual curiosity and thirst for knowledge led to the spread of Literary and Philosophical Societies and Mechanics Institutes across the country. By 1800, there were over 200 'Lit & Phil' societies, and by 1850, Yorkshire and Lancashire had over 700 Mechanics Institutes.[308] After the Napoleonic Wars, the middle classes were able to tour European capitals, and on their return they continued their education. Two hundred years later the Unitarian Mill Hill Chapel in Leeds still hosts Literary and Philosophical Society lectures.

The chapter on leisure noted the large number of reading rooms and libraries that were opened in the second half of the 19th century, and Tristram Hunt, in his book *Building Jerusalem,* quotes a visitor to Bradford, saying that it had, "a better stock of daily and periodical literature than some of the reading rooms, where officers of the army and navy, and gentlemen of the professions, resort in the fashionable town of Cheltenham."[309] Bradford, like many other northern cities, had a community of German immigrants, and in Bradford's case they had a major impact on both the commercial and cultural life of the city. The Bradford Germans were wealthy wool merchants who helped establish the Chamber of Commerce and formed the majority of the board at the School of Art. They invited Ruskin to give the inaugural lecture at the School of Design in 1859 and again in 1864 when they sought his advice on the design of a proposed Wool Exchange. In her book*, Little Germany: A History of Bradford's Germans,* Susan Duxbury–Neumann quotes a contemporary source who stated that, "their influence was out of all proportion to their numbers as reflected in the architectural parts of central Bradford and the rich cultural heritage they bestowed on the city."[310] The prosperous wool merchants built magnificent warehouses, and today Little Germany is a lasting legacy to their cultural taste.

Across the Pennines in Manchester, there was a similar thirst for learning where the News Room at the Manchester Exchange had 140 periodicals[311] and a lecturer on the historian Macaulay could charge 18p. entrance fee and fill a hall twice over with working men.[312] This intellectual drive was replicated across the towns and cities of the North.

But the business community lacked confidence when it came to art. From the docks of Liverpool through the cotton and woollen mills of Manchester and Bradford, to the engineering works of Leeds, they were accused by the *Leeds Mercury* of neglecting, "almost everything except the making of individual fortunes."[313] When Manchester asked a member of the aristocracy to lend his paintings to the Art Treasures Exhibition, he replied haughtily, "What in the world do you want with art in Manchester? Why can't you stick to your cotton spinning?"[314]

Engels attacked them, Matthew Arnold mocked them, Ruskin lectured them, Disraeli – seeking their votes – flattered them and only William Morris offered concrete support.

In 1842, a certain Mr. and Mrs. Engels, despairing of the bad company their son Friedrich was keeping with the Young Hegelians in Berlin, sent him to work in their relative's mill in Manchester. They might have sent him elsewhere if they had known that he would visit Marx on his way to Manchester, and so began one of the most famous partnerships in modern history. Engels worked in the offices of the Manchester mill, but was soon spending all his free time researching the lives of the poor. He formed a relationship with a radical young woman called Mary Burns, and she took him round the back streets and slums of Manchester and Salford to see the appalling conditions. In 1854 he published *The Condition of the Working Class in England.* Engels wrote that, "What is true of London, is true of Manchester,

Birmingham, Leeds, is true of all great towns. Everywhere barbarous indifference, hard egotism on one hand and nameless misery on the other."[315]

Engels did not attack the mill owners for lack of culture but for their refusal to acknowledge the appalling conditions of their workers in the workplace and at home. As he noted, the upper middle classes lived in the outer areas:

> ...and the finest part of this arrangement is this, that the members of the money aristocracy can take the shortest road through the middle of all the labouring districts to their places of business, without ever seeing that they are in the midst of the grimy misery that lurks to the right and the left.[316]

Only in the field of culture did Engels praise his Manchester hosts when he visited the 1857 Art Treasures Exhibition and wrote to Marx urging him to come and visit it.

Whereas Engels attacked the business community for their greed and the treatment of their workforce, Matthew Arnold attacked them for their lack of culture and their Nonconformist views. In *Culture and Anarchy,* published in 1869, Arnold labelled them Philistines, stating that:

> Philistine gives the notion of something particularly stiff-necked and perverse in the resistance to light and its children, and therein it specially suits our middle class, who not only do not pursue sweetness and light, but who prefer to them that sort of machinery of business, chapels [and] tea meetings.[317]

Arnold worked as a school inspector travelling across the country, and it was perhaps his hatred of his job that made him turn so unjustifiably against the business world. The business practices of many of the manufacturers and mill owners were not above criticism, but if Arnold had taken the trouble to attend a Literary and Philosophical meeting in Leeds, or a lecture at the Free Trade Hall in Manchester, he would have seen a devotion to lifelong learning that would have impressed a school inspector.

One person who both criticised and supported the business community was Ruskin. Today, if you were out walking in Oxfordshire and came across the Slade Professor of Fine Art building a road with his students, you might think that you had walked into a piece of performance art, short-listed for the Turner Prize. In 1875 this scenario was being played out in deadly seriousness. Ruskin, in pursuit of the dignity of labour, persuaded his students, who included Oscar Wilde and Arnold Toynbee, to build a road joining the villages of North and South Hinksey. Wilde wrote that:

> It seemed to him [Ruskin] to be wrong that all the best physique and strength of the young men of England should be spent aimlessly on cricket ground or river, without any result at all… He thought, he said, that we should be working at something by which we might show that in all labour there was something noble… So out we went, day after day, and learned how to lay levels and to break stones and to wheel barrows along a plank… a very difficult thing to do… and what became of the road? Well, like a bad lecture it ended abruptly… in the middle of a swamp.[318]

Professor of Fine Art and road builder, critic of capitalism and campaigner for art galleries, champion of the working class and elitist, Ruskin was a bundle of contradictions and the most influential figure in the art gallery building boom of the late Victorian era.

He toured the country constantly lecturing to businessmen and councillors. He attacked them for their business practices, criticised them for their taste and derided their exhibitions, yet still they invited him back and still he came. In Bradford, when invited to speak about the proposed Wool Exchange, he opened by saying, "I do not care about this Exchange of yours", castigated them for worshipping the 'Goddess of Getting–on', and went on to lecture them on taste and morality.[319] In Birmingham, in 1877, he met with leading councillors and then wrote in *Fors Clavigera* that while he was impressed with their good intentions, their inability to see the basic fault lines of capitalism doomed them to failure.[320] In Liverpool he was a major influence on the Liberal councillors campaigning for a civic art gallery. Local councillor James Picton met Ruskin, corresponded with him and exchanged books. Picton's campaign originally fell on stony ground and he and his fellow councillors were called 'art-maniacs' by the local press, but when the Conservative Councillor and wealthy brewer, Andrew Walker, put up the money for a new gallery, his magnificent Walker Gallery was opened to much fanfare.[321]

Ruskin was a key influence on the businessmen donating funds and collecting paintings, the councillors building the art galleries and the curators managing them. They invited him to their cities, listened to his lectures, read his works and formed Ruskin Societies while often misreading much of his message. And when not lecturing to the middle classes, he was putting his time and money into projects for working people, giving money to Octavia Hill to provide housing for the poor, opening a museum for working people in Sheffield, setting up sustainable farming communities and teaching drawing at the Working Men's College in London. Despite poor health, his energy was prodigious, and his books, his talks and his works had a major impact on art galleries throughout the regions. Kenneth Clark, Director of The National Gallery and later famous for his television programme *Civilisation*, stated that, "Poets may not be 'the unacknowledged legislators of the world' but Ruskin, like Rousseau, changed the world by a vision which has the intensity and innocence of poetry."[322]

One man whom Ruskin influenced greatly was William Morris. He said of Ruskin's *The Stones of Venice* that:

> ...in future days it will be considered as one of the very few necessary and inevitable utterances of the century. To some of us when we first read it...it seemed to point out a new road on which the world should travel.[323]

Morris crossed the country speaking in towns and cities, but promoting socialism more often than art. When he did speak on art, as when he lectured in Birmingham in 1879 on 'The Art of the People', he followed Ruskin's example and did not spare his audience saying, "I am among friends, who may forgive me if I speak rashly", and then went on to tell his wealthy middle-class audience, "I have never been in any rich men's houses which would not have looked the better for having a bonfire made outside of it of nine-tenths of all that it held."[324]

But Morris also gave generously of his time and expertise to promote art in the regions. In Birmingham, he was President of the Society of Arts in 1879, and Amy Woodson-Boulton notes the extent to which Morris's speeches formed the policies of the Birmingham Museum and Art Gallery.[325] Morris's artistic legacy is everywhere today, but his political career was less successful. Engels was correct when he said of Morris that he is, "a very rich art-enthusiast but untalented politician."[326]

A footnote in art history shows the pull of both Ruskin and Morris. In 1859 Ruskin filled a hall in Bradford at a charge of 2s.6d. while Tom Thumb, also in Bradford, could only charge 1s.[327] Similarly, in 1886, Morris was a sell-out in Birmingham despite being up against

Performing Fleas in the nearby Exchange Buildings.[328]

The Businessmen

Ruskin and Morris were both political animals, but it was a professional politician, unashamedly pursuing votes, who supported the allegedly Philistine businessmen of the North. Disraeli, who knew the power of flattery, never gave up trying to convert the Liberals of Manchester. In two speeches, he praised the local business community for their cultural acumen. Speaking in The Athenaeum in 1843, he said that, "the pages of history" have shown that, "literature and the fine arts… have ever discovered that their most munificent patrons are to be sought in the busy hum of industry."[329] The following year, on the Victorian version of a book-signing tour promoting *Coningsby*, he gave a speech entitled, "The Value of Literature to Men of Business" in which, while praising the local businessmen, he also encouraged them to look to Athens for inspiration.[330]

Disraeli even went so far as to stand against Ruskin and defeat him in the election for Lord Rector of Glasgow University at a time when the university had a parliamentary seat. On one famous occasion, Disraeli gave a three-hour speech to 6,000 people in Manchester's Free Trade Hall. We can only speculate on how many in the audience stayed awake for the full three hours, but we do know that Disraeli kept himself going by drinking two full bottles of white brandy.[331]

Five very different figures, Engels, Arnold, Ruskin, Morris and Disraeli, but all found the businessmen of the North keen to hear their words on matters cultural even if the outcome was not always as the speakers would have wanted.

Many of the wealthy businessmen whom Engels attacked and who funded art galleries, schools and hospitals have persuaded history to see them as self-made men and philanthropists, but it is a very mixed picture. They ruled with an iron rod, campaigned against the abolition of child labour and held out against strikes by starving the workforce back to work. The great majority were not self-made men. Historian Harold Perkin states that the Victorian myth of the self-made millionaire was, "one of the most powerful instruments of propaganda ever developed by any class to justify itself and seduce others to its own ideal."[332] Research into the background of Lancashire mill owners reveals that only 20% came from poor beginnings.[333] But while they were often second-generation mill owners, their roots were in working-class culture. Before moving out to their mansions in the country, some of them lived in houses in the mill complex, and they all spent their working lives close to the shop floor.

In Bradford, Samuel Lister is seen by many today as the self-made man who gave the city Lister Park and Cartwright Hall. The reality is somewhat different. His father was a wealthy mill owner who built a mill in Bradford for Samuel and his brother. The brothers were very successful, and when the mill was destroyed by fire, they replaced it with Manningham Mills, which is one of Europe's largest mills. Lister was neither self-made nor, given his tremendous wealth, a generous philanthropist. He sold the land for Lister Park to the Council for £40,000 and then provided £47,500 for Cartwright Hall, but when the costs overran, he insisted on the ratepayers footing the bill.[334] But as the owner of Manningham Mills, he was a cruel mill master. In December 1890, three weeks before Christmas, he informed his workforce that he was reducing their pay by 25%, and in so doing, he unwittingly paved the way for the formation of the Labour Party. The workforce came out on strike for 19 weeks and were denounced by Lister, saying that, "the women spend their money on dress and the men on drink, so that the begging bowl goes round and it matters not what wages are."[335] They were eventually forced back to work, but the strike resulted in the formation of the Bradford Labour Union and in January 1893, the Independent Labour Party held its first meeting in Bradford when Keir Hardie was elected as chair.

Lister's descendants have continued in his footsteps. Philip Lloyd-Greame, who married Lister's granddaughter and changed his name to Cunliffe-Lister to inherit her fortune, was President of the Board of Trade in Baldwin's Cabinet when it broke the General Strike and his son was Mrs. Thatcher's Chief Whip when she crushed the miners.[336]

Staying in Bradford, even Titus Salt, who more than most mill owners could be considered a true philanthropist, joined the special constables to fight striking workers.[337] Crossing the Pennines to Manchester, we have seen how Thomas Fairbairn, the driving force behind the Art Treasures Exhibition, was also determined to break the unions.

Further north in Paisley, Peter Coats, the chair of the cotton spinning company Coats and Clark, funded the local art gallery and hospital but also campaigned vigorously against changes to the laws on child labour. The mills have now been converted into apartments, but as late as 1960, when I worked there as an apprentice, the local people said of the hospital, "Coats built it and Coats fill't it." A more artistic connection was through Kenneth Clark, former Director of the National Gallery and presenter of the programme *Civilisation*, whose wealth came from Coats and Clark.

But many of the rich businessmen who funded art galleries were true philanthropists and none more than Thomas Ferens of Hull, a deeply religious man who left school at 13 and worked his way up to become joint chair of Reckitt and Company. He gave away £47,000 annually of his £50,000 income, and among many contributions to Hull, he paid for the Ferens Gallery.[338]

A key figure in Manchester and a true philanthropists was Joseph

Whitworth. He left school at thirteen and became an apprentice in a cotton mill. He soon discovered an aptitude for engineering and moved from Manchester to London where, among other jobs, he worked on Charles Babbage's Calculating Machine. He eventually returned to Manchester, where he invented the British Standard Whitworth screw thread. He gave £128,000 to fund scholarships in science and industry and in his will specified that his wealth should go to good causes, including the establishment of the Whitworth Art Gallery.

One man who was also a generous philanthropist, but granted his money with an unusual twist, was Edward Massey of Burnley Brewery, who contributed paintings and funds to the Art Gallery at Towneley Hall.[339] He wrote to the Mayor of Burnley offering £125,000 but added a caveat that every time the Magistrates refused to renew the license for one of his many public houses, he would reduce the sum by the value of the property. Furthermore, the money would be added to a gift he had made to Manchester University of £6,800; the university eventually received £10,386.[340] An equally shrewd brewer was Andrew Walker of Liverpool. As a Conservative Councillor, Walker was keen to become Mayor and so paid for the building of the magnificent Walker Gallery, duly became Mayor and had a fine statue of himself erected in the entrance. Other brewers who built galleries from beer were Alexander Laing, who funded the Laing Gallery in Newcastle, and Michael Bass, who paid for Derby's art gallery.

A wonderful story, whether true or false, lies behind Dundee's art gallery, which was funded by John Keiller of marmalade fame. In 1792 a Spanish ship loaded with oranges was blown off course and eventually sought refuge in Dundee harbour. Keiller's father, a local grocer, bought the distressed cargo of oranges, and his mother made them into a revolutionary new type of marmalade complete with peel and so funded Dundee's art gallery.³⁴¹

A town to benefit in a spectacular fashion was Accrington in Lancashire. In 1891, a local boy named Joseph Briggs set off to New York to seek his fortune. There he happened to meet Louis Tiffany, became his personal assistant and eventually rose to be head of the Tiffany Studios. The Great Depression forced Briggs into bankruptcy, but not before he had shipped 140 beautiful works of Tiffany back to England where on his death they were bequeathed to the people of Accrington and now form Europe's largest collection of Tiffany glass.³⁴²

These provincial galleries were designed for everyone to enjoy, but two galleries were specifically built for working people: Ruskin's St. George's Museum at Walkley near Sheffield and Horsfall's Art Museum in Ancoats in Manchester.

Ruskin, visiting Sheffield in 1875, came up with the idea of a museum located in the countryside which would inspire local workers. He bought a cottage at the top of a long road, hoping that visitors would be entranced by the beauty of the surrounding countryside as they walked away from the industrial city. He stated that, "The mountain home of the Museum of Walkley was originally chosen not to keep the collections out of smoke, but expressly to beguile the artisan out of it."³⁴³ Ruskin installed a former student from the London Working Men's College as curator, and the museum opened in 1876. It displayed a range of paintings, drawings and artefacts, including Turner's *View of Sheffield from the Derbyshire Lane*, which he presented to the museum.³⁴⁴

The collection was designed to uplift and inspire the working man after his walk from the hell of Sheffield to the heaven of the Dales. One visitor, a young grinder named Benjamin Creswick, was so inspired that he gave up his job, became a sculptor and produced among other works a bust of Ruskin which today is on display in Sheffield.[345] The museum was soon found to be too small and in 1890 moved to Meersbrook Hall, a large house outside Sheffield. In 1953 it closed, but the collection can now be seen at the Millennium Gallery in Sheffield.

Thomas Horsfall's Art Museum was, "formed for the purpose of giving effect to Ruskin's teaching."[346] He was in correspondence with Ruskin over the design and evolution of his project, and Ruskin gave him support, including writing an introduction to Horsfall's book *The Study of Beauty*. The museum opened in 1886 in Ancoats Hall, which was in one of the most deprived areas of Manchester. The museum was a success, providing music as well as lectures and in 1892 expanded to include a concert hall. There were also various entertainments in the evenings and on Sunday afternoons many activities for children. Horsfall believed firmly in the power of art to transform the lot of the working classes, but realised that other activities were necessary if he was to attract people to his art gallery. At the same time a University Settlement, based on the idea of Toynbee Hall in London, opened in 1901.

But Horsfall's vision went far beyond the power of art, and the Annual Report for 1904 stated that:

> It is not enough that in our rooms tired people may find pictures and other beautiful objects among which they may forget their weariness – or that from time to time Concerts, At Homes, and other gatherings bring the refreshment of music and good company to our neighbours...Alongside these other activities, therefore, we must develop and stimulate a healthy and vigorous sense of citizenship, which in time will find its expression in the work of our municipality.[347]

In 1918 the Art Museum was transferred to Manchester Council, and it closed in 1953. For nearly seventy years, Horsfall's Art Museum provided a northern version of Besant's People's Palace. That it survived until the early 1950s is a tribute to his vision.

The men who built these galleries and who left a wonderful legacy were therefore a mixed bunch, but for the most part, they made their fortunes through employment practices that gave Victorian industry such a bad name. Their aim in funding art galleries was often straightforward egotism, demonstrated in the many portraits of Victorian worthies now languishing in the stores of regional galleries. As with their London counterparts, they also believed that art would improve the working classes, teach them about design, lead to less social division and create beauty to counter the industrial environment. But, perhaps more than in London, they simply wanted to give their workers something they could enjoy. Councillor Robert Crawford, the driving force behind Glasgow's magnificent Kelvingrove Art Gallery, spoke for many a Victorian benefactor when he simply said that good art, "provided pure enjoyment of the loftiest order."[348]

The Visitors

The Victorians were great statisticians and conscientiously counted the number of people visiting their art galleries. In many cases, they even installed turnstiles to ensure that their figures were correct. Thomas Greenwood noted approvingly, when visiting Birmingham, that the numbers, "can be accurately told, as there are registering turnstiles with which there can be no tampering."[349] Unfortunately their statistics did not break down visitor numbers by class. We still have to rely on descriptions by mainly middle-class observers, but when the visitor numbers are set alongside the local population figures, it is possible to surmise that large numbers must have been from the labouring classes.

Two key primary sources are Thomas Greenwood's book *Museums and Art Galleries*[350] and Howarth and Platnauer's *Directory of Museums in Great Britain & Ireland, Together with a Section on Indian and Colonial Museums*.[351]

Greenwood was a Fellow of the Royal Geographical Society and wrote extensively on museums, art galleries and libraries. He was a self-made man in the Victorian mould. Leaving school aged 11, he went to work on W.H. Smith's bookstall at Stockport Station. By age nineteen, he was a salesman for a Sheffield hardware company, and this role allowed him to develop his passion by visiting museums and art galleries on his travels. His next job was as a librarian from where he took the step of founding a chain of business journals covering every trade from *The Hatter's Gazette to The Gas Fitter's Journal*. He campaigned extensively for free libraries, becoming known as, "the apostle of the free library movement."[352] *Museums and Art Galleries*, published in 1888, gives statistics for 166 museums and art galleries from municipal to privately owned and from those in schools to universities. In this work, he provides a fascinating commentary, and many of his ideas would seem modern today.

Elijah Howarth was curator at Manchester and Henry Platnauer at York, and both were instrumental in setting up the Museums Association in 1887. Their directory, which was commissioned by the Association and published in 1911, covers a wide range of museums and art galleries, listing visitor numbers alongside population statistics.

There is no reason to doubt Howarth and Platnauer's figures, as when they could not get reliable statistics from turnstiles, they visited museums to substantiate numbers. However, the present day numbers need to be treated with caution when compared with the figures for 1911. There have been significant changes in the world of both museums and art galleries since 1911 and many figures for the early period refer to buildings that no longer exist and have been replaced by modern galleries. In 1888 and 1911 it was also difficult to gauge the public's appetite for art as many of the museums and art galleries were joint enterprises. It is not easy to state whether visitors to Nottingham Castle Museum and Art Gallery went to see the pictures or the biggest stuffed gorilla in the country, and elsewhere did the dinosaurs detract from the drawings? Repeat visits can also give a false impression, though Greenwood takes the view that this is doubtful during holidays, when galleries were packed, "as holidaymakers were not likely, in any large percentage, to call twice in one week."[353]

Despite the caveats required by statistics, it is possible to draw conclusions from Howarth and Platnauer's alignment of visitor numbers with population numbers in many towns which were predominantly working class, such as Burnley, Bury and Bradford. Before Cartwright Hall was built, Bradford had a small gallery in the city centre, and Greenwood notes that during the Christmas holiday of 1887, 22,000 people passed through the turnstiles, giving, "a number exceeding that in any week since the opening and enormously in excess of the proportionate attendance at the great national institutes of the Metropolis."[354] Equally striking is Salford, where in 1862, in a year when the main attraction was an exhibition of paintings, there were 767,700 visits from a population of 148,740. [355] Nottingham, with a population of nearly 260,000, had over 450,000 visits in 1910 while the equally industrial Wolverhampton had 150,000 visits from a population of only 95,000.[356]

Even taking account of the caveats surrounding statistics, these extraordinary figures clearly indicate that the galleries were popular with the working classes.

As a primary source, Greenwood's statistics are impeccable; his descriptions of galleries full of wide-eyed workers are less objective. Greenwood campaigned for galleries to be free, to be open on Sundays and accessible to the working classes. He describes the labouring class in somewhat lyrical terms:

> The working man, or agricultural labourer, who spends his holiday in a walk through any well-arranged Museum cannot fail to come away with a deeply rooted and reverential sense of the extent of knowledge possessed by his fellow-men.[357]

Even more romantic:

> It is only those who come closely in contact with the more intelligent of the working-classes, who know the nobility of character and the earnest reaching out towards higher things to be found among them, who can be familiar with the intense longing to have within their reach institutions such as Museums, Art Galleries and Free Libraries.[358]

He then goes on to ask the rhetorical question, "Are these objects of art appreciated, and is the work extending? The answer is, Yes, decidedly so."[359] He praises Manchester for ensuring that its museum has been:

> ...most carefully arranged for the purpose of interesting the mass of the people, and which has been opened on the days and at the hours when working people can most easily go to it, and their work has brought them into contact with a large number of persons of all classes and ages.[360]

Many museums and art galleries were open from 10.00 a.m. till 9.00 p.m. on weekdays and for shorter hours on weekends to ensure that working people could attend. Greenwood writes here of working-class visitors in a gallery in the evening:

> I have watched minutely the faces of visitors at many an Art Gallery and Museum, especially in the evening, and the faces of the working-class visitors have provided a study in physiognomy so gratifying that I never now enter a Museum without giving some attention to the faces of the visitors....how the eyes light up at some picture...I have more than once seen a wife with a pale careworn face cling more closely to the arm of her husband as some picture of child life was being looked at.[361]

On another occasion, he describes a wide range of working-class visitors:

> Here may be seen young and old go from picture to picture with deep interest depicted on their faces. The sailor lad has been there fresh from his ship, and by his side the sweetheart about whom he no doubt dreamed when on his mid-night watch far away on the ocean wave. Boys and girls fresh from school, tripping from room to room... working men and working women were there in strong force, and many a wearied mother, as she carried her baby, brightened up as she gazed on some picture, say of a young fresh face, with blooming youth and merry eyes.[362]

Even allowing for Greenwood's misty-eyed descriptions, it is clear that evening opening attracted large numbers of working-class visitors.

Waterfield's publications on regional museums, *The People's Galleries*, *Art for the People* and his essay '*Art Galleries and the Public*', all of which this chapter draws on heavily, are a secondary source but less subjective than Greenwood.

In *The People's Galleries*, Waterfield notes that visitors to a range of regional museums in the 1890s, "appear to have been drawn from the whole population excepting only the poorest members of society."³⁶³ In *Art Galleries and the Public*, he quotes a comment on the Derby Museum in Liverpool that, "A considerable proportion of the visitors have consisted of excursionists, chiefly from the manufacturing districts, the conduct of whom has been orderly and respectable."³⁶⁴ Similarly, the *Annual Report* for Birmingham Corporation Art Gallery for 1874 notes that, "a gratifyingly large number of visitors were artisans."³⁶⁵ By 1911, Whitworth Wallis, the long-standing curator at Birmingham, could state that in twenty five years, "not a single object has ever been damaged."³⁶⁶ In summarising the situation in the late Victorian era, Waterfield states that, "In contrast to earlier museum types, they were not intended primarily for the privileged classes or for artists; to a great extent they were museums and galleries for workers."³⁶⁷

Both Greenwood and Waterfield comment on the large numbers from the working classes who attended lectures and musical events at museums and art galleries. Greenwood praises Whitworth Wallis for his popular lecture, "The Art Gallery and how to see it."³⁶⁸ Wallis himself, in a somewhat deprecating manner, estimated that, "something like 100,000 people must have been talked to…poor souls."³⁶⁹ In Liverpool, average attendance at forty-eight lectures in 1894 was over 1,240, and they were especially popular among the, "ill-educated."³⁷⁰ Leicester had an average of 400 at the Saturday morning talks, and in Leeds, even Frank Rutter, the somewhat high-minded curator who despised local councillors, lectured for the Workers' Education Association.³⁷¹

The numbers visiting the museums and art galleries, the contemporary descriptions and the location of the galleries in predominantly working-class towns demonstrate large working-class visitor numbers. The theorists of the 20th century, Gramsci, Bourdieu and

Foucault, seem determined to deny the working classes the right to simply enjoy a visit to an art gallery. They must be subjects of 'cultural hegemony', 'symbolic violence', and 'disciplinary scrutiny.' The reality was that most working-class Victorians went to art galleries because they enjoyed an outing, they enjoyed visiting the wonderful buildings and they enjoyed seeing beautiful pictures.

The Pictures

The fact that these pictures were soon to be castigated by critics and curators and relegated to the basements of galleries across the country merely illustrates the cycle of fashion. The Victorians loved a picture that told a story, depicted a beautiful landscape or showed royalty in all their glory. '*And When Did You Last See Your Father?*', which was bought by the Walker Gallery in Liverpool in 1878, is perhaps the most famous example of Victorian narrative art.

A popular subject was the harsh life of the poor. Luke Fildes was the pre-eminent master of the school of social realism, and his pictures were bought by many regional galleries. Fildes had an interesting family history that may have drawn him to portray the worst of Victorian hardship. He was looked after by his grandmother who was injured at the Peterloo Massacre in 1819, later became a Chartist and must have had an influence on her grandson. Fildes' most famous picture, *The Doctor,* was commissioned by Henry Tate. It was based on the death of Fildes' own son and shows a compassionate doctor watching over a sick child. It was shown at the Royal Academy in 1891 and was an immediate success. Agnews, fine art dealers in London, produced a print which was an instant hit and sold more than one million copies in America. Nearly sixty years later the picture was to again attain fame in America. The American Medical Association, campaigning in 1949 against Truman's plans to nationalise health care, printed 65,000 posters of the picture with the slogan *Keep politics out of this picture*. Given Fildes' family history, it seems safe to assume that he would have been appalled.³⁷²

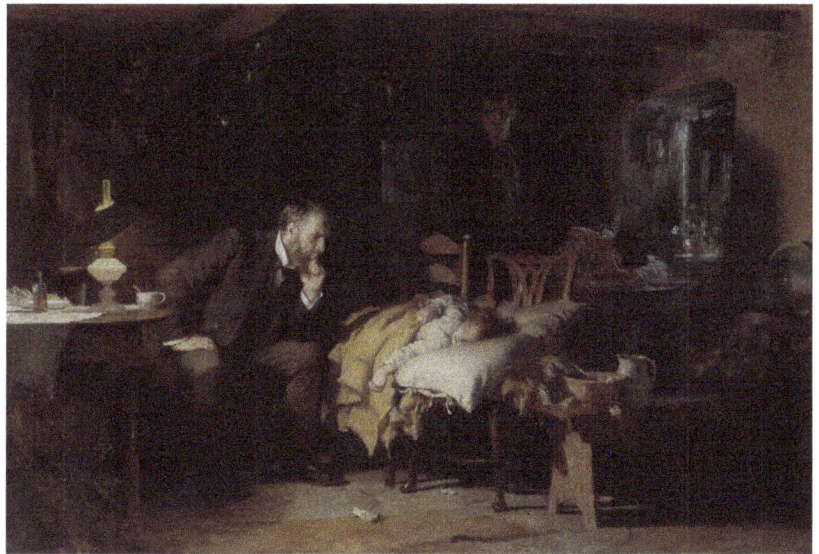

The Doctor by Luke Fildes

Less emotional were William Frith's enormous pictures of crowds at the Derby, at Paddington Station and at the seaside. Vilified by Ruskin, but bought by Queen Victoria, Frith was a tremendous success. *Derby Day* was so popular that when it was put on show at the Royal Academy, it had to be guarded by a strong policeman and an iron fence. Regional galleries were quick to buy Frith's work; the Mercer in Harrogate owned his classical Victorian family scene, *Many Happy Returns of the Day,* while Wolverhampton bought *The Rejected Poet.*³⁷³

Just as visitors to Vauxhall Gardens enjoyed Hayman's battle scenes, so the Victorians flocked to see paintings of war. The most popular were by Elizabeth Butler, one of the few women artists to be bought by regional galleries and one who did not glorify war. *The Battle of Balaclava,* which was bought by Manchester, depicts the devastated survivors of the charge of the Light Brigade in all its horror.

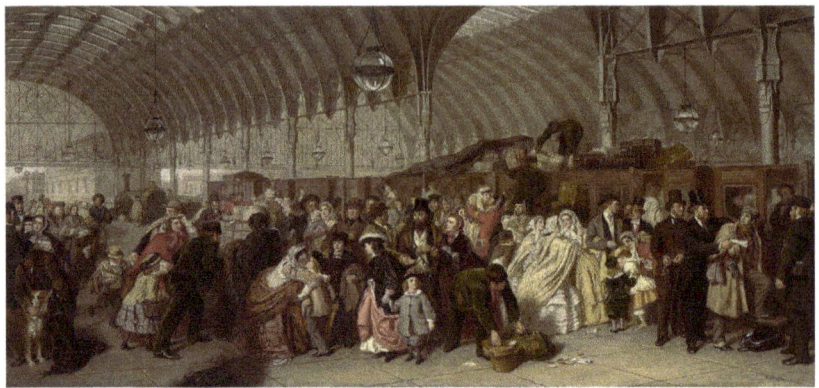

The Railway Station by William Frith

Landscapes were also popular, enabling those living and working in the appalling conditions described by Engels to have a glimpse of another world on their visit to the local gallery.

The wealthy businessmen and councillors naturally wanted their portraits on display and today, mercifully, they have been condemned to the stores. One interesting exception was in Bradford. A Mr. G.A. Gaskell was offended by the number of portraits of rich businessmen and wrote to the Museums Committee saying:

> I have observed with a feeling of dissatisfaction that while extravagant sums are readily subscribed for presentation portraits of rich men, memorial portraiture of poor men is almost entirely neglected. It occurred to me early this year that I might, if I were allowed, employ my art to rectify, in some degree, this injustice and offer to the town some portraits of men who, without being wealthy, have won for themselves an

honourable reputation in Bradford.

The offer was accepted and Gaskell presented the town, "in perpetuity, portraits of six eminent townsmen, in frames provided by friends."[374]

But despite their egotism, the councillors of the Victorian era have left us a magnificent legacy in their astute purchase of Pre-Raphaelite paintings. Manchester Town Hall, with its murals by Ford Maddox Brown and its gallery of Pre-Raphaelite paintings, is perhaps the pre-eminent collection, but many Pre-Raphaelite masterpieces can still be seen today in local galleries.

The Councillors and the Curators

The collections that were bought by local councillors and curators delighted their public. The majority of regional galleries were owned by the local council and run by the Art and Museums Committee. In many cases, the councillors on these committees were also active members of their Literary and Philosophical Societies and were committed to doing their best for their town. They built the great Victorian town halls, museums, art galleries, hospitals, stations and parks. Their enthusiasm and devotion to their cities led to a Victorian version of today's competitions to become Capital of Culture.

Just as Glasgow, in 1990, and Liverpool, in 2008, claimed that culture had regenerated their cities, so did the Victorians claim culture as the way forward. Waterfield quotes the Mayor of Bury stating that the city's collection , "had raised the status of Bury among municipalities of the kingdom" while the Annual Report of the Walker Gallery in Liverpool stated in 1896 that:

> The Gallery had already a high reputation, but it is most desirable that efforts should be made to render it as complete as possible, in order that its prestige may be in no way eclipsed or

diminished by the patriotism and munificence of the wealthy in other cities.[375]

The editor of the Liverpool *Liberal Review,* opposing civic expenditure on art, wrote that, "If we were to believe all that we are told, we should arrive at the conclusion that the world is only to be regenerated by an acquaintance with Art."[376] He would not have been surprised to discover that 150 years after he penned his opposition to, "art maniacs" that the debate was still raging. Glasgow and Liverpool, despite being Capitals of Culture, are among the most deprived cities in Britain. The jury is still out on the impact of culture on regeneration: is Glasgow now a city of low-paid waiters where once it was a city of high-paid welders?

Hunt praises the Victorian councillors for their civic pride, and compares their efforts favourably with cities today where the bid to become Capital of Culture, "is frequently the work of quangos and urban regeneration consultants rather than the organic outcome of any homegrown civic sentiment."[377] As one commentator put it in the 1980s, New Deal for Communities had become New Deal for Consultants.

The councillors' working-class roots may have been loosened over a generation, but they knew their audience because they employed them. They bought pictures that both they and their workforce could enjoy. They did not spend money on Old Masters and to them a good story was what mattered. Greenwood was correct in stating that Fildes' *Village Wedding* was, "worth more to them than all the works of Rubens in the National Gallery."[378] The councillors would make an annual trip to the Royal Academy and buy what they liked, and if visiting numbers are a measure of success, their selections were successful.

But as the professions of curator and critic developed, the role of councillors diminished. Many of the early curators, such as Howarth at Manchester and Wallis at Birmingham, worked well with their committees. Greenwood speaks highly of professional curators and warns councillors not to interfere:

> Some curators are much harassed and hindered by the captious and fault-finding tendencies of one or two members of their Committee. It is marvellous how one man in a governing body has the power to make a public servant very uncomfortable.[379]

In Birmingham, the Council had a very enlightened policy. They gave Wallis freedom to travel across Europe to purchase paintings and to spend up to £100 using his own judgement.[380] In Liverpool, ever conscious of the need to save the ratepayers' money, the opposite was the case, and the approval of full Council was required for all purchases.[381]

But a war was now erupting between councillors, who believed in buying pictures that they and the public would enjoy, and curators and art enthusiasts, who wanted to move on from Victorian narrative. Charles Rowley, who was active in artistic circles in Manchester, despaired of his time as a co-opted member of the Manchester Art Gallery Committee, as he tried to persuade the councillors to take a more modern approach, "For two years I was on the Art Gallery Committee of the Manchester Corporation. Nothing would induce me to undergo the experience again."[382] This was relatively mild compared with The Alderman in Art, which set the tone for future attacks on local councillors. In a vitriolic essay written in 1898, George Moore wrote, "that it should have ever come to be believed that twenty aldermen, whose lives are mainly spent in considering bank-rates, bimetallism, and sewage, could collect pictures of permanent value is on the face of it as wild a folly as ever tried the strength of the strait waistcoats of Hanwell or Bedlam."[383]

Moore set the bar high, but Frank Rutter was to exceed him. In his biography, *Since I Was Twenty-Five*, Rutter writes of his time at Leeds, where he became curator in 1912. He does have the decency to preface his attacks by admitting that, "I am not at all the kind of being to make a municipal officer", and that how he came to be selected was a mystery to him.[384] He writes that before going to Leeds he assumed that Moore's essay was:

> ...an amusing but gross exaggeration. After five years' experience I knew it to be a lamentable understatement of the facts... never before had I come into contact with the kind of men who become councillors and aldermen, and – with remarkably few exceptions – I was appalled at their grossness, their ignorance and general lack of manners.

He continues in the same strain but now going beyond Leeds:

> With few exceptions – among which an honourable place must be assigned to Aberdeen, Birmingham, Dublin and Glasgow – the municipal galleries of Great Britain are deplorable. They are a disgrace to the elected persons responsible for their maintenance, a laughing stock to art-loving visitors from abroad and an offence as well as a burden to the average ratepayer.[385]

Rutter was lucky in that Michael Sadler, who was the Vice-Chancellor at Leeds University, was a connoisseur and collector of international repute. Rutter wanted him to be co-opted to the Art Gallery Committee, "But was he ever co-opted to the Leeds Art Gallery Committee? No, never; Dick, Tom and Harry were co-opted, but the Vice-Chancellor of the University was left outside."[386] But Rutter and Sadler formed a partnership, and set up the Leeds Arts Collection Fund, enabling Rutter to buy pictures that the councillors would not countenance. He summed up the dilemma for a Leeds curator, "What alternative is left to an Art Director or Curator who takes his job seriously but – Murder or Suicide? I am astounded at my moderation when, my own time coming, I chose suicide."[387]

Moving forwards to 1922, a paper presented to a conference of the Royal Society of Arts on, "The Problem of Provincial Galleries and Art Museums" by the curator of the Manchester City Art Gallery, decries the purchase of paintings by committee, "Now, Committees I suppose have their purpose in this teleological world, and may even function well, especially when the constituent members of it refrain from attending meetings."[388] In the discussion following the talk, the chair deplored the manner in which many provincial curators were appointed by local councillors:

> The idea that an important gallery in a great industrial centre could be managed by some employee of the corporation who had hitherto been assistant librarian and who had perhaps married the daughter of a town councillor was a great deal too common.[389]

Whitworth Wallis, from Birmingham, commented that, "there was no committee like a committee of one, that one occupying the position of chair." He then went on to say that the only successful director must be a dictator.[390]

As the profession of curator rose with diplomas and degrees, so the role of the councillor declined. Fortunately, the basements of most regional galleries are large enough to store the worst of the councillors' purchases and the galleries spacious enough to display the many jewels that they bought and still accommodate contemporary art and temporary exhibitions.

The removal of councillors from purchasing broke the link between many galleries and their working-class populations. Whether this has contributed to the decline in working-class visitors is impossible to say, but despite the rise of Friends organisations, many galleries are today disconnected from their local communities.

A Rural Footnote

The story of art in the regions has focussed on towns and cities. Engels painted a devastating picture of conditions in cities like Manchester, but in rural areas, poverty was even more extreme. At a time when Manchester's mill workers were earning at least 16s. a week, Mrs. Gaskell's heroine in *North and South* dissuades a Manchester mill-hand from going south in search of work, "with the best will in the world you would, maybe, get nine shillings a week…you must not go to the South."[391] Pay was poor, and living conditions in rural villages often worse than in the industrial slums. Fine art was not a key issue for farming labourers, but the annual agricultural shows drew crowds of over 100,000 and each show would have a tent showing fine art. In *Jude the Obscure*, one of the few episodes when Hardy depicts Jude and his lover Sue enjoying themselves is when they go to the Art Tent at the Great Wessex Agricultural show.

The Society for the Encouragement of Agriculture, Arts, Manufactures and Commerce in the Counties of Somerset, Wilts., Gloster and Dorset and in the City and County of Bristol, or as it was better known, the Bath and West, was famous for exhibiting works by well-known contemporary artists. Sir Thomas Acland, the largest landowner in Devon and a friend of Ruskin, became closely involved with the Society. He edited its *Journal* and turned it into an important book running to 300 pages and discussing the latest developments in farming. But he was also an enthusiastic collector of contemporary art and established an Arts Section of the Show.[392] In 1859, at the Barnstaple Show, in addition to viewing livestock and machinery, visitors could view paintings, sculpture and contemporary design. The South Kensington Museum lent exhibits, and the Fine Art Section included works by Turner. The *Journal* for 1860 notes that, "some of [his] relations were actually living in Barnstaple as artisans, and came to look and wonder."[393] The Dorchester Show the following year included works by Frith and Holman Hunt. *The Strayed Sheep,* by Hunt, was especially popular and praised in the catalogue, "to each animal is given an individuality which must have been thoroughly appreciated by the sheep farmers of Dorset."[394] The Fine Art section then went into decline. In 1870, the Secretary noted that the Dorchester and Bristol Shows had been sent paintings that had not sold in London and that, "several exhibitors were persons who regularly have stalls at the Crystal Palace."[395]

In 1873, a policy of borrowing from well-known collectors was instituted and the Plymouth Show was a great success. Pictures by Reynolds, Opie, Prout, Angelica Kauffman and Sir Thomas Lawrence were all exhibited, and although many of these names are no longer well known, their pictures are held by all the major national galleries.[396] The *Journal* noted that the Fine Art Section was, "visited by eager crowds, most of whom witnessed perhaps for the first time in their lives those grand works of English art of which this country is so justly proud."[397] The new policy of showing works borrowed from established collectors worked well. One commentator, following the Southampton Show, reported that the society, "is one of the great Art teachers of the day. It brings annually before a class of society, that cannot be reached in any other way, a varied and valuable collection of oil-paintings, watercolour drawings and works of ornamental art, seldom surpassed by exhibitions of a more stationary and lasting character; thereby awakening thoughts that otherwise might not have existed."[398]

The Bath and West was one of the most successful agricultural shows and the Fine Art Section brought the best of contemporary art to an audience of agricultural labourers who would otherwise never have the opportunity to view such paintings. The Shows attracted up to 100,000 visitors, and it is safe to assume that the development of the Fine Art Section was a response to increasing numbers wanting to see the pictures.

The First World War and the Great Depression put a halt to the building of new galleries and reduced the collections budgets. Many galleries went into decline. At the same time, the rise of a new generation of curators and influential critics changed the art world dramatically. In the next chapter, we shall explore the impact of these developments and the effect of new directions after the Second World War when the middle classes hijacked the nation's art.

Chapter 8

A New World

Queen Victoria and Ruskin both died in the first months of 1901. Victoria bought Frith's paintings and Ruskin berated him, but they would both have been outraged and offended by the art of the new century.

The new Whitechapel Gallery opened on 12 March 1901 and was soon putting on shows that perplexed Canon Barnett. The Bloomsbury Group, led by the formidable duo of art critics Roger Fry and Clive Bell, drove a stake through the heart of Victorian narrative and declared it dead.

For nearly 150 years, private, public and voluntary organisations had worked to ensure access to art for all. In the commercial realm, Tyers and Bullock made money from displaying art at low prices to large numbers. Parliamentary Select Committees spent hours ensuring free access to the nation's galleries. In the regions, mill owners and manufacturers funded municipal galleries full of paintings their workers enjoyed. In London, the galleries of Barnett, Rossiter and Besant were open till 10.00 p.m. to allow the workers to appreciate fine art after a hard day's work. But as the century turned, all this would change. Public bodies were too sophisticated to deride the working classes, so they simply forgot them. In the art establishment, the Bloomsbury Group had no hesitation in labelling the masses uneducated and incapable of appreciating the new art.

The First World War and the Great Depression brought the building of new galleries to a halt, led to cuts in purchasing budgets and an overall fall in visitor numbers. There was occasional good news: the opening in the Wirral of the Lady Lever Gallery in 1922 and the new

Duveen extension to The Tate in 1926. Some galleries maintained high numbers of working-class visitors: throughout the 1930s, Bethnal Green had consistently more visitors than the Tate.[399] In 1935, the British Institute of Adult Education travelling exhibitions, *Art for the People*, toured the country and attracted thousands of visitors who did not have access to art galleries.

It was not until 1946 that the new Arts Council stemmed the decline in arts expenditure. But by then Keynes, the first chair of the Arts Council, had taken control of the arts world. As we have noted, Roy Strong's acerbic words revealed the truth: after the establishment of the Council, "the winners… were the ever burgeoning and aspiring middle classes, who found to their delight arts activities for which in the past they would have had to pay dearly now came cheap."[400]

Overlying the period of decline, from 1901 to 1946, were two dominant themes: firstly, the transfer of power in London from the old aristocracy to the new elite of the art world, and in the regions from councillors to curators; and secondly, the dominance of the Bloomsbury Group, who could hardly have been more distant from the working classes.

In his book *The State and the Visual Arts,* Nicholas Pearson devotes a chapter to the importance of Edward Poynter, who was a key figure in the late Victorian art world.[401] Poynter was an artist who at seventeen studied with Leighton in Rome and Whistler in Paris. The character Lorrimer in George du Maurier's novel *Trilby* is based on Poynter, and he is described as, "a painstaking young enthusiast, of precocious culture, who read improving books, and did not share the amusement of the quartier latin, but spent his evenings at home with Handel, Michelangelo and Dante, on the respectable side of the river."[402] Poynter went on to marry a famous beauty who had three sisters: Georgina, who married Burne-Jones; Alice, who was

Kipling's mother; and Louisa, who was Stanley Baldwin's mother. As Saumarez Smith states, he was a member of, "the purple of the Victorian art aristocracy."[403]

He painted large-scale historical paintings which can still be seen in Tate Britain and many regional galleries. His career encompassed all the key posts in the Victorian art establishment: Slade Professor of Art at University College London, Director of the Art Division at the Department of Education and Science, Principal of the National Art Training School, Director of the National Gallery and finally President of the Royal Academy. Even by Victorian standards, it was an amazing range of jobs. Today's elite directors, as they seamlessly glide between the National Gallery, the British Museum, the Royal Academy and the Arts Council, are mere amateurs in the art of career building.

But the importance of Poynter was not the posts he held but his influence on the principles underpinning the world of art as it moved towards the 20th century. Pearson describes Poynter's thinking, as the leading figures in the art world became increasingly concerned at the influence of new money on old art.[404] Poynter edited a series of textbooks on art, and in one which he wrote himself, *Classic and Italian Painting*, he set out his concerns in the preface. Poynter was worried that the class of person who was in a position to support art often lacked the necessary knowledge and taste.

In the past, the nation could rely on a small circle of cultivated members of the aristocracy to control the art world. Poynter, writing in 1880, opens his Preface by questioning public taste:

> It is no doubt the business of artists to educate the public in matters of art by raising the standard of taste...and it is equally without doubt that public opinion reacts, and not always too

favourably, upon art, by creating a demand which can but rarely be up to the required level of taste and critical knowledge.[405]

He then expresses concern that:

> Within the last few years an interest in art – not unfrequently genuine enough – has sprung up, which is very widespread, and which is increasing far beyond the circle of the few highly cultivated persons who at one time constituted the amateur classes[406]

But, "we must have in addition an acquaintance with great works of art that are standards of style; such works, that is to say, as have received the sanction of cultivated men of all times."[407] Despite his somewhat high-handed manner, Poynter had a sense of humour, mocking English noblemen who collected classical statues with broken noses.[408] As Pearson states, "Art, it is suggested, is too important to be left in the hands of Government, business, or the population at large." As we shall see, Poynter's concerns would come to the surface as the battle for control of the art world moved away from the old aristocracy and local councillors to the new professional elite.

The irony is that Poynter was a victim of the old aristocracy in one of their last attempts to maintain control. In 1904, he resigned his post as Director of the National Gallery after losing a battle with the very people he had praised in 1880. When Poynter's predecessor retired, the Prime Minister, Lord Rosebery, decided to shift the balance of power away from the Director to the Trustees. In a Treasury note of 1894, known as the 'Rosebery Minute', the Director's powers were severely curtailed. In 1902, a resolution put by the Marquis of Lansdowne reinforced the 'Rosebery Minute' and left the Director a puppet of the Trustees. Two of the leading Trustees, Lansdowne and Lord Rothschild, behaved in a high-handed and appalling manner. As Saumarez Smith states, "the 1890s were altogether a bad decade for the National Gallery" when due to Lansdowne and Rothschild's behaviour, numerous old masters either left the country or were bought by private collectors. Eventually, demoralised by the behaviour of his aristocratic Trustees, Poynter moved on to the Royal Academy.

One highlight of Poynter's period was the opening of the National Gallery of British Art, or The Tate. Henry Tate was precisely the kind of man Poynter had warned about. One of the last of the working-class, Unitarian philanthropists, he left school in Liverpool at the age of thirteen to work as a grocer and by the age of twenty had his own shop. But it was by devising the process of making sugar cubes that he was to make his fortune and build up a magnificent collection of paintings. When in 1887, he offered this collection to the nation, his love of Victorian narrative betrayed his working-class roots. Just as the establishment had misgivings about buying Angerstein's collection for the National Gallery because of his roots in Jewish banking, so Tate became known as 'the sugar boiler,' who knew much about trade and little about art. The fact that Tate owned some of the most popular and best-loved paintings of the time, notably Fildes' *The Doctor,* did not impress the elite of the art world or the London press.

The Hawk declared that, "the three pictures by Sir John Millais are the only ones the Trustees would be not only justified in, but congratulated on, selecting out of the modern section of Mr. Tate's collection," adding that, "what may be great works of art in the eye of a gentleman skilled in sugar refining are not necessarily so in the opinion of those who, knowing nothing of the sugar trade, do know something about pictures."[409] *The Society,* taking a sideswipe at Millais, was more critical:

> Tate's sugar is getting a better advertisement now than ever any soap secured, and the proprietor must chuckle at the success of his boom. But the public should discriminate between sugar and art. Because a gentleman has purveyed, 'crystal loaf' with success for many years it does not follow that he knows anything about pictures.[410]

Only *The Spectator* gave full-hearted support, stating that, "it is monstrous that a man who makes an offer like Mr. Tate's should be treated as if he were a criminal."[411]

A combination of the Treasury's reluctance to provide funds and the London art world's distaste for his paintings led to a saga whereby it took eight years from Tate offering his collection, and paying for a new building, for it to open as the new National Gallery of British Art at Millbank. Even then, the press could not hold back from criticism. *The Times* had the decency to confess that, "it seems ungrateful to criticise Mr. Tate's gift" but then went on to say, "there is something heathenish about its heavy pillars and frowning portico. This type of architecture has been happily called Gorgonesque, and no other word defines the present building more closely."[412]

When the Tate opened, in what was a working-class area, there were reports of working people visiting the gallery. The *Norwood Press* declared that:

> ...many working men and women were to be seen wandering through the rooms and gazing with interest at the pictures, for Grosvenor Road borders on a very busy working-class neighbourhood, and it seems evident that the residents there are not going to neglect the beautiful art gallery which has been placed so close to their doors.[413]

Henry Tate was perhaps the last person with truly working-class roots to present a notable collection to the nation. The next major contribution was not in the form of paintings but a generous cheque from Joseph Duveen. He was a wealthy art dealer who had already paid for a new gallery at the British Museum to house the Elgin Marbles and in 1926 funded an extension to the Tate to display modern foreign art.

Taylor sees the transformation of The Tate as another step in the direction of the middle classes. He argues that there was now a battle between different groups in the art world which:

> ...occurred not between or among classes, but in the ranks of the governing class itself: a consequence was that working-class participation in the national culture ceased to be an issue of importance in the years leading up to the opening of the new galleries at Millbank in 1926. On to centre stage now came the question of how to accommodate the 'modern art' of France, and this in turn led to a disposition to regard the arts as a culture of the professionalised middle classes alone.[414]

One concession to the working classes was to build houses for artisans on spare land behind the new gallery. Even then the Victorian press, never one to shy away from the issue of class, suggested that the houses should be for clerks, creating, "a residential colony of a class somewhat superior to the 'artisan' neighbourhood and a little more in keeping with the vicinity of this splendid national institution."[415] The homes eventually went to artisans, and in an attempt to link the new housing to the gallery, each of the fifteen homes were named after national artists.

World War I and the Great Depression understandably caused local and central government to focus on issues other than art. But the world of museums and galleries was not entirely forgotten, and in the interwar years, there were three reports into the state of regional and national galleries and a fourth into the future of the arts after World War II.

The last report was to be very influential, but the first three also warrant attention. The Carnegie United Kingdom Trust funded reports in 1928 and 1938, examined the state of regional museums and galleries, and found them wanting. Both reports criticised them for being disconnected from and uninterested in their publics. Sir Henry Miers, who carried out the 1928 investigation, asked the question, "Do museums and art galleries fulfil the function of stirring interest and exciting the imagination?" and answered in a resounding fashion that the great majority, "fail and fail lamentably."[416] He then criticised art galleries for being full of, "undesirable and inappropriate works of art."[417] He attacked councillors for paying disgracefully low salaries to curators, in some cases paying them less than their caretakers. In summary, his only praise was for the Victoria and Albert Museum's loans scheme and his solution was to employ better-qualified and better-paid staff.

Ten years later, the Carnegie Trust asked Sir Henry Markham to revisit regional galleries and his report, *The Museums and Art Galleries of the British Isles,* makes equally bleak reading. He opens by stating that, "the museum movement has little determination to make its worth known." He is even more critical of art galleries than Miers:

> ...my greatest criticisms are directed to art and ethnological exhibits and in these great fields, it is, I think, true to say that there has been little outstanding progress during the last decade... personally I suspect that the day of the old-fashioned provincial art gallery is passing...today it is true to say that the artistic level of some of the Christmas numbers of our periodicals is much higher than some of our provincial galleries.[418]

Damning criticism.

Markham lays the blame squarely at the door of councillors. He uses less colourful language than Rutter and Moore, but his message is clear.

> We find that for the main part museum and art gallery committees consist of newly elected councillors who have had no experience whatsoever of museum administration, ideals or methods...the result, therefore, is that the majority of those who control our municipal museums are men but lightly equipped for the task, and their lukewarmness is evident by the poor moral or financial support which museums receive in so many centres.[419]

He concludes that, "municipal museums are controlled by elected councillors whose enthusiasm for museums is sometimes an absent quality."[420]

Like Miers, his solution is better-trained and better-paid staff. He praises the establishment in 1933 of the Courtauld Institute degree courses for curators, but saves his savage pen for the failure of the councillors to pay adequate salaries to qualified staff. In one case in Yorkshire, he cites where an, "economically minded corporation retained the services of its curator cheaply for fifty years until he reached the age of eighty-five, and then retained him at £85 per annum as a consultant."[421]

Markham is one of many in a long line of people raising the issue of the discrepancy in funding between London and the regions. He calculated that of £1,450,000 spent annually on museums and art galleries that £1,000,000 was spent on the national galleries and £450,000 on 770 provincial museums and galleries. This becomes a repeated refrain, and with each report, the gap widens until in 2014 the annual spend per head in London was £70.00, compared with

£5.00 in the regions.[422]

The 1929 *Royal Commission on National Museums and Galleries* was a low-key report prompted by a debate in the House of Commons. Its remit was to examine whether admission charges should be introduced, to examine congestion, meaning galleries overflowing with worthless artefacts rather than people, and finally whether there should be a central, controlling authority. The recommendations were not to introduce charging, to be more discriminating about what was on display and to establish a standing commission with no powers but to discourage extravagant spending.

Like the Miers and Markham reports, the Commission criticised the museums and galleries for having, "insufficiently developed contact with the public."[423] The Commission thought that the galleries and museums were visited, "by all classes of the population, to the most learned and the least learned but that due to an excess of artefacts the public suffer from not only exhibition fatigue but with exhibition terror."[424] In an interesting submission, Dr. Schmidt Degener, of the Rijksmuseum in Amsterdam, praised the British gallery visitor, saying, "your strongest point is your British public. They have in face of the exhibits a reverence one seldom meets on the Continent."[425] This contrasts with the view of the British gallery-goer from Samuel Courtauld, who states in his book, *Ideas and Industry* that:

> I think it is true that the visual sense as a road to aesthetic enjoyment is *not* very highly developed in England. It used to be interesting to compare the comments made by a French working-class crowd at the Louvre on a Sunday afternoon, or conversations which one sometimes overheard in cafes frequented by shopkeepers, with the things one heard in similar places in this country. The Frenchmen discussed the artistic qualities and commented on them most shrewdly: the English

were almost wholly interested in subject matter and anecdote.[426]

The Royal Commission did praise the importance of evening opening at both the Victoria and Albert and Bethnal Green, where they achieved an attendance of 63,000 in 1928 on the three nights a week they were open from 5.00 p.m. till 9.00 p.m.[427] They spoke highly of Bethnal Green, which with visitor numbers of 370,000 a year from the local people was, "an oasis in a desert of dingy streets."[428]

The Miers and Markham reports and the Royal Commission reveal both national and provincial museums and galleries in a state of decline. The Royal Commission noted that whereas expenditure on universities had multiplied nineteenfold in the previous twenty-five years, that of museums and galleries had only gone up twofold, barely keeping up with inflation. In the interwar years, purchasing budgets were slashed with Birmingham boasting that it did not spend a penny of the rates on buying art.[429] All three reports paint a picture of decline, with regional museums suffering a lack of interest from their councils, purchasing budgets slashed or abolished, and unqualified staff employed on very low salaries. The Royal Commission described the regional galleries as having, "an air of stagnation",[430]

None of the above reports led to any significant action, but it was an informal report, which the civil service tried to curtail, that was to have a major influence. Building on the arm's-length model that the University Grants Committee had established, the cultural elite set about ensuring that after the war neither politicians nor the people would be involved in the publicly funded promotion of the arts.

Anna Upchurch, in her paper, "'*Missing' from policy history: The Dartington Hall Arts Enquiry 1941–1947*", argues that while the Visual Art section of this report was not published till 1946, its thinking and recommendations were well know to the small but influential circle who established the Arts Council.[431] The Dartington Report was originally linked to the Nuffield College Social Reconstruction Survey led by G.D.H. Cole, the left-wing historian. This survey was funded by the Treasury, but by 1943, the Civil Service was increasingly concerned at Cole's interference in an area that they considered the Government's responsibility and stopped his grant. The Dartington Report was then funded by Dorothy and Leonard Elmhirst, who were the founders of the Dartington Hall Centre for the Arts in Devon. Originally intended to provide proposals for post-war reconstruction in all the arts, only the report entitled *The Visual Arts* was significant and influential. As the following quotes show, it took forward the now well-established denigration of local councillors, "few in England can feel that the visual arts are accorded the recognition and encouragement they need";[432] "purchases by local galleries have been spasmodic and indiscriminate";[433] "many[municipal] galleries have been used as dumping grounds for collections of no value";[434] "[councillors] have very little interest in art; very rarely is there any knowledge";[435] "municipal art collections are for the most part neither interesting nor valuable";[436] "no more than a dozen galleries in the provinces have an annual attendance of more than 100,000."[437]

The glory days of both national and regional galleries attracting one million people were over. It was a mixed picture, with Bethnal Green still attracting large numbers of local people and the national galleries in London just about holding their own. There were exceptions: in 1935, Sheffield held an exhibition of contemporary paintings from Ingres to Picasso, and Liverpool and Leicester were displaying both Impressionist and Post-Impressionist artists. But the days of barriers to hold back visitors from popular paintings and of local councillors bringing back showstoppers from the Royal Academy were over.

The overall picture is very dark, but what is important about the Dartington Enquiry is the key recommendation: namely the establishment of an autonomous arts council. The enquiry, had similar concerns as Poynter over sixty years earlier about the art world falling into the wrong, uneducated hands. Under the heading, 'Painter, Sculptor and Patron', the report states that:

> The earlier tradition of informed patronage was largely replaced by a competitive demand for the work of popular mediocrities, and high prices were paid, partly for the sake of ostentation and partly to assuage the conscience of the age. The essentials of art were no longer generally recognised either by artists or by patron. But nineteenth century values, established mainly under the authority of the Royal Academy, were at last shown to be false; and the pictures and sculptures whose purchase they had prompted proved a bad investment.[438]

Like Poynter, the enquiry approved of the role of aristocratic patrons and was dismissive of the new collectors who, "paid increasingly huge prices in competition for works of the most popular artists."[439] As we have seen when considering John Martin and William Frith, in the language of the art world, the word 'popular' means second-rate. Indeed, Kenneth Clark wrote in his autobiography, "Popular taste is bad taste, as any honest man with experience will agree."[440]

One of the key aspects of the Dartington Enquiry is that it was written by a group who remained anonymous.[441] This was an elite group made up of people such as Kenneth Clark, Philip Hendy, a future director of the National Gallery; John Rothenstein, Director of the Tate; and prominent practitioners, such as Henry Moore. The group were part of a London-based circle who were to make up the post-war art establishment and who did not want either politicians or the people interfering in their world. Their report put forwards three proposals: a Ministry of Art, a Department of Art within a Ministry or an autonomous body with its own board of governors. It is no surprise that they recommended the third option.

Nor is it a coincidence that this recommendation was in line with the thinking of Keynes and others as they developed the idea of the Arts Council. Keynes was friendly with the Dartington Elmhirsts, and Kenneth Clark shared the ongoing workings of the enquiry with Keynes and R.A. Butler, the President of the Board of Education.[442]

In the British tradition, the establishment knew the answer before they had formulated the question.

The Arts Council's autonomous position in the Whitehall hierarchy stemmed from the Dartington Report, but as an organisation it developed out of the Council for the Encouragement of Music and the Arts (CEMA). This was a body which was set up during the war to bring culture to the people, alongside the Entertainments National Service Association (ENSA), which brought entertainment to the troops.

One of the last major initiatives that still recognised that the majority of people of all classes enjoyed art did not come from the art world but from the British Institute of Adult Education (BIAE). The BIAE had a very dynamic Welsh director, Bill Williams, who in 1935 launched *Art for the People*. With the help of the Director of the Courtauld Institute, he persuaded many private collectors to lend paintings for touring exhibitions to towns without galleries.

Three very different towns were used as a pilot: Swindon, a railway town; Barnsley, a coal mining community; and Silver End, which is in Essex and was predominantly agricultural but had a large steel window factory. The paintings covered French and English art of the 19th and 20th centuries and works ranged from Cézanne, Gaugin, Van Gogh and Matisse to Stanley Spencer, Paul Nash, Ben Nicholson and Duncan Grant. The exhibitions were accompanied by a panel of experts who gave talks and also by guides who gave lectures.

At a total cost of only £300 each the exhibitions were a great success. The following years saw *Art for the People* travel to towns across the country, and when war broke out, CEMA funded the tours and Bill Williams joined the Council. The exhibitions now went to factories and canteens with artists such as Graham Sutherland, John Piper and Duncan Grant providing free murals to enliven the canteens in a project known as 'Art for the British Restaurants'. In 1940, 300,000 people visited exhibitions in 80 different locations, and the following year the figure came to over 360,000.[443]

CEMA was the brainchild of Dr. Tom Jones, who had an extraordinary career. Born in a Welsh mining village, he left school aged fourteen. Mary Glasgow, secretary of CEMA, described him as a, "formidable little pyramid of a figure, with a small head and long pointed nose."[444] Tom Jones, despite becoming Deputy Cabinet Secretary under Lloyd George, never forgot his roots. During the Depression, he chaired the South Wales Coalfield Distress Committee, was on the Unemployment Assistance Board and still found time to establish Coleg Harlech, the Welsh equivalent to Ruskin College for mature students.[445] Despite his valley background, Jones was a member of the 'Cliveden Set' who led the campaign for appeasement in the 1930s. In 1935, he was sent to meet Hitler and came back claiming that, "Hitler does not seek war with us. He seeks our friendship."[446]

But bringing art to the people was Jones' main passion, and when John Christie, the owner and founder of the Glyndebourne Opera, began lobbying Neville Chamberlain to allow him to create a National Council to promote music and the arts, Chamberlain passed the proposal to Jones and asked him to respond. Jones, ever the Welsh valley boy, was not about to let Christie and the Glyndebourne Set seize control of the arts world and successfully killed off Christie's proposals and launched his own scheme.

Yet another of Jones' positions was secretary to the Pilgrim Trust, which was an American funded charity supporting the arts. Through the Pilgrim Trust, Jones saw an opportunity to create a new project to bring art and music to the masses. Using his formidable contacts, he persuaded the Treasury to match a Pilgrim Trust grant of £25,000. He then set up a board chaired by Lord Macmillan, Minister of Information, and including such luminaries as Kenneth Clark, but also Bill Williams of the BIAE and on 19 January 1940 CEMA held its first meeting.

CEMA quickly developed regional offices and in partnership with the BIAE provided theatre, art and music across the country. When CEMA discovered that ENSA (Every Night Something Awful) was also providing highly popular classical concerts and not just light music, battle lines were drawn and the Ministry of Labour had to arbitrate. Eventually peace broke out and the list of future stars who worked for CEMA ranged from Benjamin Britten and Peter Pears to Violet Carson, better known as Ena Sharples of *Coronation Street* fame.[447]

A subplot taking place in the evolution of both CEMA and the Arts Council was a long-running battle between Keynes and Christie as each tried to gain the high cultural ground, and more importantly get government funding for their own projects. The one thing they had in common is that their wives were both theatrical. Christie's wife was an opera singer and Keynes' wife a ballet dancer, and they both unashamedly promoted their wives' careers. Christie paid for the original Glyndebourne Opera House, which opened in 1934 with Audrey Mildmay, better known as Mrs. Christie, singing the role of the servant in *Figaro*. Two years later, the Cambridge Arts Theatre, funded by Keynes, opened with a ballet gala night starring Lydia

Lopokova, better known as Mrs. Keynes.[448] Kenneth Clark summed up their relationship when he said that, "Keynes had an ancient implacable hatred for John Christie which Christie returned with interest."[449]

But in the battle between the Glyndebourne Set and the Bloomsbury Group, the Glyndebourne Set were out-numbered and out-gunned from the start. In the 1930s, the Glyndebourne Set was essentially a one-man band consisting of John Christie. He was a wealthy businessman who created a magnificent legacy in founding Glyndebourne Opera, but in the world of politics and the corridors of power, he was no match for Keynes and his friends.

The lasting impact of the Bloomsbury Group can be debated, but in the first half of the 20th century, they had a tremendous influence in the world of high culture. The group had at its core circle Virginia and Leonard Woolf, Clive Bell and Roger Fry, Lytton Strachey and E.M. Forster and Duncan Grant and John Keynes. They were infamous for their disregard of sexual norms with men and women all swapping partners with gay abandon. As the poet Dorothy Parker famously said they, "Lived in squares, painted in circles and loved in triangles." But their influence on literature and art was to break many barriers when Virginia and Leonard Woolf established the Hogarth Press. They published her radical novels, Eliot's poetry, Bell and Fry's art criticism and the first English version of the complete works of Freud.

Beyond the core membership were many other influential associates, such as Kenneth Clark, who wrote in his biography, "Roger [Fry] was a Bloomsbury. He had been the lover of Virginia Bell and his biography was written by Virginia Woolf. You can't be more Bloomsbury than that."[450] Clark goes on to describe a visit to Garsington, one of the week-end haunts of the Bloomsbury Group:

I wandered among the box hedges till I discovered a timid-looking man wearing a straw hat. As he appeared to be as embarrassed as I was, I spoke a few meaningless words. He answered with some hesitation, in a grave, low voice; he said his name was Eliot and that he worked in the City. In contrast to the birds of brighter plumage on the upper terrace he was most sympathetic, and I could not help wondering what this kind man was doing there. A few weeks later my friend Eddy Sackville-West pressed into my hand a copy of a poem that had just been published called *The Waste Land,* and my question was answered.[451]

One of the Bloomsbury Group's more fascinating habits, and they had many, was to put themselves in their fiction, and in turn, they featured in many novels. Virginia Woolf put her sister Vanessa Bell in several of her books while she features in novels by Wyndham-Lewis and Christopher Isherwood and Shaw's play *Heartbreak House.* Roger Fry stars as Martin Whitby in E.M. Forster's unfinished masterpiece *Arctic Summer*, and Forster appears as Benjamin Dexter in Graham Greene's *The Third Man.* Finally, and appropriately, Duncan Grant is Duncan Forbes in *Lady Chatterley's Lover.*

By 1942, Lord Macmillan and Tom Jones were losing a battle over the direction of CEMA. Macmillan and Jones saw their mission as taking art, music and theatre to the people. Clark and his friends were more concerned with promoting and funding national centres of excellence, preferably in London. Macmillan and Jones eventually ceded defeat and retired. R. A. Butler, President of the Board of Education, offered Keynes a peerage and appointed him chair. Keynes immediately took a very firm grip of the organisation and together with the formidable secretary, Mary Glasgow, he began to lay the foundations of the Arts Council. Ever the elitist, one of Keynes' first decisions was to halve the grant of £10,000 to *Art for the People* with a view to finding funds for opera and the ballet. Bill Williams and Kenneth Clark resisted and a cut of £2,500 was finally agreed, but this was an important signal of the direction that Keynes wanted to take CEMA and eventually the Arts Council.

Keynes was an extraordinary man. At Cambridge, he was famous not just for his formidable intellect but also for his sexual stamina. Openly homosexual, he was known as, "the iron copulating machine."[452] As a keen and accomplished climber, Keynes conquered many difficult routes in both Wales and the Alps, and through the climbing world, he met and lusted after the young George Mallory of Everest fame. In his usual frank and explicit manner, Keynes and his colleagues vied with each other in their desire to bed the beautiful Mallory. Keynes, who was friendly with the pre-eminent climber George Young, wrote of how, "I tried to get up an affair between him [Young] and George Mallory with the greatest possible success."[453] Sex, climbing and art all came together when in 1914 the Alpine Club staged an exhibition of paintings by Duncan Grant, Keynes's lover, Vanessa Bell and Roger Fry.[454]

Keynes moved on from Cambridge to become the most influential economist of the 20th century: an intellectual giant who revolutionised economics, a supporter of equal pay for women, chair of the Eugenics Society, a lover and supporter of the arts and a generous philanthropist who supported impoverished young artists. Together with Samuel Courtauld, a wealthy industrialist, he set up the London Artists Association, supporting new artists such as Henry Moore and Paul Nash. He was also a discriminating collector of modern French art. When attending the Treaty of Versailles talks in Paris, he bought a Cézanne, but when he got back to Charleston, the Bloomsbury Group's country home, he found it too heavy to carry from the taxi to the house and left it in the ditch.[455] When he died, he left his collection of over 150 paintings to Kings College, Cambridge, and many can be seen today in the Fitzwilliam Museum.

Even before he became chair of CEMA, Keynes wielded enormous influence. On a summer evening in 1940, he summoned Mary Glasgow to his house in Gordon Square. She describes how, lying propped up on pillows on his sofa, he proceeded to berate her. In his view, CEMA was spending money in village halls rather than national centres of excellence. At this time, Mary Glasgow still had loyalties to Tom Jones' philosophy of art for all and she writes that she came away, "battered but exhilarated."[456]

Keynes had clear views on the need for the state to be involved in creating a better society. In 1936, he wrote an article for *The Listener*, as part of a series on Art and The State, extolling the role of the state in funding the arts.[457] He firmly believed that private patronage would be killed off by, "economic egalitarianism."[458] Mary Glasgow was even more vociferous, writing after the War that, "the State has destroyed the patron by heavy taxation and has itself to step in."[459] They may not have approved of the Young British Artists and the works of Tracey Emin and Damien Hirst, but they would have been delighted at Charles Saatchi's patronage of the arts forty years later.

Through his many years at the Treasury, Keynes was a master of the corridors of power, and while he advocated state funding of the arts, he worked hard to ensure that the proposed Arts Council would be neither managed by Whitehall nor accountable to Westminster. When he said in his broadcast on the creation of the Arts Council that, "it had happened in a very English, informal, unostentatious way-half-baked if you like", he was being disingenuous.

Keynes' extraordinary drive and stamina saw him commuting across the Atlantic during the war to negotiate the Lend-Lease settlement with the Americans but while focussing on post-war economics he was also formulating his proposals for the future Arts Council. As early as February 1943, he was corresponding with R. A. Butler, proposing that the new body be called The Royal Council of the Arts. Then a month later, he was debating with Butler, "how far we should be an operating body, running our own concerns."[460] Despite attending the Bretton Woods Conference in America in August 1944, and suffering a heart attack, Keynes delivered his proposals for what he called a Permanent Peace Time Body. His ideas were then worked on by civil servants and colleagues, such as Kenneth Clark, over the next nine months. While Keynes was delivering his proposals to Butler, they were both being kept informed of the ideas emanating from the anonymous elite who were writing the Dartington Report.

The outcome was the creation of the Arts Council of Great Britain as an independent body. The official formation of the Council was announced to Parliament in June 1945 by Sir John Anderson, Chancellor of the Exchequer, but better remembered for the eponymous Anderson Shelters which saved many lives during World War II. Keynes and the Bloomsbury Group had pulled off the trick of obtaining taxpayer funding while remaining completely unaccountable.

Keynes was appointed the first chair and set out his vision in a radio broadcast. In it, he emphasised the importance of the arts flowering throughout the country, and even went as far as to declare that:

> Nothing can be more damaging than the excessive prestige of metropolitan standards and fashions. Let every part of Merry England be merry in its own way. Death to Hollywood. But it is also our business to make London a great artistic metropolis, a place to visit and to wonder at.[461]

Keynes' actions belied his words, and the final sentence carried more weight than the rest of the paragraph. Not one to be concerned about conflicts of interest, Keynes, as Chair of the Arts Council, and also chair of Covent Garden Opera Trust, secured a grant of £25,000 for Covent Garden and fifty years later, there was no change. As Robert Hewison notes, in *Cultural Capital,* one of the first major grants of The National Lottery, launched in 1994, was £78.5 million for Covent Garden. He comments:

> It also happened that in 1996, the chairman of the Arts Council's advisory Lottery panel that had made the award, the public relations magnate Lord Chadlington, brother of a Conservative minister, moved over to become chairman of the Covent Garden Trust. One favour deserves another.[462]

In *The State and the Visual Arts,* Pearson has a section entitled 'The Erasure of Politics'. Keynes had achieved the depoliticisation of arts funding, but when people talk of taking something out of politics, what they mean is maintaining the status quo in their favour. In this case the people concerned were the metropolitan elite of the art world. Art was now safe in the hands of the experts, but as Raymond Williams noted:

> ...the Council is politically and administratively appointed, and its members are not drawn from arts practice and administration but from the vaguer category of, "persons of experience and goodwill," which is the State's euphemism for its informal ruling class.[463]

In short, these are the very elite whom sixty years earlier Poynter was praising. Upchurch cites Christopher Madden who discusses the rationale for the arm's-length body due to fear of experts being, "deterred by the aggressive world of local politics" and, "the need to protect public administration from the cut and thrust of day-to-day politics."[464] To people like Keynes and his successors, the cut and thrust of politics was one of the joys of life.

When it came to the appointment of experts, Keynes maintained a very strong grip. Being an expert bridge player, he played his cards both ways. When Sir Edwin Lutyens complained in March 1943 about the lack of Academicians on the Arts Panel of CEMA, Keynes, in his usual robust style, told Butler that it was inadvisable, "to start so early in our life on the vicious practice of filling up with respectable dunderheads."[465] A year later, when another group of Academicians complained of CEMA's modernising tendencies, Keynes replied that the Art Panel, "had as mixed a bunch of fogeys of repute as you could reasonably hope to collect."[466] But as Leventhal states in his paper on state sponsorship in the arts,, "a common set of priorities within the arts establishment ensured that Keynes's own image of high culture would dominate its appointments and its agenda, nurturing the national companies at the expense of local activity."[467]

It is not the purpose of this chapter to comment on the performance of the Arts Council, but it is the purpose to demonstrate that after 1946, a new elite dominated the arts world and controlled the public money that flowed from the taxpayer to the Arts Council. They made such a good job of embedding the 'arm's-length' model that thirty years later, when Lord Redcliffe-Maud carried out an investigation into the funding of the arts he thoroughly endorsed the autonomous model. By today's standards of accountability and transparency, Redcliffe-Maud's endorsement is astonishing.

> By self-denying ordinance, the politicians leave the Council free to spend as it thinks fit. No minister needs to reply to questions in Parliament about the beneficiaries or about unsuccessful applicants for an Arts Council grant.[468]

But in apparently bestowing this freedom, the politicians and the civil servants knew what they were doing. Raymond Williams, who served on the Arts Council, noted that:

> The British State has been able to delegate some of its official functions to a whole complex of semi-official or nominally independent bodies because it has been able to rely on an unusually compact and organic ruling class. Thus, it can give Lord X or Lady Y both public money and apparent freedom of decision in some confidence, subject to normal procedures of report and accounting that they will act as if they were indeed state officials.[469]

And it was the politicians, on the advice of the civil servants, who appointed Lord X and Lady Y. When Lord Keynes died, Kenneth Clark noted in his biography, *The Other Half,* that

> ...the Treasury have a principle that a volatile chairman, and in Keynes' case a brilliant one, should be succeeded by what the eighteenth century used to call 'a man of bottom'; and they discovered an amiable example in Sir Ernest Pooley...who having no interest in the arts he could be relied on not to press their claims too strongly.[470]

Since 1946, the Arts Council has had fifteen chairs of whom only two did not go to public school and Oxbridge. John S. Harris, in *Government Patronage of the Arts in Great Britain,* notes that, "Between 1945–46 and 1966–67, sixty-eight persons served on the Arts Council. Although family data are incomplete, they indicate a preponderance of middle and upper-class families, almost none from the working class."[471] He then analyses the different composition of the Council under Conservative and Labour Governments and shows that the only difference is that under Labour more Council members came from the best known prestige, "public schools."[472]

Andrew Sinclair, who was commissioned to write a history of the first fifty years of the Arts Council, notes that in 1992, "Curiously, the three leading figures in the world of politics and the arts were Old Etonians. Timothy Renton, the Conservative Minister for the Arts, Mark Fisher, the Labour Shadow Minister, and Lord Palumbo, the Chair of the Arts Council."[473] Not curious at all.

Kenneth Clark, chair of the Arts Council from 1953 to 1960, was one of the few members of the art world to have actually studied art history. He was the son of an immensely wealthy family, who made their fortune from the cotton spinning mills of Coats and Clark in Paisley. He spent his childhood holidays on yachts in Monte Carlo, and when he married, his father gave him a hotel as a wedding present.[474]

Moving seamlessly between the different elites at the early age of 31, he became Director of the National Gallery where his style led him to be described, by the Earl of Crawford, "as a very arrogant chap, but clever as a monkey."[475] On a tour of regional galleries, he was astonished to discover that not a single Town Clerk had seen an original picture, and he writes of how his wife Jane, "who always accompanied me, dressed in exquisite Lanvin clothes, gave immense pleasure to the local Mayors."[476] He was one of the anonymous group of experts who wrote the Dartington Report and was a close ally of Keynes in the running of CEMA and the foundation of the Arts Council.

Like Keynes, he was also a generous philanthropist and supported many young artists. He antagonised the Royal Academy by buying contemporary art for the National Gallery, and Gerald Kelly, a notable Academician, was sent to ask him to stop buying the works of young artists. Clark dismissed Kelly, telling him that the young painters lived on £85 a year while Kelly had £80,000 and, "his only problem was whether to lay down Château Lafite or buy Château Batailley that was ready for drinking."[477]

Clark was passed over as Chair of the Arts Council when Keynes died because the Treasury wanted the malleable Ernest Pooley, but he succeeded Pooley in 1953. He and Bill Williams, who was now Secretary General of the Council, did not get on. Williams made clear who was in charge, "I am the captain of this ship. You are the Admiral. I pipe you aboard with full honours. But I run the ship."[478] In 1947 Clark had ensured that the Arts Council was well housed by locating their offices in the former London home of the Astors. When Williams refused to let Clark have any power, he retreated to a room which he had fitted out with furniture borrowed from the Astors, and would sit in front of the fire and read and write.[479] Writing in his memoirs of his time at the Arts Council, he states, "I can't remember a single thing I did there."[480] Like Keynes, Clark, who was an ardent supporter of Covent Garden, would not see a conflict of interest if it hit him on the head. While at the Arts Council, he proudly noted that his daughter was the first woman on the board of Covent Garden while his wife was on the board of Sadler's Wells.[481] Keep it in the family.

Clark was a great innovator and communicator. He opened the National Gallery at 7 a.m. on Cup Final mornings and also instituted evening openings. He is now best remembered for the television series *Civilisation* when he achieved record viewing figures for an arts programme. It was in the world of television that his arrogance and confidence came through. Despite not owning a television and stating that, "It was obvious that Commercial Television would produce a cloaca maxima [great drain] of rubbish", he took on the chairmanship of the Independent Television Authority in 1954.[482] On this occasion he came up against his own elite, as when his appointment became known he was publicly booed when he took dinner at his club, the Athenaeum.

Clark was firmly on the side of the elite fearing that after the war we would see, "the disappearance of an independently wealthy leisure class steeped in inherited convictions about the sanctity of the fine arts."[483] If Clark's post-war experience was typical of the leisured elite, he need not have worried. In 1953, he bought Saltwood Castle, complete with battlements, a moat, a secret garden, a gatehouse, a ghost and a mere 300 acres. By today's standards, Clark, like Keynes, had no time for either the middle classes or the working classes. James Stourton, in his biography of Clark, quotes a letter to Edith Wharton in which Clark complains that while on a cruise, "There was not one person on board who spoke English with an educated accent and in most cases the lack of polish went deeper than pronunciation."[484] On a final note, one of Clark's lesser-known claims to fame was that he introduced John Betjeman to Miss Joan Hunter Dunn who was to become his muse. Working at the Ministry of Information during the War, he said to Betjeman, "John you must go up to the canteen. A most ravishing girl has just appeared there... clear brown complexion, dark eyes, wearing a white overall...she's called Miss Joan Hunter Dunn."[485]

The fact that the Arts Council was run by an elite, upper-class group with no accountability does not mean that it did not meet its objectives. What is revealing, even taking into account the long lens of history, is the extent to which these people distanced themselves from and openly denigrated the people they should have been serving. Keynes had a vision of a society that would soon conquer economic insecurity and where everyone could enjoy a culture-rich leisure life. In his 1946 broadcast, he stated that, "We look forward to a time when the theatre and the concert hall and the gallery will be a living element in everyone's upbringing."[486] But as Chair of the Eugenics Society, he supported contraception because the working class was, "too drunken and ignorant to keep its numbers down"[487] and famously stated that, "The class war will find me on the side of the educated bourgeoisie."[488] Bill Williams, said of Keynes, "there was, also, in this great scholar and art connoisseur, a streak of donnish superiority and singular ignorance of ordinary people."[489]

As a member of the Bloomsbury Group and living in the refined atmosphere of London and Cambridge in the 1930s and 1940s, Keynes' attitude would not have been considered offensive. What is surprising is that the attitude of Arts Council members continued to be out of touch and offensive up until the 1980s. In 1961, we find the Annual Report stating that:

> the paramount trusteeship of the arts in Britain today is vested in that percentage of the population which rejects the assumption that sessions of bingo and capers on the Costa Brava are the be-all and end-all of our new leisure.[490]

In 1974, the chairman, Patrick Gibson (Eton and Oxford), gave a speech focussing on the arts as a vehicle to bring different classes together.[491] Three years later, Richard Hoggart commented that, "most of the new money is going towards subsidising and improving the artistic pursuits of those who already know and enjoy the arts. To them that hath is being given."[492] As Hutchinson states, "Studying the Arts Council it is easy to see what Marx and Engels meant when they denounced the state as a committee for the management of the affairs of the bourgeoisie."[493]

In 1946 the new aristocracy of the art world secured a model which was to serve them and their colleagues well for over fifty years. Hewison writes that an opportunity was missed:

> ...to define the arts so as to embrace a wider range of activities

and to include a broader definition of the audience for them... falling back on older definitions of culture and conservative habits of thought.⁴⁹⁴

"We've won", exclaimed Clive Bell on the opening night of the Second Post-Impressionist Exhibition in 1912. While one half of the Bloomsbury Group had secured control of the money, the other half, led by Fry and Bell, had secured control of the aesthetic high ground.

In 1906, a very bored Treasury official was interviewing Roger Fry for the job of Director of the National Gallery when his patience snapped, "Yes, but isn't there *anyone* whose name we know who could tell us about you?" Fry answered, "Perhaps my father, Sir Edward Fry." "What," interrupted the civil servant, "why didn't you say at once?" End of interview.⁴⁹⁵ Unfortunately for British art, Fry never took up the post. Due to a delay in confirming the appointment, he felt obliged to keep a commitment to the Metropolitan Museum in New York and for a short time advised them from across the Atlantic.

But all this was to change when one of the great partnerships of British art was forged on a train from Cambridge to London when Fry and Bell first met by complete chance. Fry had already curated a highly influential Post-Impressionist exhibition in 1910, but it was on this train that plans were laid for the second and even more influential Second Post-Impressionist exhibition of 1912 with pictures by Manet, Matisse, Gauguin and Van Gogh, among others.

Fry was a thoughtful intellectual with a first class degree from Cambridge. If he was the scholar behind the revolution in British taste, Bell was the salesman.

They both despised Victorian art, describing the Victorian age as one of 'vulgarity', stating that, "what the Victorians made and called art was almost always rubbish [and] Victorian taste was almost always vile." Prince Albert was, "an earnest provincial intellectual and as an educated bourgeois [he was] a cultivated Philistine." The Queen was even worse, "neither cultivated nor a Philistine, she was what Matthew Arnold would have called a Barbarian."[496] As for the paintings which the Queen and her people so enjoyed, they were written off as sentimental, "Descriptive Paintings." Frith and Fildes came in for especial venom. "*Paddington Station* contains several pretty passages of colour and is by no means badly painted [but] it is not a work of art." '*The Doctor*, by Fildes, is described as the most flagrant example of unpleasant painting.[497]

Fry and Bell were quite clear that, "the normal man cannot know if a work of art is beautiful" because, "judgment in a matter of taste requires a degree of sensibility higher than that which the normal voter has been blessed."[498]

And just as the elite are the only people who have the sensibility to manage the Arts Council, so the elite must decide the nation's art. Bell, at his most provocative, writes that civilisation requires the existence of a leisured class supported by the taxpayer. "That only the leisured class will produce a highly civilised and civilising elite is an opinion supported by what seem to me incontrovertible arguments borne out by history."[499] One of the problems facing the leisured class is the tax system, which in taxing unearned income penalises the elite.

> Those who have never had to earn money know how to spend it. That the basic principle of taxation should be the squeezing out of the leisured class for the benefit of the great and small wage earners is typical of a half-civilised society.[500]

As E.M. Forster wrote in *Two Cheers for Democracy*: "In came the nice fat dividends, up rose the lofty thoughts."[501] This was one area where Keynes, who wrote of the 'euthanasia of the rentier' would have fervently disagreed with his Bloomsbury friends.

Fry and Bell were not mere theorists. Fry's 1910 exhibition, *Manet and the Post Impressionists*, was not the first exhibition of French paintings as Brighton Public Art Gallery had staged an exhibition in 1909, but Fry's was the most influential. As Lisa Tickner states, "Fry's was nevertheless the most extensive, well publicised and influential exhibition, a watershed in the public awareness of continental art."[502] Kenneth Clark said of Fry, "In so far as taste can be changed by one man, it was changed by Roger Fry."[503]

But it was not just the Bloomsbury Group who were leading the way. In Whitechapel, Charles Aitken, the first Director of the Barnetts' new gallery, moved on to the Tate in 1911 and was succeeded by his young assistant, Gilbert Ramsay. He managed to persuade the Trustees to allow him to curate an exhibition without the supervision of an advisory panel of Trustees. It was a decision they were to regret. *Twentieth Century Art: A Review of Modern Movements* was to be a turning point for the Whitechapel Gallery. Henrietta Barnett asked Ramsay:

> ...not to get too many examples of the extreme thought of this century, for we must never forget that the Whitechapel Gallery *is intended for the Whitechapel people*, who have to be delicately led and will not understand the Post-Impressionists', or the Futurists' methods of seeing and representing things.[504]

Perhaps Ramsay believed that the working class of Whitechapel, "had as much right to be informed, infuriated, excited or baffled by new developments as any other."[505]

Ramsay moved on to be Director at Kelvingrove in 1914, but was tragically struck by a shell and killed at Gallipoli one year later.

Modern paintings were now reaching regional collections. Clark, praising the Leicester Gallery in his autobiography, writes of the night before the Matisse Exhibition in 1919, "I could hardly sleep for excitement."[506] Leicester also held the first one-man shows of Cézanne, Van Gogh, Pissarro and Picasso. In Leeds, Rutter had managed to circumvent his councillors and raise money to buy modern art, and Liverpool and Sheffield held exhibitions of the French Impressionists.

But whereas in the past two hundred years, there had always been a voice supporting art for the people, after 1945 the new elite controlled the funds and the new curatorial elite controlled the galleries. There were, of course, exceptions. In 1948, in partnership with the Welsh Miners Welfare Commission, the Arts Council funded a theatre tour of over 100 Welsh towns and villages. Similarly, Victorian narrative did not completely vanish from the walls of either the Tate or regional galleries. And not everyone was a modernist. Evelyn Waugh was no supporter of Fry and Bell. In *Brideshead Revisited,* he has Sebastian Flyte reading Bell's seminal work *Art* and pouring cold water on his philosophy.[507] But the working-class taxpayers were increasingly paying for the middle-class gallery-goers to indulge their passions.

The world of fine art is one arena where the post-war consensus never existed, and there are many similar areas where inequality has grown since 1945. As austerity continues to punish the less well off, the final chapter will show why the exclusion of the working classes from the world of art matters.

Chapter 9

Conclusion

This story has covered 250 years: for the first 200 working-class people went to art galleries. Today the nation's galleries are the preserve of the middle and upper classes, entrenching gross inequalities as the elite of the art-world exercise their influence to maintain their dominant position. For example, the London art-world gets £21per head while the South West Region gets £4.50[508] and over one billion of capital funding has been spent in London since 2010 while over 173 art galleries and museums in the regions have closed.[509] The majority of taxpayers fund art for the few while the rich can use their art collections to offset their taxes. And worst of all in denying working-class children access to art they are being denied access to cultural capital which is a crucial component in education and life chances. When researching this book I was regularly told that the working-classes are not interested in art . Not so. The data shows that when galleries mount exhibitions of contemporary, narrative art they are packed out with people from all classes.

Today class is an issue that polite people prefer not to discuss, and yet in a 2016 survey, 60% of people stated that they were working class.[510] The change over the last 250 years is that for the first 200 of those, class was not a taboo topic, and in the art world, those in power recognised the working classes' appetite for art.

Jonathan Tyers attracted all classes to Vauxhall Gardens. The Society of Arts held firm to their policy of free admission to their exhibitions. The millhands in the North crowded into their local art galleries while the farmhands in the South flocked to the Art Tent at the agricultural shows. In the centre of London, the National Gallery was full of working-class families enjoying a day out, and in the East

End, the Rev. Barnett had to limit the numbers wanting to get into his exhibitions. From 1740 to 1940, 'Art for All' was not a cliché but a reality. But then highbrow CEMA (Council for the Encouragement of Music and the Arts) became the state-funded Arts Council, and lowbrow ENSA (Entertainments National Service Association) was scrapped.

Tyers lived in a mansion in Surrey housing the country's best collection of contemporary art. Many 19th-century mill owners and M.P.s lived in a similar style, but both entrepreneurs and politicians were in constant contact with their working-class populations. Tyers knew his working-class visitors and made a fortune showing them art. The Victorian M.P.s infuriated Queen Victoria by rejecting plans to move the National Gallery from working-class central London to middle-class South Kensington. Henry Cole opened his new museum in Bethnal Green in 1872, and in the first six months, it was packed out with East Enders. Despite their lifestyle, the entrepreneurs, politicians and museum professionals were all firmly grounded in working-class culture. The birth of the Arts Council and the rise of the curators saw a major rift open up between those who enjoyed art and those who controlled art. Today this gap is wider than ever.

In their book *The Blunders of our Governments,* Anthony King and Ivor Crewe coin the term, 'cultural disconnect', to explain the gap between politicians and civil servants and the rest of the country. Cultural disconnect occurs when the assumptions that politicians and civil servants make are radically wrong and, "when men and women in Whitehall and Westminster unthinkingly project onto others values, attitudes and whole ways of life that are not remotely like their own." In short, "The man in Whitehall not only did not know best: he did not know that he did not know that which he badly needed to know."[511]

Three examples illustrate the cultural disconnect that exists in the nation's galleries today.

If you managed to get a ticket for the 2016 V&A Summer Party, you would have been transported to a world far removed from the everyday reality of regional galleries struggling to meet their cuts. Posing before a wall of pink peonies, the stars ranged from Kate Moss to Kylie Minogue and Andrew Lloyd Weber to Ben Elton. No need for 'selfies'. Queen Victoria would not have been amused to see her beloved Albert's museum turned into a show-stopper party, starring among others, Jenna Coleman, aka Queen Victoria in the eponymous television drama. Underwritten by Harrods to the tune of £200,000 and with tickets costing over £100, those unfortunate enough to have to buy their own tickets would have been amused to hear the V&A chairman, and publisher of *Vogue,* state that, "We thought that there were a lot of good fundraising events in London put on by arts institutions, but we wanted to do something more egalitarian."[512] Two weeks later, if you left the V&A and walked up Exhibition Road and into Hyde Park, you would find the Serpentine Gallery Party in full flow, though, as Kate Spicer commented, it would be, "an exhausting hobble in £800 Manolo Blahniks."[513] Described by *Vogue* as, "a highlight of London's social calendar", you would have met the same set who were at the V&A party.

The second example of cultural disconnect involves the former Chancellor of the Exchequer, George Osborne. In his final days in office, before being ruthlessly sacked by the Prime Minister, the man who told the country that, "we're all in this together" authorised a one-off Treasury payment of £19 million to keep a painting in the National Gallery. The painting is *A Portrait of a Young Man in Red Cap* by the 16th-century Florentine artist Jacob Pontormo. The National Gallery already has six Pontormos, yet the man who brought austerity to the masses and the closure of galleries and museums across the country had no qualms in allocating £19 million of taxpayer's money on yet another Pontormo rather than using these funds to throw a lifeline to struggling regional galleries that had been starved of funding.[514]

Staying with the National Gallery, if in these difficult times for the art world you offered to help as a volunteer, you would discover that, "Unfortunately, as the Gallery is a comparatively small organisation we lack the space and other facilities to offer voluntary work and only very rarely have any opportunity for work experience."[515] The National Gallery has 600 staff: the European definition of a Small and Medium Enterprise is one which employs less than 250 people. At a time when it is difficult for even well-qualified post-graduates to get work in the art world, evidence of volunteering can be crucial to career progression. By contrast the outstanding Peace Museum in Bradford has two part-time staff, but like most small museums it welcomes and trains both volunteers and work experience pupils.

The national galleries all work hard to attract children and run events to address gender, race and disability. But the examples I have given illustrate the cultural distance between London and the rest of the country, and as the number of working-class visitors continues to fall, so the cultural distance between galleries and communities continues to grow.[516]

It is no coincidence that our three examples are in London. The ability of the capital to drain funds from the rest of the country is a major factor in preventing working-class people from accessing art.

In a debate on funding the National Gallery in 1833, William Cobbett, who was then M.P. for Oldham, "objected to the whole population of the country being taxed to pay for the erection of metropolitan buildings."[517] One hundred years later, as we have seen, Sir Henry Markham noted that of £1,450,000 spent on art galleries and museums, £1 million went to London while the remaining £450,000 funded 770 provincial museums and galleries.[518] Keynes said he wanted to see art flourish throughout the country, but then poured money into Covent Garden.

Following his death, the Arts Council continued the focus on London. In the 1951 Annual Report, Bill Williams, who was now the all-powerful General Secretary, and who had moved steadily from left to right across the political spectrum as his career progressed, made an extremely disingenuous comment:

> The Arts Council did not decide to give half of its money to London; it resolved to act as patron to certain institutions already established, and of these the most meritorious and representative were situated in London. If any provincial city had assumed the responsibility for creating and maintaining, say, Sadler's Wells, the Arts Council would gladly have become its patron.[519]

In this same report, Williams abandoned CEMA's policy of, 'the best for the most', and replaced it with, 'few but roses'. The man who had set up *Art for the People* was now firmly on the side of the elite. Three years later, the body charged with promoting the arts took the theme of centralisation forwards with an amazing attack on local councils, stating in the 1954 Annual Report, "Certain local authorities have shown an excess of zeal by providing concerts and plays under their own management."[520] Centralisation was finally achieved when the last of the regional offices, set up by CEMA, was closed in 1956. A note in the Annual Report for that year presages the best of today's spin doctors by commenting that, "These changes do not represent, as some critics have declared, any doctrine of 'centralisation'…the closure of the regional offices implies no change in the direction of Council policy."[521] Even George Orwell would have been shocked at their use of 'newspeak'.

It took the formidable team of Harold Wilson and his visionary Minister of Arts, Jennie Lee, to reverse the dominance of London in their White Paper, *A Policy for the Arts*. Even then the hidden hand of the establishment tried to rewrite the paper to reinforce London's position. In a briefing note to the Prime Minister, Burke Trend, the powerful Cabinet Secretary who had been introduced to opera by Keynes, complains that, "the great national institutions", such as Covent Garden, "are not singled out for any degree of special mention" and that they are important to the whole country and not just London, "because they are at the apex of the pyramid."[522] A more famous Cabinet Secretary, Sir Humphrey Appleby, put it more succinctly, saying that the subsidy of the arts, "Is not to be given to what people want! It is for what people don't want but ought to have."[523] Fortunately, Harold Wilson ignored Burke Trend.

After nearly 200 years of handwringing, the imbalance between London and the regions is still scandalous despite the moves by the Arts Council to redress the balance in 2023. In 2013 an important piece of research by Stark, Gordon and Powell (GPS Culture) finally exposed the facts in plain English. In 2013 the spend on arts per head of population in London was £70.00 compared with £5.00 in the regions.[524] Equally inequitable was the lottery spend. The people of Westminster spent £14.5 million on lottery tickets between 1995 and 2013, and their arts organisations received £408 million.[525] In the same period, the people of County Durham spent £34 million and received a return of only £12 million. Using a different approach, Stark and his colleagues calculated the 'regional premium', or cost of living outside London. A Leeds family of two adults and two children, visiting London at half-term and using rail cards, the cheapest hotels and eating frugally would spend £947 on a three-day visit. The same family living in Cambridge would spend £333 and a family from outer London only £185.10. A difference between London and Leeds of £761.90.[526]

The imbalance is not accidental. In response to the work of GPS, Melvyn Bragg stated that, "London is simply eating up resources, which are limited, and is therefore starving the rest of the country. This is wrong, short-sighted and undoubtedly unfair."[527] Governments of all parties and the Arts Council have long argued that new money would be required to fund the regions without damaging London. But as GPS comment, new money did arrive and in large numbers. Since 1994, the Lottery has provided an extra £3.5 billion, but this has merely meant more money for London.[528] As we have seen the first major lottery grant was to Covent Garden. The determination of the government and the Arts Council to continue supporting London against the regions is demonstrated in the failure to use the Lottery money which had been diverted to the Olympics but returned to the Lottery Boards in 2013. As GPS note, an Arts Council shift of this post-Olympics money amounted to only an extra 0.25p. per head going to the regions.[529] Not only does London get an unfair share, but it is the organisations which attract the middle and upper classes, and which receive 82% of all private donations, who get the biggest share of the cake. The Royal Opera House, the Royal National Theatre, English National Opera, Sadler's Wells and the Southbank Centre have received more Lottery funding since 1995 than the 33 councils where communities are least engaged with the arts.[530]

London also benefits at the expense of the regions due to the sacrosanct issue of free admission to national galleries and museums. As we have seen this expensive policy has merely resulted in the middle-class visitors making repeat visits while the number of working-class visitors has declined. While London goes free, regional galleries get cuts. Arguing for a return to charging in London, Tristram Hunt wrote in 2011 of the costs facing local museums:

But not in London. This metropolitan, club-class government has made sure that our global cultural icons are immune from pressures hitting their regional colleagues and, even more perversely, in the case of Tate Modern, continue to enjoy secure funds for major capital projects.[531]

When, in 2017, Tristram Hunt moved from being Member of Parliament for Stoke to Director of the V&A, the press office put out a release explaining that he no longer supported charging though he was still passionate about supporting museums in the regions.[532]

Finally, all galleries and museums have stores, but in 2015, the Government gave the V&A, the British Museum and the Science Museum £150 million to improve their storage facilities. If Henry Cole had been given these funds, he would have used them to send artefacts and paintings to museums and galleries across the country rather than lock them away in yet more stores in London.

But it is not just a case of London draining money from the rest of the country. In 2015, The Science Museum decided to transfer the core of the National Science and Media Museum's (NSMM) photographic collection from Bradford to London.

Bradford is a city which has been hard hit by recession. The closure of the woollen mills in the 1970s was followed by the closure of the district's manufacturing industry. In the 1980s, unemployment stood at record levels and to reverse the decline the Council launched a tourism initiative based on Haworth and the Brontes, the city's curry houses, the NSMM and its heritage of Victorian buildings. One of these buildings is Manningham Mills, built by Samuel Lister and his brother in 1873, but which was now derelict. In 1983, in partnership with the V&A, the Council put on an exhibition of South Asian art entitled *Petals of the Lotus*. Out of this came a proposal to lend the Council some of the V&A's extensive collection of Asian art, 95% of which was stored in a warehouse in Battersea, to create an exhibition in Manningham Mills.

But the Council underestimated the power of the London museum mafia. Despite warm words from the Director, Roy Strong, and his successor Elizabeth Esteve-Coll, despite support from Mrs. Thatcher's indomitable press secretary, Bernard Ingham, and despite the offer of space in an ideal setting, the V&A Trustees refused to let any of the collection leave the store in Battersea.[533] Move forwards thirty years, and the V&A is still hoarding its Asian collection, but in a power grab reminiscent of the original looting of art from the Indian Sub-Continent, the Science Museum has decided that 400,000 of the most important photographs from Bradford's National Science and Media Museum be transferred to the V&A. In a meeting in London in 2015 the Science Museum Board, made up of the great and the good and with no connections to Bradford, took a unilateral decision to transfer the Royal Photographic Society (R.P.S.) collection to London. The move was opposed by the National Media Museum board in Bradford, but their views were of no consequence. In a statement the Head of the NSMM, Jo Quinton-Tulloch, stated that, "the R.P.S. collection would find a home where they can be accessed and enjoyed by public and researchers alike."[534] Yet more people now have to travel to London in an age when digital access is increasingly available and when cities like Bradford need every visitor they can get.

Since 2014, there have been positive moves to reverse the imbalance, but arts groups in the regions are not holding their breath as much of their funding comes from hard-hit local authorities. Here again the North/South divide is equally stark. In Liverpool, one of the most deprived areas in the country, council spend per head has been reduced by £390 between 2010 and 2016. In Elmbridge in Surrey, known as the English Beverly Hills because of the number of super-rich residents from the world of film and television, the reduction is only £8.14.[535] Between 2010 and 2021, local councils had cut spending on the arts by as much as 75%.

GPS have done an important job in shining a light on the Government and the Arts Council and holding them to account for the disparity between London and the regions. The Arts Council now has a clear strategy of re-balancing expenditure across the country with a ministerial instruction directing the Arts Council to move funding of £24 million from London to the regions with the decision to force English National Opera to move out of London dominating the headlines.[536]

We shall have to wait and see if the declarations from the Arts Council that they will now move money to the regions holds up. If so, with the exception of Jennie Lee's period, this will be the first time since Cobbett gave his impassioned speech in 1833.

The figures from London and the regions illustrate one small aspect of the inequality that exists in Britain today. Visiting art galleries will not be high on your list of priorities when you are struggling to make ends meet, but that does not mean that you should be denied the opportunity and it does not mean that you should pay for the well-off to visit them.

Three examples will suffice to show how the working classes subsidise the cultural life of the middle classes.

First on the list is admission to art galleries. At first sight, entrance to the national galleries is free but not to the key exhibitions and the big blockbusters. Take the National Gallery as an example. There are concessions, but even then the cost for two people is £44, though if you are a member you go free. So if you can afford to pay £119 upfront, then you and your partner get free admission, and if you can pay by Direct Debit, this is reduced to £109. If you are on unemployment benefit, or to use the correct Orwellian term Job Seekers Allowance, you will be unable to find such a large sum, and so by paying on the door, you are subsidising the better off. The trustees of the national galleries have introduced a two-tier system, and this is one reason why despite free admission, the number of working-class visitors is in decline.[537] The national galleries are now introducing a range of concessions for those on benefit but if you are on the Real Living Wage you will still be unable to pay the entrance charge of £44 per couple.

Secondly, an increasing proportion of arts funding now comes from the lottery and while it is a 'voluntary tax' there is an inverse relationship between educational attainment and spending on lottery tickets. Those with the highest education, who tend to visit art galleries, buy fewer tickets than those with a poor education who do not visit art galleries. We saw above how the people of County Durham subsidise the well-off in Westminster.

Lastly, the poor are by definition not going to pay high rates of Income Tax, Inheritance Tax or Capital Gains tax, and they will not be spending time worrying about Corporation Tax. But this does not mean that reductions in these taxes, available to wealthy individuals and private companies, should be used to reinforce their cultural capital. Under the Government's Cultural Gifts and Acceptance in Lieu Schemes, it is possible to gift paintings and objects to the nation and receive substantial reductions in the above taxes. Elements of the scheme are even known as a 'douceur' or 'sweetener'. As a consequence, many companies have an incentive to invest in art, and over 150 companies in the U.K. have corporate art collections.[538] It would be misleading to state that companies only collect art to reduce their taxes as many sponsor young artists. When the Vanquis Banking Group was Provident Finance it had a major art collection and worked with a wide range of schools. Harris notes that 60% of company collections are available for the public to visit by appointment, but in reality these major collections are but one example of the nation's 'Hidden Art'.[539] One other bastion of 'Hidden Art' is the universities. In 2015 a BBC Freedom of Information request revealed that universities in England had spent £20 million on art in the previous five years. As the union Unison stated, this was at a time when many universities paid their staff less than the living wage. What price culture?[540]

Between 2011 and 2021, the Treasury forewent £284 million under the Art in Lieu scheme[541]. In March 2015, the Churchill family settled a £9.4 million tax bill by gifting 37 paintings by Churchill to the Government. All but two of the paintings will remain in Churchill's former home at Chartwell.[542]

Staying with the Churchill family, one way to avoid tax is to state that members of the public can visit your home to view items that would otherwise have been taxed. Mark Thomas, the social-activist comedian, took a group of people to visit the home of Sir Nicholas Soames, Churchill's grandson, to view heirlooms he had been left including, "a lovely three-tier mahogany buffet with partially slender balustrade upright support." Soames was so surprised and outraged at this invasion that he contacted the Inland Revenue and paid the tax.[543] Paintings and objects are allocated to galleries across the country, but in 2021, the great majority of the 36 'gifts' went to galleries and houses in the South East of England. Given the distribution of wealth in Britain this is not surprising, but the corollary is that the majority of the working classes live outside the South East. Consequently, £284 million, which could have paid for schools and hospitals, was foregone, and the outcome was to reinforce the cultural capital of the middle classes.

The Institute for Public Policy and Research 2004 report, *For Art's*

Sake, is worth quoting at length as it gives a striking example of the tax benefits:

> The National Gallery was recently given £11.5 million from the Heritage Lottery Fund to help keep Raphael's *Madonna of the Pinks* in the U.K. The cost will be around £21 million, and the money will go to the Duke of Northumberland, one of the richest men in the country. The Duke will not be taxed on the sale of the painting if it remains in the U.K. Art and the arts have a value. Hard choices have to be made.

The £11.5 million grant is equal to:

- 695 newly-qualified staff nurses for one year
- 635 newly-qualified teachers for one year
- 687 newly-qualified prison officers for one year.[544]

In a final twist to the tale, it now appears that the painting may not be an original. Two experts, Professor James Beck of Columbia University and Antonio Natale of the Uffizi, both believe it is a copy.[545]

The working classes are not only paying for the cultural activities of the middle and upper classes but in being denied access to art, are being denied access to cultural capital.

In *Social Class in the 21st Century,* Mike Savage draws on the work of the French sociologist, Pierre Bourdieu, to show the importance of cultural capital. Bourdieu states that cultural capital is as important as economic and social capital.[546] Cultural capital is what we would call highbrow culture: art, music, opera and literature and in particular those works that feature in the western canon. If you do not have access to cultural capital, your life chances are radically reduced.

Bourdieu argues that the middle classes use their knowledge and familiarity with highbrow culture to differentiate themselves from the working classes. They use cultural capital to maintain and retain their dominant position in society, and Bourdieu describes this as 'symbolic violence', examples of which would be television programmes that stigmatise and denigrate the working classes.

Two examples from Savage illustrate the importance of gaining and maintaining cultural capital: firstly, graduates from the elite universities, who earn significantly more than those from other universities, score very highly on cultural capital. Secondly, only three of the top twenty local authorities, ranked by cultural capital, are outside the wealthy enclave of London and the South East.[547]

Recent work on the importance of cultural capital in education indicates that in both Europe and America, cultural capital is an important determinant of educational success. Cultural capital is a key factor in determining admissions to Oxford University; an important element in the General Certificate of Secondary Education in England; and a determining factor in Belgium, Denmark and Norway in secondary schools, while studies in America have come to similar conclusions.[548] The Social Mobility Commission report *The childhood origins of social mobility: socio-economic inequalities and changing opportunities* emphasises the importance of cultural capital, and it is a key factor leading to a gap on average of £7,000 per year between people from working-class backgrounds in the same professions as those from the middle classes.[549]

Savage states that highbrow culture may be an outdated concept limited to older generations: witness the grey heads at the opera. An emerging culture may be replacing it consisting of contemporary music, computer games, social media and the gym. But using Bourdieu's analysis, the dominant classes would be quite capable of defining and refining the emerging culture to preserve their position in society.

The research all carries many caveats, but the importance of cultural capital is now firmly established as a key factor in educational success and future earnings.

Bourdieu and Savage both highlight the role of cultural capital in maintaining inequality in society, and in this book we are concerned with access to art, which is just one aspect of highbrow culture. The following stark statistic shows the grip that the dominant classes have across the cultural field: for every £1 spent by the Labour Government in 2008 on brass bands, it spent £1,113 on opera.[550] Staying with music, the difference between Glyndebourne, well-off, middle-aged opera-goers in their evening dress, and Glastonbury, cash-strapped young people in their wellingtons, shows the power of the middle classes. Glyndebourne is a charity and as such benefits from tax relief. Glastonbury, rather than being a charity, generates over £1 million a year for charity, paid for by the young people buying unsubsidised tickets. [551]

Access to the arts is also increasingly seen as a factor adding to the quality of life. In her paper, *'Raising our quality of life: the importance of investment in arts and culture,'* Abigail Gilmore lists a range of studies showing how people's quality of life benefits from participation in cultural activities.[552] She cites the Arts Council report *The Value of Arts and Culture to People and Society,* which states that, "Research has evidence that a high frequency of engagement with arts and culture is generally associated with a high level of subjective well-being," but also notes that, "those who are most actively involved with the arts and culture that we invest in tend to be from the most privileged parts of society."[553] Similarly, GPS, in their 2016 document *The Next Steps?,* emphasise the role of the arts and culture, "in supporting and enhancing individual and community wellbeing" and the need to ensure that taxpayers' money is used to help individuals and communities in the greatest need.[554]

In summary, the working classes are not only paying for the cultural activities of the middle classes but in being denied access to art, they are being denied the capital that Savage shows is a crucial component in driving our increasingly unequal society. As stated earlier what was once, "art for the many not the few" has now become, "from the many to the few."

The subtitle of this book is, '*How the middle classes hijacked the nation's galleries*'. When I was writing the book, many people, especially those who work in art galleries, denied the issue of class and accused me of concocting a conspiracy theory. The figures speak for themselves. The latest statistics from the Government show a continuing decline in the number of people from the working classes visiting the major national galleries in London.[555] To add to this, Dorling and Hennig show in their paper, "London and the English desert – the geography of cultural capital in the U.K.", that between 2012 and 2014 self-direct school visits to the major galleries and museums in London fell by 13.3 % and outreach activities by 21.5%. They conclude that, "any argument that the increased concentration of arts funding in these few major institutions is resulting in more outreach and visits from schools would be wrong."[556]

At the same time there has been a dramatic drop in the money spent on the arts by schools. In a Times Education Supplement survey in 2022, 68% of schools report cuts to art education.[557]

But a significant fact is that the Department of Culture, Media and Sport (DCMS), has stopped collecting information on class from the major galleries and museums.[558] Until 2010 the Performance Indicators from the major galleries and museums included the number of visitors from the National Statistics Socioeconomic Classification groups 5–8, or in plain English, working class. A well-known tactic of all governments is that when statistics do not suit their purpose they merely stop collecting them.

One way of looking at the art world is through the lens of power. In his seminal book, *Power: A Radical View,* Steven Lukes lists three dimensions of power.[559] The first is straightforward power, such as that of a parent over a child; the second is where power is maintained by controlling the agenda, or to be more precise by keeping things off the agenda. The third is where people are persuaded to support actions that are not in their true interest, similar to false consciousness. The second dimension applies to the world of art.

As we have seen, the guardians of the nation's galleries have deliberately taken class off the agenda. As the number of working-class visitors continues to fall, they have decided to remove this issue from their statistical returns and to make it very difficult for anyone else to analyse what is happening. Significantly, trading figures have not been dropped. Exit through the shop. Another example of, "non-decision" making is given by GPS in their paper, *Rebalancing Our Cultural Capital*:

> It can be argued that the Arts Council's unwritten 'policy of response' that operated by default until 1984, and which established and consolidated the major patterns of funding, evaded responsibility to their ultimate paymasters, Britain's taxpayers.[560]

A key feature of 'non-decision' making is lack of transparency. Within three weeks of David Cameron becoming Prime Minister in May 2010, he wrote to all government departments calling for greater transparency and setting out clear guidelines. One year later, campaigners made a Freedom of Information request to the Tate to find out how much they received from the oil company BP. A three-year legal battle ensued, with the taxpayer-funded Tate refusing to release the information until forced to do so by the Information Tribunal in January 2015.

By establishing the arm's-length model, Keynes quite deliberately ensured that art and culture were not on the agenda of either Whitehall or Westminster. He had seen how successful his colleagues in the university world had been in establishing the University Grants Committee and making sure that universities continued to be funded by the taxpayer but were free from government control. The arm's-length approach is a classic model of non-accountability.

The dominance of London provides a clear example. Despite nearly two centuries of hand-wringing, the mandarins in Whitehall (Eton and Oxbridge) and the masters of the Arts Council (Eton and Oxbridge), who seamlessly move from the board of the Opera House to the National Gallery and on to Sadler's Wells, and who all live in London, successfully kept the issue off the agenda. Until GPS did the heavy lifting and exposed the hard facts, nothing would have changed. As noted above, since 1995 £35 billion of new funding only led to London receiving yet more of the 'percentage take'. GPS support the arm's-length principle but remark that it does not stop the government setting overall policy. They then go further and state that due to a lack of transparency, "guidance that Lottery funding should benefit the whole nation – particularly the least engaged and most disadvantaged – appears to have been ignored."[561]

In the previous chapter, we noted the dominance of former public-school pupils and Oxbridge graduates on the board of the Arts Council from the 1950s to the 1980s. In 1990 Noel Annan, a one-time leading light of the intellectual elite, wrote in his autobiography of the end of the elite, of the 'death of the dons', in dominating British culture. In 2008 Dave Griffiths, Andrew Miles and Mike Savage set out to investigate whether Annan was correct.[562] In *The end of the English cultural elite?*, they analyse the membership of the boards of the DCMS and conclude that the Arts Council and the major London galleries and museums are still dominated by people who went to the same elite public schools, went to Oxbridge and were members of the same London clubs. In short, no real change in the art world. They note how in 1946 Keynes, "succeeded in placing his Bloomsbury contacts on the commissioning panels"[563] of the Arts Council and in 2007 a closed circle of intellectuals still dominated the arts world. They state that, "the Arts Council remained, on the eve of the millennium, very much an 'establishment' agency strongly influenced by a male, Oxbridge-educated, academic/literary elite."[564] The same holds true of the so-called 'National' galleries and museums, "London museums, such as the V&A, the Science Museum, the Imperial War Museum, the Tate and the National Portrait Gallery are very well connected through having members from the same [elite public] schools."[565] The same institutions score highly on the other dimensions of university attended and membership of 'Gentlemen's' clubs. Griffiths et al. conclude that while there has been some change at the Arts Council and the London institutions, its impact has been negligible, and they question, "whether the national boards are really national given how closely they are all connected to London-interest groups and how simultaneously distant they are from the rest of the U.K."[566]

A second report in 2008, entitled *You've been Quango'd,* came to the same conclusion. The New Local Government Network examined the residential addresses of 1,000 quango members and revealed that, "the six most London-centric Public Bodies are all from the cultural sector."[567] They concluded:

Our survey demonstrates beyond doubt that it is Londoners who drive forwards the UK's cultural decisions and policies. The capital city reigns not only in terms of political power, but especially when it comes to decisions on media, broadcasting, fine art and music. Despite 2008 seeing Liverpool as the European Capital of Culture, the city sends none of its residents to the boards of these prestigious cultural bodies.[568]

In 2023 the boards of the National Gallery, the Tate and the V&A were completely dominated by Trustees based in London with no councillors or museum managers from the regions on any of the 'National' boards.

Any change in the governance of the national galleries has been to increase the number of trustees from the world of finance. O'Brien et.al., in their paper *Who runs the arts in England? A social network analysis of arts boards.*, note that there has been a shift away from trustees with an arts or academic background to those from the world of business and in particular finance although England has not yet reached the heights of the Metropolitan Museum of Art in New York where there are nine billionaires on the board.[569] And it is worth asking why the National Portrait Gallery has two Conservative Members of Parliament on the board in addition to the trustees with a financial background?

In recent years there has been a move to transfer local authority museums and art galleries to local trusts but it is significant that these trusts are dominated by local people who have a relationship with their communities and it is no coincidence that these are the galleries which show contemporary, dramatic narrative and achieve record visitor numbers.

The world of social science has seen an increase in the study of elites in recent years and it is no coincidence that the art world provides plentiful material. From the dominance of the elite Bloomsbury Group in the post-war period to the dominance today of wealthy financiers the only change has been from one elite to another.

But it is not just the governing bodies of the major galleries and museums, which are dominated by an unrepresentative elite. Today jobs in the arts are simply not accessible to people from the working classes. Three recent reports reveal the stark statistics. In a survey carried out by Goldsmiths University in 2015, 90% of respondents stated that they had been obliged to work for free at some point in their career. More than 25% earned less than £5,000, and 38% did not have a proper contract. Welcome to the world of middle-class internships. Hadrian Garrard, Director of Create, who were involved in commissioning the research, puts it bluntly when stating that, "we are in danger of returning to the pre-1950s when art was considered to be largely the preserve of the rich."[570]

The report of The Warwick Commission, *Enriching Britain: Culture, Creativity and Growth,* sums up the evidence when stating that, "children born into low-income families with low levels of educational qualifications are the least likely to be employed and succeed in the Cultural and Creative Industries." In the world of volunteering, often seen as a route into work in the cultural industries, the situation is similar, "once again participation correlates with a more comfortable socio-economic background."[571]

Finally, in 2017, in a report on internships, the Institute for Public Policy Research noted that across the economy, 44% of the working population had a breadwinning parent from a managerial or professional job whereas in the creative industries the figure is 64%.[572]

Two initiatives which came after the above reports are *Panic!2018 It's an Arts Emergency* and Museums as Muck.

The first of these uses a range of approaches to investigate inequality in the cultural workforce while Museums as Muck describes itself as, "a supportive network of working-class museum people and active agents for change" using their, " lived experience and sector expertise to address issues of inequity in museums and galleries."

As part of the overall Panic! Project academics from Edinburgh and Sheffield Universities drew up a report entitled *Social Class, Taste and Inequalities in the Creative Industries*.[573] This report examines significant inequalities in the cultural and creative industries but more significantly it looks at the scale of inequalities and provides a clearer understanding of how these inequalities operate.

The Panic! Project and the establishment of Museums as Muck are important steps forward as for the first time working-class people in the creative industries are not only involved in research but are creating change.

Waldemar Januszczak, art critic for *The Sunday Times*, arguing from a different angle, reaches a similar conclusion, describing contemporary curators:

> These people think alike, act alike, travel alike, reward alike and decide alike. Whereas artists, in my experience, are all very different, curators, in my experience, are all pretty much the same. They read the same magazines, attend the same conferences, and graduated from the same curatorial courses. They write the same, look the same. And, most destructively of all, they think the same.[574]

It is difficult to campaign for change when the government and the large London galleries stop collecting key statistics, when the arm's-length principle leads to a lack of transparency, when the majority of people on the boards of the national institutions are all based in

London and when jobs in art galleries and museums are dominated by the middle classes.

It is sometimes argued that the working classes do not go to art galleries because they are not interested in art. If this is the case, why were galleries full of working-class visitors in the past? One reason is that the galleries were full of pictures that people liked. Not just pictures for the working classes but pictures for everyone. Victorian narrative paintings, telling dramatic stories, covered the walls.

Across the centuries, dramatic narrative has been the key driving force behind all successful entertainment; from Dickens to Dan Brown in literature; from Browning to Betjeman in poetry and from Frith and Fildes to Hopper and Vettriano in art. It drives great cinema and is the force behind today's television blockbusters.

In their research, Bennet et.al. found that people who do not go to art galleries prefer portraits and landscape to modern art. Even among gallery-goers, Turner's The *Fighting Temeraire* was significantly more popular than Hockney's *Paper Pools* and Renaissance art was preferred to modern art.[575] In short, people like narrative art and especially those who do not go to art galleries.

But going back to Fildes and Frith, by the 1880s, they had both made a fortune from prints and seen their paintings hung in the national galleries. Fildes was knighted in 1918. Frith would have been knighted if he had not hidden portraits of his mistress in paintings such as *The Railway Station*, which included his wife and family. As we have seen, *Chatterton* was the most popular painting at the Manchester Art Treasures Exhibition, and a fence was required to hold back the crowds.

In the 20th century, artists did not stop producing narrative paintings, but those who controlled the galleries hung the newly fashionable, dramatic Victorian paintings in exhibitions with an entry charge, but refused to hang modern narrative work. As Bennett notes, "art is defined by where objects are displayed, whence their consecration, and these places are often controlled by individuals in privileged positions."[576]

A group of unskilled workers, interviewed by Bennett, describe the situation better than the statistics:

> Who tells us what is a good picture and what isn't? Who decides what gets hung up somewhere? Those who've got the say. I don't know who they are, do I. I'll tell you they're not from around here though.[577]

In the same survey, 52% of working-class respondents agreed that, "The arts funded by the government aren't really designed for ordinary people."[578]

We have seen that for many people the very cost of going to an exhibition is prohibitive, especially if you live outside London or the exhibition has an admission charge, but these quotes illustrate that cost is not the only factor. New Labour coined the term Social Exclusion and set up a Social Exclusion Unit. Galleries and museums were given targets aimed at increasing the number of working-class visitors though the term 'working class' was never used. But it was a classic case of blaming the victim. When on very rare occasions, galleries hang modern narrative paintings, the visitor numbers break all records.

Absent from 20th-century art history and absent from the national galleries are the artists whose paintings hang above the mantelpiece in a million homes. Artists who are best sellers but whose paintings are banned from public galleries. Artists who achieve record sales and record prices. Artists who are loved by the working classes but loathed by the elite. Mention Vladimir Tretchikoff, he of *The Green Lady* and one of the world's bestselling artists, in the National Gallery, and you would be very politely shown the door.

In his book *Just Above The Mantelpiece,* Wayne Hemingway, one-time fashion designer, collector of popular prints and now Professor of the Built Environment, tells how he was brought up living in an art gallery: 15 Thirlemere Drive, Morecambe, his grandmother's house. "Not for her the Mayfair Galleries or Sotheby's and Christie's auction rooms. She bought through Freeman's and Littlewood's catalogues, Argos....and the myriad of promenade gift shops." He goes on to argue that:

> Value deserves to be restored to a genre derided by certain members of the art elite and respect should be given to artists whose work broadened the horizons of collecting to reach the working classes, making this art form available to a wider public than ever before.[579]

When the BBC made a documentary about Tretchikoff's famous painting, *The Green Lady,* the prominent art critic, William Fever, described it as, "arguably the most unpleasant work of art to be published in the 20th century."

Today Tretchikoff, who has works hanging in a million homes, has been replaced by Jack Vettriano. The sale of his prints has made Vettriano a millionaire, but unlike Fildes and Frith, you will not find his paintings in the national galleries. In yet another example of non-decision making, top curators refuse to explain why Vettriano is disparaged by the elite. Like John Martin he is loved by the public but loathed by the critics. When Melvyn Bragg made a programme about Vettriano for the South Bank Show the Director of Tate Galleries, Sir Nicholas Serota, and the Director of the Scottish National Galleries,

Sir Timothy Clifford, were approached, but both knights of the realm were too busy to comment. Ask them to appear on the prestigious South Bank Show and talk about any other artist and they would have cleared their diaries.[580]

Two hundred and fifty years after Vauxhall Gardens, we shall not see the working classes flock to the high-end exhibitions in London's parks, and today the National Gallery does not need to worry about miasma from middle-class visitors damaging the paintings.

But change is in the air. London's dominance is being challenged. Thanks to the Freedom of Information Act, more light is being cast on the decisions of the elite boards of the national galleries. The House of Commons Digital, Culture, Media and Sport Select Committee has a long way to go to meet the vigorous questioning of the Victorian select committees about access to art, but a start has been made.

In 2002 Cartwright Hall in Bradford held a blockbuster exhibition with a difference. The gallery was full of working-class visitors admiring the works that hung on their walls at home. The nation's best-loved paintings had been brought in from the cold and were hanging in a prestigious gallery. In 2007, the Baltic Centre for Contemporary Art was full of people admiring paintings by Beryl Cook, she of the fat ladies. In 2009, people queued for up to six hours to see Banksy in Bristol with a record attendance of 300,000. In 2013, Jack Vettriano filled Kelvingrove Galleries in Glasgow. The people in Bradford could still see *The Brown Boy* by Reynolds and paintings by Hockney; in Gateshead the Baltic still had leading edge contemporary art; in Bristol, they could see works from Constable to Pissarro and in Glasgow the French Impressionists and Dali's famous *Christ of Saint John of the Cross*. But they were also able to see paintings they loved.

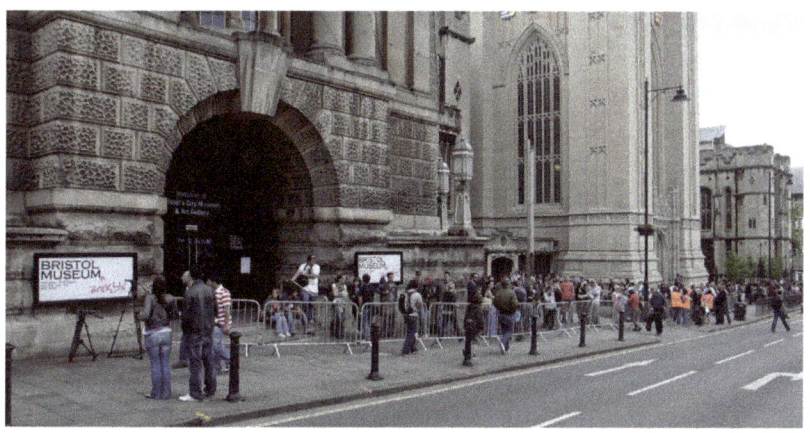

Banksy Exhibition, Bristol, 2009 - courtesy of SWNS

The children of working-class families in Bradford, Gateshead and Bristol saw paintings from their homes in an art gallery, laughed with Beryl Cook at her fat ladies and conspired with Banksy. In short they could enjoy modern, dramatic narrative and in so doing they became familiar with art galleries. When these galleries were welcoming children to their exhibitions they were also opening them to cultural capital and although no one outside academia would use such a term they were in a small way levelling the gap between the working-class children and their middle-class peers.

Is the tide turning?

Bibliography

Adams, R. (2010) *The V&A: empire to multiculturalism?* Museums and Society.

Addison, P. (1981) 'Jingo Joe' *London Review of Books*

Allan, D.G.C. (1979) *William Shipley: Founder of the Royal Society of Arts*. London: Scolar Press.

Allen, B. (1987) *Francis Hayman*. New Haven: Yale University Press.

Allen, B. (1995) *Towards a Modern Art World*. New Haven: Yale University Press.

Altick, R.D. (1978) *The Shows of London*. London: The Belknap Press.

Andersen, P., & Hansen, M.N. (2011) *Class and Cultural Capital: The case of class inequality in educational performance* in European Sociological Review

Appleton, J. (2001) *Museums for 'The People'?* London: Academy of Ideas.

Archer, J.H.G. (1986) *Art and Architecture in Victorian Manchester*. Manchester: Manchester University Press.

Arnold, D. (2004) *Art History: A very short introduction*. Oxford: Oxford University Press.

Arnold, M. (1869) *Culture and Anarchy*. Kindle Edition.

Arts Council of Great Britain (1961) *Partners in Patronage: Sixteenth annual report*. London: Arts Council.

Arts Council (2023) *Cultural Gifts Scheme & Acceptance in Lieu* 2013-23. London. Arts Council.

Atkinson, W. (2015) *Class*. Cambridge: Polity.

Austen, J. (1813) *Pride and Prejudice*. New York: Anchor Books.

Bailey, P. (1978) *Leisure and Class in Victorian England: Rational recreation and the contest for control 1830–1885.* London: Routledge & Kegan Paul.

Barlow, P., & Trodd, C. (2000) *Governing Cultures: art and institutions in Victorian London.* Aldershot: Ashgate.

Barnes, J. (2015) *Keeping an Eye Open: Essays on art.* Kindle Edition Location 434.

Barnett, H. (1918) *Canon Barnett: His Life, Work and Friends. Vol.II.* London: John Murray.

Barringer, T. (2005) *Men at Work, Art and Labour in Victorian Britain.* New Haven: Yale University Press.

Barringer, T., Rosenfeld, J., & Smith, A. (2012) *Pre-Raphaelites: Victorian avant-garde.* London: Tate Publishing.

Bell, C. (1938) *Civilization.* London: Pelican Books.

Bell, C. (1987) *Art.* Oxford: Oxford University Press.

Bennett, T. (1995) *The Birth of the Museum.* London: Routledge.

Bennett, T. Savage, M. Silva, E. Warde, A. Gayo-Cal, M., & Wright, D. (2009) *Culture, Class, Distinction.* London: Routledge.

Berger, J. (1972) *Ways of Seeing.* London: Penguin.

Besant, W. (1902) *The Autobiography of Sir Walter Besant.* New York: Dodd Mead.

Besant, W. (1997) *All Sorts and Conditions of Men.* Oxford: Oxford University Press.

Bills, M. (ed.) (2012) *Dickens and the Artists.* London: Yale University Press.

Black, J. (1987) *The English Press in the Eighteenth Century.* London:

Croom Helm.

Boddy, K. *Bloomsbury in Bloom.* Article in the UCL Leverhulme funded Bloomsbury Project website www.ucl.ac.uk/bloomsbury project. Accessed 26 April 2017.

Bonython, E. and Burton, A. (2003) *The Great Exhibitor: The life and work of Henry Cole.* London: V&A Publications.

Borzello, F. (1987*) Civilising Caliban: The Misuse of Art 1876–1980.* London: Routledge & Kegan Paul.

Bottero, W. (2009) 'Class in the 21st Century' in *Who Cares about the White Working Class?* Ed. Sveinsson, K.P. London: Runnymede Trust. p.7.

Boulton, A.W. (2012) *Transformative Beauty: Art museums in industrial Britain.* Stanford: Stanford University Press.

Bourdieu, D. (1984) *Distinction: A social critique of the judgement of taste.* London: Routledge.

Bourdieu, D., & Darbel, A. (1991) *The Love of Art.* Cambridge: Polity Press.

Bowton Luminary. (1857) *Bobby Shuttle and his Woife Sayroh's Visit to Manchester un-th Greight Hert Treasures Place Owd Traffort.* Manchester: John Heywood.

Bradley, I.C. (1990) *Titus Salt: Enlightened entrepreneur* in *Victorian Values: Personalities and perspectives in nineteenth-century society*

Breakwell, I. (2000) in *The Whitechapel Art Gallery Centenary Review 2001.* Manchester: Cornerhouse Publications..

Bronte, C. (1849) *Shirley.* London: Penguin (1981).

Buckley, P. (2009) *The National Lottery: Is it progressive?* London: Theos Think Tank.

Cannadine, D. (2000*) Class in Britain.* London: Penguin.

Carbonneau, J.B.C., Linton, W.J., Linton, H.D., & Morton, W. (1857) *The Art Treasures Examiner: A pictorial, critical and art historical record of the Art Treasures Exhibition at Manchester in 1857.* Manchester: A. Ireland.

Carey, J. (1992) *The Intellectuals and the Masses.* London: Faber and Faber.

Carey, J. (2005) *What Good Are the Arts?* London: Faber and Faber.

Chapple, J.A.V., & Pollard, A. (1966) *The Letters of Mrs. Gaskell.* Manchester: Manchester University Press.

Clark, K. (1964) *Ruskin Today.* London: Penguin.

Clark, K. (19740 *Another Part of the Wood: A self-portrait.* London: John Murray.

Clark, K. (1977) *The Other Half: A self-portrait.* London: John Murray.

Clark, K. (1980) *Civilisation.* London: BBC and John Murray.

Coke, D., & Borg, A. (2011) *Vauxhall Gardens: A history.* Yale: Yale University Press.

Cole, H. (1857) *The Functions of the Science and Art Department.* London: Chapman and Hall.

Cole, H. (1884) *Fifty Years of Public Work.* London: George Bell.

Conlin, J. (2006) *The Nation's Mantelpiece: A history of the National Gallery.* London: Pallas Athene.

Conlin, J. (2013) *The Pleasure Garden from Vauxhall to Coney Island.* Philadelphia: University of Pennsylvania Press.

Courtauld, S. (1949) *Ideals and Industry: War-time papers.* Cambridge: Cambridge University Press.

Cowling, J. (2004) *For Art's Sake: Society and the arts in the 21st century.* London: Institute for Public Policy Research.

Crewe, T. (2016) *The Strange Death of Municipal England* in London

Review of Books December 2016

Cruickshank, D. (2010) *The Secret History of Georgian London.* London: Random House Books.

Cunningham, H. (2014) *Time, work and leisure: Life changes in England since 1700.* Manchester: Manchester University Press.

Curl, J.S. (2010) *Spas, Wells & Pleasure Gardens of London.* London: Historical Publications.

Dakers, C. (2011) *A Genius for Money.* New Haven: Yale University Press.

Damrosch, L. (2005) *Jean Jacques Rousseau: Restless genius.* Boston: Houghton Mifflin.

Dartington Hall Arts Enquiry (1946)

Davenport-Hines R. (2015) *Universal Man: The seven lives of John Maynard Keynes.* London: William Collins.

Davis, W. (2012) *Into The Silence: The Great War, Mallory and the conquest of Everest.* London: Vintage Books.

De Tocqueville, A. (1958) *Journeys to England and Ireland*

Dickens, C. (1836) *Sketches by Boz.* London: Penguin.

Dickens, C. (1854) *Hard Times.* London: Penguin.

Dickens, C. (1857) *Household Words.* London: Bradbury and Evans.

Disraeli, B. (1845) *Sybil.* London: Penguin (1980).

Dorling, D., & Hennig, B.D. (2016) *London and the English Desert: The geography of cultural capital in the U.K.* London: Cultural Trends.

Duncan, C. (1995) *Civilizing Rituals Inside Public Art Museums.* Oxford: Routledge.

Duxbury-Neumann, S. (2015) *Little Germany: A history of Bradford's*

Germans. Stroud: Amberley Publishing.

E.T.B. (1857) *What to See and Where to See It or the Operatives Guide to the Art Treasures Exhibition.* Manchester: Abel Heywood.

Engels, F. (1845) *The Condition of the Working Class in England.* London: Penguin (1987).

Evans, B.I., & Glasgow, M. (1949) *The Arts in England.* London: The Falcon Press.

Fawcett, T. (1974) *The Rise of English Provincial Art: Artists, patrons and institutions outside London, 1800–1830.* Oxford: Clarendon Press.

Finke, U. (1986) *The Art Treasures Exhibition*

Fischer, E. (1971) *The Necessity of Art: A Marxist approach.* London: Pelican.

Fisher, M (2004) *Britain's Best Museums and Galleries.* London: Allen Lane.

Fitzgibbon, T. (1970) *A Taste of Scotland in Food and Pictures.* London: Pan Books.

Flanders, J. (2006) *Consuming Passions: Leisure and pleasure in Victorian Britain.* London: Harper Press.

Flanders, J. (2012) *The Victorian City: Everyday life in Dickens' London.* London: Atlantic Books.

Forgan, S., & Gooday, G. (1994) 'A Fungoid Assemblage of Buildings.' *History of Universities* (1994) 13: 153–192

Forster, E.M. (1951) *Two Cheers for Democracy.* London: Penguin.

Foss, B. (2007) *War Paint: Art, war, state and identity in Britain 1939–1945.* New Haven: Yale University Press.

Fraser, D. (1979) *Urban Politics in Victorian England.* London: Macmillan.

Fraser, D. (1980) *A History of Modern Leeds.* Manchester: Manchester University Press.

Freedland, J. (2012) *Eugenics: The skeleton that rattles loudest in the left's closet.* In The Guardian 17 February 2012.

Friedman, S. and Laurison, D. (2019) *The Class Ceiling. Why is Pays to be Privileged.* Bristol. Policy Press.

Friedman, S., Laurison, D., Macmillan, L. (2017) *Social Mobility, the Class Pay Gap and Intergenerational Worklessness: New insights from the labour force survey.* London: Social Mobility Commission.

Fry, R. (1981) *Vision and Design.* London: Oxford University Press.

Gaskell, E.C. (1975) *North and South.* London: Dent.

Gattrell, V. (2013) *The First Bohemians: Life and art in London's Golden Age.* London: Allen Lane.

Geddes Poole, A. (2010) *Stewards of the Nation's Art. Contested Cultural Authority 1890–1939.* Toronto: University of Toronto Press.

Gilmore, A. (2016) *Raising Our Quality of Life: The importance of investment in arts and culture.* London: Centre for Labour and Social studies.

Glasgow, M. (1975) 'The Concept of the Arts Council' in *Essays on John Maynard Keynes* ed. Milo Keynes. London: Cambridge University Press.

Golby, J.M., & Purdue, A.W. (1984) *The Civilisation of the Crowd: Popular culture in England 1750–1900.* Stroud: Sutton Publishing.

Gombrich, E.H. (1984) *The Story of Art.* Oxford: Phaidon.

Greenwood, T. (1888) *Museums and Art Galleries.* London: Simkin, Marshall.

Griffiths, D., Miles, A., & Savage, M. (2008) 'The end of the English cultural elite?' *Sociological Review.*

Gutting, G. (2005) *Foucault: A short introduction.* Oxford: Oxford University Press

Hadden Parkes (1864) *Window Gardens for the People and Clean and Tidy Rooms.* London: S.W. Partridge.

Hardman, M. (1986) *Ruskin and Bradford: An experiment in Victorian cultural history.* Manchester: Manchester University Press.

Harris, A. (2010) *Romantic Moderns: English writers, artists and the imagination from Virginia Woolf to John Piper.* London: Thames & Hudson.

Harris, J. (1970) *Government Patronage of the Arts in Great Britain.* Chicago: The University of Chicago Press.

Harris, P. (2002) Corporate Art Collections-Opportunities on a grand scale. *Arts Professional* www.artsprofessional.co.uk accessed 19 April 2017.

Haskell, F. (2000*) The Ephemeral Museum: Old Master paintings and the rise of the art exhibition.* New Haven: Yale University Press.

Hawthorne, N. (1883) *Our Old Home and English Note-Books*

Haythornthwaite, J. *Roller Coasters and Helter Skelters, Missionaries and Philanthropists: A history of patronage and funding at the Whitechapel Art Gallery* in *The Whitechapel Art Gallery Centenary Review* (2001)

Heffer, S. (2013*) High Minds: The Victorians and the birth of Modern Britain.* London: Random House Books.

Hemingway, W. (2000) *Just Above the Mantelpiece: Mass-market masterpieces.* London: Booth-Clibborn Editions Limited.

Hewison, R. (1981) *In Anger: Culture in the Cold War 1945–60.* London: Weidenfeld and Nicolson.

Hewison, R. (1995) *Culture & Consensus England: Art and politics since 1940.* London: Methuen.

Hewison, R. (2014) *Cultural Capital: The rise and fall of creative Britain.*

London: Verso.

Hill, K. (2005) *Culture and Class in English Public Museums, 1850–1914*. Aldershot: Ashgate.

Hills, J. (2015) *Good Times, Bad Times: The welfare myth of them and us*. Bristol: Policy Press.

Hitchcock, T., Shoemaker, R., Emsley, C., Howard, S., McLaughlin, J., et al. *The Old Bailey Proceedings Online 1674–1913* www.oldbaileyonline version7.1 April 2013.

Hoggart, R. (1958) *The Uses of Literacy*. Middlesex: Penguin.

Hoggart, R. (1989) Introduction in Orwell,G. (1989) *The Road to Wigan Pier* London. Penguin

Horrocks, C. (2009) *Introducing Foucault*. London: Icon Books.

Howarth, E., & Platnauer, H.M. (1911) *Directory of Museums in Great Britain and Ireland together with a section on India and Colonial museums*. London: Museums Association.

Hudson, D., & Luckhurst, K. (1954) *The Royal Society of Arts 1754–1954*. London: John Murray.

Hudson, K. (1972) *Patriotism with Profit: British agricultural societies in the eighteenth and nineteenth centuries*. London: Hugh Evelyn.

Hudson, K. (1975) *A Social History of Museums*. London: Macmillan.

Hudson, K. (1976) *The Bath & West*. Bradford-on Avon: Moonraker Press.

Hunt, T. (2004) *Building Jerusalem: The rise and fall of the Victorian city*. London: Weidenfeld & Nicolson.

Hunt, T., & Whitfield, V. (2008) *Art Treasures in Manchester 150 Years On*. Manchester: Manchester Art Gallery.

Hunter, D. (2015) *The Lives of George Frideric Handel*. Woodbridge: The

Boydell Press.

Hurd, D., & Young, E. (2014) *Disraeli, or, The two lives*. Kindle Edition.

Hutchison, E.M. (1971) *Aims and Action in Adult Education*. London: National Institute for Adult Education.

Hutchison, R. (1982*)* *The Politics of the Arts Council*. London: Sinclair Brown.

Jackson, K. (2011) *The Works of John Ruskin*. London: Pallas Athene.

Januszczak, W. (2014) *Talking 'bout a revolution*. The Sunday Times 12 January 2014.

Januszczak, W. (2015) *Sunday Times* 21 June 2015.

Jerrold, W.B. (1857) *How to See the Art Treasures Exhibition*. Manchester: A. Ireland.

Jevons, M. (1882) *Methods of Social Reform and Other Papers*. London: Macmillan.

Jevons, W. S. (1882) 'The Use and Abuse of Museums' in Jevons (1883)

Johnston, C., & Hartnell, J. (2015) *Cotton to Gold: Extraordinary collections of the industrial North West*. London: Two Temple Place.

Jones, C. (2015) *Universities in England spend £20 million on art work* BBC www.bbc.co.uk/news/uk-england-34677443.

King, A., & Crewe, I. (2014) *The Blunders of Our Governments*. London: Oneworld.

Kingsley, C. (1848) *Politics for the People*. London: Francis Lincoln.

Kingsley, C. (1849) *Alton Locke*. London: Penguin.

Lambert, R.S. (1938) *Art in England*. London: Penguin.

Langan, P. (2007) '*Prejudiced mill owner drove his workers into the unions'* in *Wharfedale Observer*

Lansley, S., & Mack, J. (2015) *Breadline Britain. The rise of mass poverty* London: Oneworld.

Lawson, D. (2013) *Why is free admission to art galleries and museums sacrosanct, when free swimming is not?* @indyvoices Monday 25 February 2013 www.independent.co.uk/voices. Accessed on 17

Leslie, C., & Dallison, O. (2008) *You've been Quango'd.* London: New Local Government Network.

Leventhal, F.M. (1990) 'The Best for the Most' CEMA and State Sponsorship of the Arts in Wartime, 1939–1945. In *Twentieth Century British History* Vol.1, No.3, 1990 p.289–317.

Lewis, G. (1989) *For Instruction and Recreation: A centenary history of the Museums Association.* London: Quiller Press.

Lukes, S. (1974) *Power: A radical view.* London: Macmillan.

MacCarthy, F. (1994) *William Morris: A life for our time.* London: Faber & Faber.

Macleod, D.S. (1996) *Art and the Victorian Middle Class: Money and the making of cultural identity.* Cambridge: Cambridge University Press.

Markham, S.F. (1938) *The Museums and Art Galleries of the British Isles.* Dunfermline: Carnegie United Kingdom Trust.

Marsden, G. (1990) *Victorian Values: Personalities and perspectives in nineteenth-century society.* London: Longman.

Marx, K., & Engels, F. (1983) *Collected Works.* London: Lawrence Wishart.

Miers, H. (1928) *Report on Public Museums of the British Isles.* Dunfermline: Carnegie United Kingdom Trust.

Minihan, J. (1977) *The Nationalization of Culture: The development of state subsidies to the arts in Great Britain.* London: Hamish Hamilton.

Morris, E. (2001) *Public Art Collections in North-West England.* Liverpool: Liverpool University Press.

Morris, T. (1857) *The Painters and Their Works: An historical, descriptive and directorial handbook to the Art Treasures Exhibition.* Manchester: Abel Heywood.

Myrone, M. (2012) *John Martin: Apocalypse.* London: Tate Publishing.

Neumann, S.D. (2015) *Little Germany: A history of Bradford's Germans.* Stroud: Amberley.

Nord, D.E. (2013) 'Night and Day' in Conlin, J. (2013) *The Pleasure Garden from Vauxhall to Coney Island.* Philadelphia: University of Philadelphia Press

Obama, B. (2007) *Dreams from My Father.* London: Canongate.

O'Brien,D., Griffiths,R., Taylor M., (2022) *Who runs the arts in England? A social network analysis of arts boards.* London. Poetics.

Old Bailey Proceedings Online 2003–2013 Version 7.1 April 2013 ISBN 978-0-9557876-0-7. www.oldbaileyonline.org6/5/2014

Orwell, G. (1989) *The Road to Wigan Pier.* London: Penguin.

Oxford Dictionary of National Biography (2004). Oxford: Oxford University Press.

Oxford Dictionary of National Biography (2020)

Parkes, S.H. (1862) *Flower Shows of Window Plants for the Working Classes of London.* London: Emily Faithfull.

Parkes, S.H. (1864) *Window Gardens for the People.* London: S.W. Partridge.

Paxman, J. (2009) *The Victorians: Britain through the paintings of the age.* London: BBC Publishing.

Peake, F. (1908) *Has Sunday Opening of Museums, Art Galleries and Libraries been a success?* London: Lord's Day Observance Society.

Perkin H., (1969) *Origins of Modern English Society* London. Routledge.

Pearson, N. (1982) *The State and the Visual Arts.* Milton Keynes: Open University Press.

Pergam, E. A. (2011) *The Manchester Art Treasures Exhibition of 1857: Entrepreneurs, connoisseurs and the public.* Surrey: Ashgate.

Pointon, M (ed.) (1994) *Art Apart.* Manchester: Manchester University Press.

Poynter, E.J. (1880) *Classic and Italian Painting.* London: Sampson Low, Marston, Searle, & Rivington.

Prior, N. (2002) *Museums and Modernity.* Oxford: Berg.

Putnam, R. (2015) *Our Kids: The American Dream in Crisis.* New York: Simon & Schuster.

Report of the Select Committee on Arts and their Connexion with Manufactures (*1836*).

Report of the Select Committee on National Monuments and Works of Art (1839)

Report of the Select Committee on the National Gallery (1850)

Report of the Select Committee on the National Gallery Site (1857)

Report of Select Committee (1853)

Richards, L., Garrat, E., Heath, A.F., Anderson, L., & Altintas, E. (2016) *The Childhood Origins of Social Mobility: Inequalities and changing opportunities.* London: Social Mobility Commission.

Roberts, C. (2017) *The Inbetweeners: The new role of internships in the graduate labour market.* London: Institute for Public Policy Research. p.29.

Robertson, B. (2004) 'The South Kensington Museum in Context: An alternative history.' *Museum and Society* March 2004 2(1) 1–14.

Rogers, C. (1857) *A Peep at t'Manchester Art Treasures Exhebishan.* London: T.W. Grattan.

Rose, J. (2002) *The Intellectual Life of the British Working Classes.* New Haven: Yale University Press.

Rosslyn, H. (2013) *Bought with Love. The Secret History of British Art.* BBC.

Royal Commission on National Museums and Galleries (1929). London: His Majesty's Stationary Office.

Royal Society of Arts. (1760) *Minute Book.* London: Royal Society of Arts.

Ruskin, J. (1864) *Traffic.* Kindle Edition.

Rutter, F. (1927) *Since I Was Twenty-Five.* London: Constable.

Sabbach, K. (2001) *Power into Art: The Making of Tate Modern.* London: Penguin.

Sandell, R. (2002) *Museums, Society, Inequality.* London: Routledge.

Sandford, F.R. (1881) *Report on the System of Circulating art Objects on Loan from the South Kensington Museum.* London: South Kensington Museum.

Saumarez Smith, C. (2009) *The National Gallery. A Short History.* London. Frances Lincoln.

Saumarez Smith, C. (2012) *The Company of Artists: The origins of the Royal Academy of Arts in London.* London: Modern Art Press.

Savage, M. (2015) *Social Class in the 21st Century.* London: Penguin.

Scharf, G. (1858) *On The Manchester Art Treasures Exhibition, 1857.*

Siegel, J. (2008) *The Emergence of the Modern Museum.* Oxford: Oxford

University Press.

Sinclair, A. (1995) *Arts and Cultures: The history of the fifty years of the Arts Council of Great Britain.* London: Sinclair-Stevenson.

Skidelsky, R. (2001) *John Maynard Keynes. Volume Three: Fighting for Britain 1937–1946.* London: Macmillan.

Smith, D. (2004) *He's our favourite artist. So why do the galleries hate him so much?* The Guardian 11 January 2004.

Southworth, G.S. (1941) *Vauxhall Gardens: A chapter in the social history of England.* New York: Columbia University Press.

Spicer, K. (2016) *Heavyweight clash over summer bash.* London: The Sunday Times

Stark, P., Gordon, C., Powell, D. (2014) *Rebalancing Our Cultural Capital.* www.gpsculture.co.uk

Stark, P., Gordon, C., Powell, D. (2014) *The Place Report: Policy for the lottery, the arts and community in England.* www.gpsculture.co.uk

Steadman Jones (1984) *Outcast London: A study in the relationship between classes in Victorian Society.* London: Penguin Books.

Steegman, J. 1970) *Victorian Taste: A study of the arts and architecture from 1830–1870.* London: Nelson's University Paperbacks.

Stourton, J. (2016) *Kenneth Clark: Life, Art and Civilisation.* London: William Collins.

Strong, R. (1999) *The Spirit of Britain: A narrative history of the arts.* London: Hutchinson.

Sullivan, A. (2001) *Cultural Capital and Educational Attainment* in Sociology

Taylor, B. (1999) *Art for the Nation: Exhibitions and the London public 1747–2001.* New Jersey: Rutgers University Press.

The Whitechapel Centenary Review (2001). London: The Whitechapel Gallery.

Tickner, L. (2000) *Modern Life and Modern Subjects: British art in the early twentieth century.* Yale: Yale University Press.

Times Higher Education Supplement. (1977).

Uglow, J. (2002) *Hogarth: A life and a world.* London: Faber & Faber.

Upchurch A.R. (2011) 'Keynes's legacy: an intellectual's influence reflected in arts policy.' In *International Journal of Cultural Policy*. Vol.17, No.1 January 2011, 69–80.

Upchurch, A.R. (2004) 'John Maynard Keynes, The Bloomsbury Group and the Origins of the Arts Council Movement' in *International Journal of Cultural Policy* Vol.10, No. 2, 2004. ISSN 1028-6632.

Upchurch, A.R. (2012). *'Missing from policy history: The Dartington Hall Arts Enquiry'* in *International Journal of Cultural Policy* 19 (5) 610–622.

Veblen, T. (2009) *The Theory of the Leisure Class.* Oxford: Oxford University Press.

Vergo, P. (ed.) (1989) *The New Museology.* London: Reaktion Books.

Victoria and Albert Museum. *The Story of Music Hall* (2015)

Waagen, G.F. (1857) *A Walk through The Art Treasures Exhibition at Manchester.* London: John Murray.

Warwick Commission. (2015) *Enriching Britain: Culture, creativity and growth.* Coventry: University of Warwick.

Waterfield, G. (1998) 'Art Galleries and the Public' in *Art Treasures of England: The Regional Collections.* London: The Royal Academy.

Waterfield, G. (2016) *The People's Galleries: Art museums and exhibitions in Britain 1800–1914.* New Haven: Yale University Press.

Waterfield, G. (ed.) (1994) *Art for the People.* London: Dulwich Picture Gallery.

Waterfield, G., & Clifford, T. (eds.) (1991) *Palaces of Art.* London: Dulwich Picture Gallery.

White, E.W. (1975) *The Arts Council of Great Britain.* London: David-Poynter.

Whitehead, C. (2004) *The Public Art Museum in Nineteenth Century Britain: The development of the National Gallery.* Aldershot: Ashgate.

Willes, M. (2014) *The Gardens of the British Working Class.* New Haven: Yale University Press.

Williams, E. (1971) *The Pre-History of the Arts Council* in *Aims and Action in Adult Education 1921–1971* ed. by Hutchinson, E.M. London: National Institute of Adult Education.

Williams, R. (1979) *Culture and Society 1780–1950.* London: Penguin.

Wilson, A.N. (2003) *The Victorians.* London: Arrow.

Witts, R. (1998) *Artists Unknown: An alternative history of the Arts Council.* London: Warner Books.

Wolf, J., & Steed, J. (1988) *The Culture of Capital: Art, power and the nineteenth century middle class.* Manchester: Manchester University Press.

Woodson-Boulton, A. (2012) *Transformative Beauty: Art museums in Industrial Britain.* Stanford: Stanford University Press.

Woolf, V. (1919) *Roger Fry.* London: Penguin.

Newspapers and Magazines

Apollo

Daily Chronicle

Edinburgh Literary Journal

Frasers Magazine

Lloyds Newspaper

London Illustrated News

London Review of Books

Manchester Guardian

Norwood Press

Nottingham Evening Post

Punch

South Yorkshire Times

The Art Journal

The Art Newspaper

The Art Treasures Examiner

The Bradford Observer

The Hawk

The Independent

The Listener

The Spectator

The Times

Wharfedale Observer

York Herald

Endnotes

1. Hewison,R. (2014) Cultural Capital. London. Verso p.77
2. Edinburgh Literary Journal (1829) quoted in Myrone M., (2011) John Martin. Apocalypse. London. Tate Publishing p.11
3. Ibid p.13
4. Ibid p.13
5. Bell, C., (1938) Civilization. London. Pelican Books. P.124.
6. Op.Cit. Hewison p.22
7. Strong, R. (1999) The Spirit of Britain. A narrative history of the arts. London. Hutchinson p.641
8. Op.Cit. Hewison p.77
9. Ibid. p.77
10. Sharp, R. Britain's Hidden Art New Statesman 19 February 2009
11. Friedman, S. and Laurison, D. (2019) The Class Ceiling. Why it pays to be privileged. Bristol. Policy Press. p.209.
12. Hoggart, R. (1989) Introduction in Orwell, G. (1989) The Road to Wigan Pier. London: Penguin. p.vii.
13. Savage, M., (2015) Social Class in the 21st. Century London. Penguin.
14. Music Halls Available at vam.ac.uk/content/articles/t/the -story -of-music-halls.
15. Golby, J.M. and Purdue A.W. (1999) The Civilisation of the Crowd: Popular Culture in England 1750-1900. Stroud: Sutton Publishing p.106
16. London v Regions Costs. Dorries, N. (Secretary of State for Digital, Culture, Media and Sport) quoted in The Art Newspaper 25 February 2022
17. Museum Closures Candlin, F. How to march out in a Blaze of glory. The Guardian 10 May 2019.
18. Rosslyn, H. (2013) Bought with Love: The Secret History of British Art. BBC 4 July 2013.
19. This section draws heavily from the above BBC4 programme and also from Coke and Borg's work on the history of Vauxhall Gardens.
20. Austen, J. (1813) Pride and Prejudice. New York: Anchor Books (2007). p.444.
21. Januszczak, W. (2015) Sunday Times 21 June 2015.
22. Coke, D. and Borg, A. (2011) Vauxhall Gardens: A history. Yale: Yale

	University Press. p.29.
23	Uglow, J. (2002) Hogarth: A life and a world. London: Faber & Faber. P.315
24	Leeds WIKI HIST2530. Building the literate nation: the historical debate. https://wiki.leeds.ac.uk accessed on 2 April 2017.
25	Op. cit. Coke, D., & Borg, A. p.85.
26	Ibid. p.2 & 86.
27	Ibid. p.2.
28	Ibid. p.220.
29	Ibid. p.220.
30	Ibid. p.43.
31	Ibid. p.250.
32	Nord, D.E. (2013) Night and Day in Conlin, J. (2013) The Pleasure Garden from Vauxhall to Coney Island Philadelphia. University of Pennsylvania Press. p.179.
33	Southworth, G.S. (1941) Vauxhall Gardens: A Chapter in the Social History of England. New York: Columbia University Press quoted in Conlin, J. p.179.
34	Hunter, D. (2015) The Lives of George Frideric Handel. Woodbridge: The Boydell Press. p.79.
35	Conlin, J.(2012) The Pleasure Garden, from Vauxhall Gardens to Coney Island Philadelphia, University of Philadelphia p.13.
36	Ibid. p.186
37	Dickens, C. (1836) Sketches by Boz. 'Vauxhall Gardens by Day' Chapter 14.
38	Black, J. (1987) The English Press in the Eighteenth Century. Beckenham: London: Croom Helm p.14.
39	Damrosch, L. (2005) Jean-Jacques Rousseau: Restless genius. Boston: Houghton Mifflin. p.432.
40	Gatrell, V. (2013) The First Bohemians: Life and art in London's Golden Age. London: Allen Lane. p.389.
41	Foundling Hospital Exhibition 2014.
42	Cruickshank, D. (2009) The Secret History of Georgian London: How the wages of sin shaped the capital. London: Random House. p.34.
43	Heffer, S. (2013) High Minds: The Victorians and the birth of Modern Britain. London: Random House. p.113.

44	Taylor, B. (1999) Art for the Nation: Exhibitions and the London public 1747–2001. New Jersey: Rutgers University Press. p.4.
45	Ibid. p.4.
46	Op. cit. Gatrell p.xxii.
47	Royal Society of Arts (R.S.A.) London: Minutes March 1760.
48	Op. cit. Taylor p.10.
49	Saumarez Smith, C. (2012) The Company of Artists: The origins of the Royal Academy of Arts in London. London: Modern Art Press. p.31.
50	Op. cit. Taylor p.10.
51	R.S.A. Minutes May 1760.
52	R.S.A. Minutes May 1760.
53	R.S.A. Minutes February 1761.
54	Op. cit. Taylor p.11.
55	Ibid. p.11.
56	Ibid. p.14.
57	Hudson, K. (1975) A Social History of Museums: What the visitors thought. London: Macmillan. p.4.
58	Altick, R.D., (1878) The Shows of London. London, Belknap Press p3.
59	Ibid. p.102
60	Ibid p.105
61	www.royalcollections.org.uk/collection/paintings-and-miniatures/paintings. Accessed 13 March 2017.
62	Op. Cit. Altick p.3.
63	Ibid. p.102.
64	Ibid. p.105.
65	Ibid. p.101.
66	Ibid. and quotation from Barnes, J. (2015) Keeping an Eye Open: Essays on art. Kindle Edition Location 434.
67	Louvre website.
68	Op. cit. Altick p.410.
69	Op. Cit. Altick p.502
70	Minihan, J. (1977) The Nationalization of Culture. London: Hamish Hamilton. p.7.
71	Taylor, B. (1999) Art for the Nation: Exhibitions and the London public 1747–2001. New Jersey: Rutgers University Press. p.30.
72	Ibid. p.31.

73	Ibid. p.502.
74	Op. cit. Altick p.406.
75	Heffer, S. (2013) High Minds: The Victorians and the birth of Modern Britain. London: Random House Books. p.xiii.
76	Ibid. p.xvi.
77	Siegal, J. (2008) The Emergence of the Modern Museum: An anthology of nineteenth century sources. Oxford: Oxford University Press. p.74.
78	Op. cit. Minihan p.20.
79	Ibid. p.21.
80	Op. cit. Taylor p.37.
81	Ibid. p.36.
82	Conlin (2006) The Nation's Mantelpiece: A history of the National Gallery. London: Pallas Athene. p.53.
83	Op. cit. Taylor p.37.
84	Ibid. p.40.
85	Op. cit. Minihan p.32.
86	Ibid. p.39.
87	Op. cit. Conlin p.60.
88	Ibid. p.68.
89	Disraeli, B. (1845) Sybil. London: Penguin. (1980 Edition.) p.96.
90	Putnam, R. (2015) Our Kids: The American Dream in crisis. New York: Simon and Schuster. p.263 (This general point was brought to my notice in an article by Matthew D'Ancona).
91	Bennett, T. (1995) The Birth of the Museum. London: Routledge. p.70.
92	Report of the Select Committee on Arts and their Connexion with Manufactures 1836. p.v.
93	Ibid. p.x.
94	Evidence of Mr. C.H. Smith p.51 para 662.
95	Evidence of John Martin and Mr. Papworth p.iii.
96	Report of the Select Committee on National Monuments and Works of Art 1841 p.133 para 2584.
97	Ibid. p.136 para 2643–2644.
98	Ibid. p.91 paras 1845–1851.
99	Report of the Select Committee on the National Gallery (1850) p.68.
100	Ibid. p.37 para 544.
101	Ibid. p.40 para 607.

102	Ibid. p.6 para 82.
103	Ibid. p.6 para 83.
104	Ibid. p.44 para 657.
105	Ibid. p.45 para 664.
106	Report of the Select Committee on the National Gallery Site (1857) p.93 para 2415.
107	Op. cit. Taylor p.61.
108	Quoted in Minihan p.59 William Makepeace Thackeray, 'Strictures on Pictures' in Critical Papers in Art (1904) London: Macmillan. p.4.
109	Report of Select Committee (1857) p.95 para 2458.
110	Ibid. p.170 Appendix No. III Returns from Employers.
111	Report of Select Committee (1853) p.495 paras 7013 and 7017.
112	Quoted in Conlin p.80.
113	Report of Select Committee (1857) p.68 para 1662.
114	Saumarez-Smith, C. (2009) The National Gallery: A short history. London: Frances Lincoln. p.78.
115	Op. cit. Taylor p.54.
116	Kingsley, C. (1848) Politics for the People. 6 May p.6 John W. Parker London. Google Books from original in Princeton Library.
117	Quoted in Taylor p.57.
118	Bonython, E. and Burton, A. (2003) The Great Exhibitor: The life and work of Henry Cole. London: V&A Publications. p.2.
119	Ibid. p.1.
120	Ibid. p.75.
121	Flanders, J. (2006) Consuming Passions: Leisure and pleasure in Victorian Britain. London: Harper Press. p.9.
122	Waterfield, G.W. (2015) The People's Galleries: Art museums and exhibitions in Britain, 1800–1914. New Haven: Yale University Press. p.98.
123	Op.Cit. Flanders p.29
124	Forgan, S. and Gooday, G. (1994) 'A Fungoid Assemblage of Buildings'. History of Universities 13:153–192 p.160. Quoted in Robertson, B. (2004) 'The South Kensington Museum in context: An alternative history.' Museum and Society March 2004 2(1) 1–14 p.5.
125	Op. cit. Bonython p.143.
126	Heffer, S. (2013) High Minds: The Victorians and the birth of Modern Britain. London: Random House Books. p.294.

127	Flanders. p.29.
128	Ibid. p.30.
129	Op. cit. Bonython p.148.
130	V & A www.vam.ac.uk Accessed 28 March 2017.
131	Macleod, D. S. (1996) Art and the Victorian Middle Class: Money and the making of cultural identity. Cambridge: Cambridge University Press. p.57.
132	Ibid. p.57.
133	Lloyds Newspaper 5 July 1857 p.6.
134	Cole, H (1857) The Functions of the Art and Science Department. London. Chapman and Hall p24 and 26.
135	Draft of an Art and Science Department Minute (1862) quoted in Bonython p.209.
136	The Times (14 June 1858) p.9 Quoted in Bonython and Burton p.184
137	Sandford, F.R. (1881) Report on the System of Circulation of Art Objects on Loan from the South Kensington Museum (1881). London: South Kensington Museum quoted in Siegel, J. (2008) The Emergence of the Modern Museum: An anthology of nineteenth-century sources. Oxford: Oxford University Press. p.265.
138	Ibid. p.267.
139	Ibid. p.275.
140	Jevons, W. S. (1882) 'The Use and Abuse of Museums' in Jevons (1883) Methods of Social Reform and Other Papers. London: Macmillan. Quoted in Siegel p.284.
141	'Lord Stanley on Schools of Art' Art Journal (1863) p.225 quoted in Bonython p.215.
142	Op. cit. Bonython p.155.
143	Op. cit. Waterfield p.136.
144	Ibid. p.90.
145	Op. cit. Bonython p.147.
146	Cole, H. (1884) Fifty Years of Public Work. London: George Bell. p.347 (Completed by Henrietta and Alan S. Cole after Cole's death).
147	Hill, O. (1875) Homes of the London Poor. P .7. Quoted in Borzello, F. (1987) Civilising Caliban: The misuse of art 1875–1980. London: Routledge & Kegan Paul. p.38.
148	Barnett, H. (1918) Canon Barnett: His life, work, and friends. Vol.I. London: John Murray. p.76 quoted in Borzello p.36.
149	Barnett, H. (1918) Canon Barnett. His life, work and friends Vol.II.

London: John Murray. p.153.
150 Ibid. p.157.
151 Ibid. p.161.
152 Ibid. p.158.
153 Ibid. p.151.
154 Ibid. p.103.
155 Ibid. p.152.
156 Ibid. p.103.
157 Peake, F. (1908) Has Sunday Opening of Museums, Art Galleries and Libraries Been a Success? London: Lord's Day Observance Society.
158 Ibid.
159 Quoted in Barnett p.173.
160 Obama, B. (2007) Dreams from My Father. London: Canongate. p.293.
161 Op. cit. Barnett p.155 and 161.
162 Ibid. p.156.
163 Ibid. p.176 and 179.
164 Ibid. p.174.
165 Ibid. p.161.
166 Op. cit. Borzello p.60.
167 Op. cit. Barnett p.162 and 174.
168 Ibid. p.161.
169 Ibid. p.162.
170 Haythornthwaite, J. Roller Coasters and Helter Skelters, Missionaries and Philanthropists: A history of patronage and funding at the Whitechapel Art Gallery in The Whitechapel Art Gallery Centenary Review (2001) p.19. from the Glasgow Evening News 12 December 1938.
171 Waterfield G. (1994) Art for the People. London. Dulwich Picture Gallery p13
172 Ibid. p.13
173 Ibid p13
174 Ibid. 13
175 Op. cit. Borzello p.90 and 91.
176 Besant, W. (1902) Autobiography of Sir Walter Besant. New York: Dodd Mead. p.243 Library of Congress Digitized Internet Archive.
177 Op. cit. Borzello p.81.

178	Besant, W. (1884) 'The Amusements of the People' The Contemporary Review quoted in Small, H. Preface to All Sorts and Conditions of Men (1997) Oxford: Oxford University Press.
179	Op. cit. Borzello quote from the Echo 'Art Culture in the East End' 7 September 1891.
180	Op. cit. Besant p.xxii.
181	Ibid. p.xxv.
182	Ibid. p.xviii.
183	Op. cit. Borzello p.82.
184	Ibid. p.98.
185	Golby, J.M. and Purdue A.W. (1999) The Civilisation of the Crowd: Popular culture in England 1750–1900. Stroud: Sutton Publishing. p.106.
186	Flanders, J. (2006) Consuming Passions: Leisure and pleasure in Victorian Britain. London: Harper Press. p.207.
187	Cunningham, H. (2014) Time, Work and Leisure: Life changes in England since 1700. Manchester: Manchester University Press. p.105.
188	Waterfield, G. (2015) The People's Galleries: Art museums and exhibitions in Britain 1800–1914. New Haven: Yale University Press. p.123.
189	Op. cit. Golby p.170.
190	Ibid. p.137.
191	Tate Gallery The Derby Day William Powell Firth 1856–1858. www.tate.org.uk/art/artworks/frith-the-derby-day-n00615. Accessed on 12 April 2017.
192	Op. cit. Flanders p.450.
193	York Herald 23 February 1888.
194	Nottingham Evening Post 5 May 1879.
195	Ibid. 168.
196	Bailey, P. (1978) Leisure and Class in Victorian England: Rational recreation and the contest for control, 1830–1885. London: Routledge & Kegan Paul. p.132.
197	Op. cit. Golby p.166.
198	Ibid. quoted in Golby p.79.
199	Ibid. p.166.
200	Ibid. p.181.
201	Op. cit. Bailey p.135.

202	Victoria and Albert Museum. The Story of Music Hall 2015 Online (Accessed 19 September 2015.) Available from www.vam.ac.uk/page/m/music-hall.
203	Ellis-Peterson, H. Save London's Live Music Venues: City-wide campaign launched. The Guardian 20 October 2015.
204	Op. cit. Golby p.70.
205	Op. cit. Cunningham p.81.
206	Op. cit. Flanders p.301.
207	Ibid. p.297.
208	Ibid. p.297.
209	Op. cit. Golby p.106.
210	Op. cit. Cunningham p.143.
211	Op. cit. Golby p.116.
212	Ibid. p.104 and 178.
213	Willes, M. (2014) The Gardens of the British Working Class. New Haven: Yale University Press. p.113.
214	Parkes, S.H. (1864) Window Gardens for the People. London: S.W. Partridge. p.62.
215	Ibid. p.24.
216	Parkes, S.H. Flower Shows of Window Plants for the Working Classes of London (London Emily Faithfull 1862) quoted in Boddy, K. (2011) University College London Bloomsbury in Bloom project. Online (Accessed 15 September 2015) Available at www.ucl.ac.uk/bloomsbury-project/articles.
217	Op. cit. Parkes (1864) p.46.
218	Boddy, K. Bloomsbury in Bloom. Article in UCL Leverhulme funded Bloomsbury Project website p.14 www.ucl.ac.uk/bloomsbury project.
219	Op. cit. Flanders p.185.
220	Ibid. p.31.
221	Rose, J. (2002) The Intellectual Life of the British Working Classes. New Haven: Yale University Press. p.75.
222	Op. cit. Flanders p.165.
223	Ibid. p.139.
224	Op. cit. Waterfield p.124.
225	Marx, K. and Engels, F. (1983) Collected Works. London: Lawrence Wishart p.131.
226	Carbonneau, J.B.C., Linton, W.J., Linton H. D., & Morton, W. (1857)

	The Art Treasures Examiner: a pictorial, critical and art historical record of the Art-Treasures Exhibition at Manchester, in 1857. Manchester: A. Ireland.
227	Macleod, D.S. (1996) Art and Victorian Middle Class: Money and the making of cultural identity. Cambridge: Cambridge University Press. p.107.
228	Engels, F. (1987) The Condition of the Working Class in England. London: Penguin. p.92.
229	Steed, J. (1988) Commerce and the Liberal Arts in Wolf, J., & Seed, J. (1988) The Culture of Capital: Art, power and the nineteenth-century middle class. Manchester: Manchester University Press. p.67.
230	De Tocqueville, A. (1958) Journeys to England and Ireland. Ed. Meyer, J.P. London: Faber and Faber. Quoted in Hunt, T. (2004) Building Jerusalem: The rise and fall of the Victorian city. London: Weidenfeld & Nicolson. p.20.
231	Uglow, J. (1993) Elizabeth Gaskell: A habit of stories. London: Faber and Faber. p.555 and Hunt (2004) p.29.
232	Op. cit. Steed p.57.
233	Pergam, E.A. (2011) The Manchester Art Treasures Exhibition of 1857: Entrepreneurs, connoisseurs and the public. Surrey: Ashgate. p.23.
234	Scharf, G. (1858) On The Manchester Art Treasures Exhibition, 1857. Address to the Historic Society of Lancashire and Cheshire. p.324.
235	Op. cit. Pergam p.250.
236	Dickens, C. (1857) Household Words Vol.XVI. 10 October 1857 London: Banbury Evans. p.349.
237	Op. cit. Scharf. p.317.
238	The Art Journal (1857) p.279.
239	Op. cit. Morris p.13.
240	Ibid. p.9.
241	Ibid. p.10.
242	"Circular No.1: Exhibition of Art Treasures of the United Kingdom" quoted in Pergam p.246.
243	Ibid. p.246.
244	Op. cit. Scharf p.327.
245	Finke, U. (1986) 'The Art Treasures Exhibition' in Art and Architecture in Victorian Manchester. Archer, J.H.G. (ed.) (1986) Manchester: Manchester University Press. p.110.
246	Burger, W. Tresors d'Art en Angleterre (1857) p.v–vi quoted in Haskell,

	F. (2000) The Ephemeral Museum: Old Master paintings and the rise of the art exhibition. New Haven: Yale University Press. p.82.
247	Op. cit. Pergam p.1.
248	Ibid. p.36.
249	Ibid. p.38.
250	Ibid. p.159.
251	Ibid. p.159 and Scharf p.284.
252	Op. cit. Scharf p.289.
253	Op. cit. Pergam p.180.
254	Op. cit. Macleod p.128.
255	Op. cit. Haskell p.86.
256	Fry, R. (1981) Vision & Design. London: Oxford University Press. p.41.
257	Op. cit. Hunt (2004) p.168.
258	Quoted in Haskell p.6.
259	Chapple, J.A.V. and Pollard, A. ed. (1966) The Letters of Mrs. Gaskell. Manchester: Manchester University Press. p.452.
260	Ibid. p.476.
261	Op. cit. Pergam p.201.
262	Ibid. p.201.
263	Bradford Observer 24 September 1857.
264	The Art Treasures Examiner (1857) Manchester p.252.
265	Bradford Observer 24 September 1857.
266	Ibid.
267	Op. cit. Pergam p.253.
268	Ibid. p.257.
269	Op. cit. Art Treasures Examiner p.252.
270	Op. cit. Pergam p.128.
271	Quote from Executive Committee Report in Hunt, T., & Whitfield, V. (2007) p.25.
272	Waagen, G.F. (1857) A Walk through the Art-Treasures Exhibition at Manchester. London: John Murray.
273	Op. cit. Pergam p.104.
274	Anonymous (1857) A Peep at the Pictures or a catalogue of the principal objects of attraction in the Manchester Art Treasures Exhibition. London: John Heywood. p.1.

275	Ibid. pages 9, 19 and 15.
276	Ibid. p.25.
277	Op. cit. Pergam p.105.
278	Jerrold, W.B. (1857) How to See the Art Treasures Exhibition. Manchester: A. Ireland.
279	Morris, T. (1857) The Painters and Their Works, an Historical, Descriptive and Directorial Handbook of the Art-Treasures Exhibition. Manchester: Abel Heywood.
280	E.T.B. (1857) What to See and Where to See It or the Operatives Guide to the Art Treasures Exhibition. Manchester: Abel Heywood.
281	Ibid. p.1.
282	Rogers, C. (1857) A Peep at t'Manchester Art Treasures Exhebishan London: T.W Grattan.
283	"Bowton Luminary" (1857) Bobby Shuttle and his Woife Sayroh's Visit to Manchester un-th Greight Hert Treasures Palace Owd Traffort. Manchester: John Heywood.
284	Op. cit. Rogers p.6.
285	Hawthorne, N. (1883) Our Old Home and English Note-Books. 2 Vols. Boston: Houghton, Mifflin and Company II: 535. Quoted in Pergam p.204.
286	Dickens, C. (1857) The Manchester School of Art in Household Words Vol XVI 10 October 1857.
287	Dickens, C. (1880) Letters of Charles Dickens Vol. 2: 1857–1870. p.23.
288	Frasers Magazine p.394.
289	Art Journal (1857)
290	Op. cit. Scharf p.34.
291	Op. cit. Art Treasures Examiner p.40.
292	Ibid. p.176.
293	Op. cit. E.T.B. p.17.
294	Op. cit. Art Treasures Examiner p.40.
295	Op. cit. Art Journal p.394.
296	Waterfield, G.W. (2015) The People's Galleries: Art museums and exhibitions in Britain 1800–1914. New Haven: Yale University Press. The next chapter draws heavily on Giles Waterfield's wonderful book The People's Galleries.
297	Waterfield, G. (2016) The People's Galleries: Art museums and exhibitions in Britain, 1800–1914. New Haven: Yale University Press. p.3

298	Ibid. p.124
299	Ibid. p.124
300	Association of Leading Visitor Attractions 2015 Report
301	Email from Bradford Council 18 July 2016
302	Conlin, J. (2006) The Nation's Mantelpiece: A history of the National Gallery. London: Pallas Athene. p.98 and 100.
303	Geddes Poole, A. (2010) Stewards of the Nation's Art: Contested cultural authority 1890–1939. Toronto: University of Toronto Press. p.227.
304	Addison, P. (1981) 'Jingo Joe' London Review of Books Vol 3 No12 2 July 1981.
305	Op. cit. Waterfield p.263.
306	Ibid. p.81.
307	Fraser D. (1980) Politics and Society in Fraser D. (ed.) A History of Modern Leeds. Manchester: Manchester University Press. p.287 and Fraser D. (1979) Urban Politics in Victorian England. London: Macmillan. p.149.
308	Hunt, T. (2004) Building Jerusalem. London: Weidenfeld & Nicolson. p.120.
309	Ibid. p.128.
310	Duxbury-Neumann, S. (2015) Little Germany: A history of Bradford's Germans. Stroud: Amberley Publishing p.24.
311	Op. cit. Hunt p.128.
312	Ibid. p.129.
313	Ibid. p.144.
314	Hunt, T. and Whitfield, V. (2008) Art Treasures in Manchester: 150 years on. Manchester: Manchester Art Gallery.
315	Engels, F. (1845) The Condition of the Working Class In England. Kindle Edition p.29.
316	Ibid. p.44.
317	Arnold, M. (1869) Culture and Anarchy. Kindle Edition Location 1279.
318	Barringer, T. (2005) Men at Work. New Haven: Yale University Press. p.71.
319	Ruskin, J. (1864) Traffic. Kindle Edition p.1.
320	Quoted in Woodson-Boulton A. (2012) Transformative Beauty: Art museums in industrial Britain Stanford: Stanford University Press. p.28.

321	Ibid. p.37 and 39.
322	Clark, K. (1982) Ruskin Today. London: Penguin. p.270.
323	MacCarthy, F. (1994) William Morris: A life for our time. London: Faber and Faber. p.69.
324	Ibid. p.420 and 421.
325	Op. cit. Woodson-Boulton, A. p.26.
326	Ibid. p.494.
327	Hardman, M. (1986) Ruskin and Bradford: An experiment in Victorian cultural history. Manchester: Manchester University Press.
328	Op. cit. MacCarthy p.539.
329	Quoted in Hunt, T. (2004) p.161.
330	Ibid. p.149.
331	Hurd, D. and Young, E. (2014) Disraeli: or, The two lives. Kindle Edition Location 3456.
332	Harold Perkin (1969) Origins of Modern English Society London. Routledge p.453 quoted in Macleod p.6.
333	Macleod, D.S. (1996) Art and the Victorian Middle Class: Money and the making of cultural identity. Cambridge: Cambridge University Press. p.6.
334	Oxford Dictionary of National Biography (2004) Oxford: Oxford University Press. Vol 33 p.992.
335	Langan, P. (2007) 'Prejudiced mill owner drove his workers into the unions' in Wharfedale Observer 18 October 2007.
336	Ibid.
337	Bradley, I.C. (1990) Titus Salt: Enlightened entrepreneur in Victorian Values: Personalities and perspectives in nineteenth-century society (1990) Marsden, G. (Ed.) London: Longman. p.74.
338	Op. cit. Oxford Dictionary of National Biography Vol 19 p.337.
339	Johnston C. and Hartnell J. (2015) Cotton to Gold: Extraordinary collections of the industrial North West London: Two Temple Place. p.44.
340	BBC Lancashire Massey's: Burnley's famous brewers 24 November 2009 news.bbc.co.uk/local/lancashire/hi/people_
341	Fitzgibbon, T. (1970) A Taste of Scotland in Food and Pictures. London: Pan Books. p.42.
342	Op. cit. Johnston p.72.
343	Ruskin at Walkley http://www.ruskinatwalkley.org/page.php?hotspots=off&level0=119&type=loc Accessed 13 March 2017.

344	Op. cit. Barringer p.239.
345	Ibid. p.239.
346	Eagles, Stuart (2009) 'Thomas Coglan Horsfall, and Manchester Art Museum and University Settlement' www.infed.org/settlements/manchester_art_museum_and_university_settlement.htm p.2. Accessed 13 March 2017.
347	Ibid. p.7.
348	Op. cit. Waterfield p.257.
349	Greenwood, T. (1888) Museums and Art Galleries. London: Simkin. Marshall and Co. p.49.
350	Ibid.
351	Howarth, E. and Platnauer, H.M. (1911) Directory of museums in Great Britain & Ireland together with a section on India and Colonial museums. London: Museums Association.
352	Op. cit. Oxford Dictionary of National Biography (2004) Volume 23.
353	Greenwood p.61.
354	Ibid. p.60.
355	Ibid. p.90.
356	Op. cit. Howarth p.170 and 239.
357	Op. cit. Greenwood p.26.
358	Ibid. p.27.
359	Ibid. p.48.
360	Ibid. p.131.
361	Ibid. p.174.
362	Ibid. p.274.
363	Waterfield G. (1994) Art for the People. London: Dulwich Picture Gallery. p.35.
364	Waterfield G. (1998) Art Galleries and the Public: A survey of three centuries. In Art Treasures of England Royal Academy, London p.44.
365	Op. cit. Waterfield (2016) p.137.
366	Ibid. p.129.
367	Op. cit. Waterfield (2016) p.139.
368	Op. cit. Greenwood p.49.
369	Op. cit. Waterfield (2016) p.230.
370	Ibid. p.45.
371	Ibid. p.240.

372	The Atlantic (2009) http://www.the atlantic.com/technology/archive/2009/06/to-the ama-its-not-about-you/19303. Accessed 13 March 2017.
373	Paxman, J. (2009) The Victorians: Britain through the paintings of the age. London: BBC. p.37 and 39.
374	Op. cit. Greenwood p.61.
375	Op. cit. Waterfield (2016) p.128.
376	Op. cit. Woodson-Boulton p.38.
377	Op. cit. Hunt (2004) p.346.
378	Op. cit. Greenwood p.176.
379	Ibid. p.362.
380	Op. cit. Boulton p.93.
381	Ibid. p.97.
382	Ibid. p.102.
383	Op. cit. Waterfield (2016) p.254.
384	Rutter, F. (1927) Since I Was Twenty-Five. London: Constable. p.200.
385	Ibid. p.201.
386	Ibid. p.203.
387	Ibid. p.206.
388	Op. cit. Haward p.637.
389	Ibid. p.639.
390	Ibid. p.640.
391	Gaskell, Mrs. (1854) North and South Kindle Edition p 310
392	Op. cit. Hudson p.100.
393	Ibid. p.103.
394	Ibid. p.104.
395	Ibid. p.104.
396	Ibid. p.106.
397	Ibid. p.106.
398	Ibid. p.108.
399	Royal Commission on National Museums and Galleries (1929) London. H.M.S.O. p.81.
400	Strong, R. (1999) The Spirit of Britain: A narrative history of the arts. London: Hutchinson. p.641.
401	Pearson, N. (1982) The State and the Visual Arts. Milton Keynes: Open University Press. p.39.

402	Saumarez Smith (2009) The National Gallery: A short history. London: Frances Lincoln. p.96.
403	Ibid. p.95.
404	Op. cit. Pearson p.39.
405	Poynter E. (1880) Classic and Italian Painting. London: Sampson. Low, Marston, Searle & Rivington. p.ix.
406	Ibid. p.x.
407	Ibid. p.xii.
408	Ibid. p.xix.
409	Taylor, B. (1999) Art for the Nation Exhibitions and the London Public 1747–2001.Manchester: Manchester University Press. p.108.
410	Ibid. p.110.
411	The Spectator 13 February 1892.
412	Op. cit. Taylor p.116.
413	Ibid. p.124.
414	Ibid. p.132 and 133.
415	Ibid. p.266.
416	Miers, H. (1928) Report on Public Museums of the British Isles. Dunfermline: Carnegie United Kingdom Trust. p.38.
417	Ibid. p.45.
418	Markham, S.F. (1938) The Museums and Art Galleries of the British Isles. Dunfermline: Carnegie United Kingdom Trust. p.90.
419	Ibid. p.23.
420	Ibid. p.32.
421	Ibid. p.60.
422	Stark, P. Gordon, C., & Powell, D. (2014) Research Conclusions: A Summary. London: GPS Culture.
423	Royal Commission on National Museums & Galleries (1929). London: His Majesty's Stationary Office. p.12.
424	Ibid. p.40.
425	Ibid. p.39.
426	Courtauld, S. (1949) Ideals and Industry. Cambridge: Cambridge University Press. p.53.
427	Op. cit. Royal Commission p.51.
428	Ibid. p.62.
429	Ibid. p.11.

430	Ibid. p.44 and 42.
431	Upchurch, A.R. (2012) '*Missing from policy history: The Dartington Hall Arts Enquiry, 1941–1947.*' International Journal of Cultural Policy, 19 (5) 610-622 (13) ISSN 1028-6632. See also Upchurch, A.R. (2004) 'John Maynard Keynes, The Bloomsbury Group and the Origins of the Arts Council Movement'. International Journal of Cultural Policy Vol. 10, No.2, 2004.
432	The Visual Arts (1946) London: Oxford University Press. p.9.
433	Ibid. p.12.
434	Ibid. p.23.
435	Ibid. p.24.
436	Ibid. p.104.
437	Ibid. p.145.
438	Ibid. p.11.
439	Ibid. p.12.
440	Quoted in Foss, B. (2007) War Paint: Art, war, state and identity in Britain 1939–1945. New Haven: Yale University Press. p.173.
441	Upchurch (2012) p.11.
442	Ibid. p.10.
443	Williams, W.E. (1971) 'The Pre-history of the Arts Council' in Aims and action in adult education 1921–1971 edited by Hutchinson, E.M. London. National Institute of Adult Education. p.20.
444	Witts, R. (1998) Artists Unknown: An Alternative History of the Arts Council. London: Warner Books. p.37.
445	Ibid. p.37.
446	Ibid. p.37.
447	Ibid. p.59.
448	Ibid. p.13 and 17.
449	Clark, K. (1977) The other half: a self-portrait. London: John Murray. p.131.
450	Clark, K. (1974) Another part of the wood: a self-portrait. London: John Murray. p.iii.
451	Ibid. p.111.
452	Davis, W. (2012) Into the Silence: The Great War, Mallory and the conquest of Everest. London: Vintage Books. p.171.
453	Ibid. p.176.
454	Ibid. p.183.

455	Davenport-Hines, R. (2015) Universal Man: The seven lives of John Maynard Keynes. London: William Collins. p.267.
456	Glasgow, M. (1975) 'The Concept of the Arts Council' in Essays on John Maynard Keynes. (1975) Keynes, M. Cambridge: Cambridge University Press. p.262.
457	White, E.W. (1975) The Arts Council of Great Britain. London: David Poynter. p.21.
458	Skidelsky, R. (2001) John Maynard Keynes. London: Macmillan. p.288.
459	Evans, I.B., & Glasgow, M. (1949) The Arts in England. London: The Falcon Press. p.16.
460	Leventhal F.M. (1990) 'The Best for the Most CEMA and State Sponsorship of the Arts in Wartime, 1939–1945'. In Twentieth Century British History Vol.1 No 3 p.315.
461	Hewison R. (1995) Culture and Consensus: England, art and politics since 1940. London: Methuen. p.44.
462	Hewison, R. (2014) Cultural Capital: The rise and fall of creative Britain. London: Verso. p.25.
463	Quoted in Pearson p.73.
464	Quoted in Upchurch, A.R. (2011) 'Keynes's legacy: an intellectual's influence reflected in arts policy.' International Journal of Cultural Policy Vol.17, No1, January 2011 p.74.
465	Quoted in Leventhal p.311.
466	Op. cit. Skidelsky p.293.
467	Leventhal p.317.
468	Op. cit. Hewison (1995) p.32.
469	Ibid. p.33.
470	Op. cit. Clark, K. (1977) p.129.
471	Harris, J.S. (1970) Government Patronage of the Arts in Great Britain. Chicago: The University of Chicago Press. p.52.
472	Ibid. p.53.
473	Sinclair, A. (1995) Arts and Cultures: The History of the Fifty Years of the Arts Council of Great Britain. London: Sinclair Stevenson. p.357.
474	Op. cit. Conlin p.155.
475	Quoted in Conlin p.154.
476	Op. cit. Clark (1977) p.77.
477	Ibid. p.23.

478	Stourton, J. (2016) Kenneth Clark. London: William Collins. p.254.
479	Ibid. p.253 and 255.
480	Op. cit. Clark (1977) p.145.
481	Ibid. p.134.
482	Ibid. p.137.
483	Leventhal p.174.
484	Op. cit. Stourton p.111.
485	Ibid. p.184.
486	Quoted in White p.60.
487	Quoted in Freedland, J. (2012) Eugenics: The skeleton that rattles loudest in the left's cupboard. The Guardian 17 February 2012.
488	Op. cit. Davenport-Hines p.128
489	Ibid. p.38.
490	The Arts Council of Great Britain (1961) Partners in Patronage-Sixteenth Annual Report. London: Arts Council of Great Britain. p.9. Quoted in Pearson p.60.
491	Quoted in Pearson p.82.
492	Hoggart, R. (1977) Times Higher Education Supplement (1977) 'We must bridge theory and practice in study of the arts.' Quoted in Hutchinson, R. (1982) The Politics of the Arts Council. London: Sinclair Browne. p.79.
493	Op. cit. Hutchinson p.151.
494	Op. cit. Hewison (1995) p.48.
495	Woolf, V. (1919) Roger Fry. London: Penguin. p.114 Originally published by Hogarth Press in 1940.
496	Bell, C. (1938) Victorian Taste in Art in England (1938) ed. R.S. Lambert. London: Penguin. p.43 and 46.
497	Bell, C. (1987) Art. Oxford: Oxford University Press. p.18 and 19 Originally published in 1914.
498	Bell, C. (1928) Civilization. London: Penguin. p.123.
499	Op. cit. Bell (1928) p.181.
500	Ibid. p.184.
501	Forster, E.M. (1951) Two Cheers for Democracy. London: Penguin. p.65.
502	Tickner, L. (2000) Modern Life and Modern Subjects: British art in the early twentieth century. Yale: Yale University Press. p.221.
503	Quoted in Woolf (1919).

504	Quoted in Tickner p.7.
505	Ibid. p.6.
506	Op. cit. Clark (1975) p.77.
507	Harris, A. (2010) Romantic Moderns: English writers, artists and the imagination from Virginia Woolf to John Piper. London: Thames & Hudson. p184.
508	Op.cit. Dorries
509	Op.cit Candlin
510	Butler, P. (2016) Results of survey quoted in The Guardian 29 June 2016. www.theguardian.com. Accessed on 17 January 2017.
511	King, A., & Crewe, I. (2014) The Blunders of Our Governments. London: Oneworld. p.244.
512	Spicer, K. (2016) Heavyweight clash over summer bash. London: The Sunday Times 12 June 2016.
513	Ibid.
514	Marks,T. (2016) What price for a Pontomoro Apollo 19 December 2016
515	National Gallery Website. www.nationalgallery.org.uk. Accessed 6 January 2017.
516	Hewison, R. (2014) Cultural Capital. The rise and fall of creative Britain. London: Verso. p.77.
517	Minihan, J. (1977) The Nationalization of Culture. London: Hamish Hamilton. p.58.
518	Markham, H. (1938) The Museums and Galleries of the British Isles. Dunfermline: Carnegie United Kingdom Trust. p.90.
519	Quoted in Stark (2014) p.62.
520	Quoted in Pearson (1982) The State and the Visual Arts. Milton Keynes: The Open University Press. p.60.
521	Ibid. p.58.
522	Op. cit. Stark (2014) p.62.
523	Quoted in Lawson, D. (2013) Why is free admission to art galleries and museums sacrosanct, when free swimming is not? @indyvoices Monday 25 February 2013 www.independent.co.uk/voices. Accessed on 17 January 2017.
524	Stark, P. et.al. (2014) Research Conclusions: A summary. London GPS Culture.
525	Stark, P. et.al. (2014) The PLACE Report Policy for the Lottery, the Arts and Community in England. London: GPS para.6.4.

526	Op. cit. Stark (2014) p.58.
527	Bragg, M. (2014) quoted in Stark et al.
528	Op. cit. Stark (2014) p.18.
529	Stark, P., Gordon, C., & Powell, D. (2016) A Policy for the Arts and Culture in England: The Next Steps? London: GPS. p.9.
530	Stark, P., Gordon, C., & Powell, D. (2014) The Place Report: Policy for the Lottery, the Arts and Community in England. London: GPS.
531	Hunt, T. (2011) We need to start charging for museums and galleries again. The Guardian 6 March 2011.
532	Brown,M. (2017) V & A reiterates commitment to free entry after Tristam Hunt appointment The Guardian 13 January 2017
533	Perraudin, F., (2016) The Guardian 26 March 2016
534	Quoted in The Guardian.
535	Crewe, T. (2016) The Strange Death of Municipal England in London Review of Books December 2016.
536	*Arts Council Annual Report and Accounts 2022-23.*
537	Op. cit. Hewison p.77.
538	Harris, P. (2002) Corporate Art Collections-Opportunities on a grand scale. Arts Professional www.artsprofessional.co.uk accessed 19 April 2017.
539	Ibid. p.2.
540	Jones, C. (2015) Universities in England spend £20 million on art work BBC 31 December 2015 www.bbc.co.uk/news/uk-england-34677443. Accessed 19 April 2017.
541	Arts Council (2023) *Cultural Gifts Scheme & Acceptance in Lieu 2013-23.* London. Arts Council.
542	Brown M., (2015) *Winston Churchill paintings accepted for nation in lieu of tax.* The Guardian 10 March 2015
543	The Independent 31 October 2015 www.independent.co.uk › Accessed on 16 April 2017.
544	Cowling, J. (2004) For Art's Sake: Society and the arts in the 21st century. London: Institute for Public Policy Research. p.5.
545	Palmer, A. (2005) A lot of pounds for a few pinks. The Daily Telegraph 24 October 2005.
546	Bourdieu, P. (1984) Distinction: A social critique of the judgement of taste. London: Routledge.
547	Savage, M. (2015) Social Class in the 21st Century. London: Penguin. p.254 and 293.

548	Sullivan, A. (2001) Cultural Capital and Educational Attainment in Sociology November 2001 Vol35 No 4 893-912; Andersen, P., & Hansen, M.N. (2011) Class and Cultural Capital: The case of class inequality in educational performance in European Sociological Review 28(5) May 2011.
549	Richards, L., Garratt, E., Heath, A. F., Anderson, L., & Altintas, E. (2016) The Childhood Origins of Social Mobility: inequalities and changing opportunities. London: Social Mobility Commission p.38 and Friedman, S., Laurison, D., Macmillan, L. (2017) Social Mobility, the Class Pay Gap and Intergenerational Worklessness: New insights from the labour force survey. London: Social Mobility Commission. p.i.
550	South Yorkshire Times 28 January 2008.
551	www.glastonbury festivals.co.uk
552	Gilmore, A. (2016) Raising Our Quality of Life: The importance of investment in arts and culture. London: Centre for Labour and Social Studies.
553	Quoted in Gilmore (2016).
554	Stark et.al. (2016) The Next Steps?
555	DCMS (2010–11) Performance indicators of DCMS sponsored museums and galleries.
556	Dorling, D., & Hennig, B.D. (2016) London and the English Desert: The geography of cultural capital in the U.K. London: Cultural Trends.
557	Times Educational Supplement 2022.
558	Department of Culture Media and Sport (2013) Sponsored Museums: Performance Indicators 2012/13. Statistical release Annex A Background Note.
559	Lukes, S. (1974) Power: A Radical View. London: Macmillan.
560	Op. cit. Stark (2014) p.62.
561	Stark et.al. (2014) Hard Facts to Swallow. www.gpsculture.co/hardfacts. Accessed 8 January 2017.
562	Griffiths, D., Miles, A., & Savage, M. (2008) The end of the English cultural elite? The Sociological Review May 2008 Vol. 56 Issue 1. Supplement.
563	Ibid. p.192.
564	Ibid. p.198.
565	Ibid. p.202.
566	Ibid. p.206.
567	Leslie, C., Dallison, O. (2008) You've Been Quango'd. London: New

	Local Government Network. p.20.
568	Ibid. p.20.
569	O'Brien,D., Griffiths R., Taylor,M. (2022) Who runs the arts in England? A social network analysis of arts boards.Poetics Volume 29 Part A June 2022
570	Ellis-Petersen, H. (2015) Middle class people dominate arts, survey finds. London: The Guardian.
571	The Warwick Commission (2015) Enriching Britain: Culture, creativity and growth. Coventry: University of Warwick. p.15.
572	Roberts, C. (2017) The Inbetweeners: The new role of internships in the graduate labour market. London: Institute for Public Policy Research. p.29.
573	Brook,O.,O'Brien,D., and Taylor,M.(2019) Social Class, Taste and Inequalities in the Creative Industries https://www.researchgate.netpublication/333508087
574	Januszczak, W. (2014) Talking 'bout a revolution. The Sunday Times 12 January 2014.
575	Bennett, T., Savage, M., Silva, E., Warde, A., Gayo-Cal M., & Wright, D. (2009) Culture, Class, Distinction. London: Routledge. p.129 and115.
576	Ibid. p.122.
577	Bennett (2009) p.204.
578	Ibid. p.210.
579	Hemingway, W. (2000) Just Above The Mantelpiece: Mass-market masterpieces. London: Booth-Clibborn Editions Limited. p.6.
580	Smith, D. (2004) He's our favourite artist. So why do the galleries hate him so much? The Guardian 11 January 2004.

Appendix Currency Conversion

In the appendix to her book *Consuming Passions. Leisure and Pleasure in Victorian Britain* the social historian, Judith Flanders, takes the view that as relative values have altered so substantially that attempts to convert nineteenth- century prices into contemporary ones are usually futile. I am therefore following her lead and rather than attempting to convert prices I have given the price of a loaf of bread or a weekly wage. For readers wanting to do the conversion she recommends: http://www.ex.ac.uk/~RDavies/arian/current/howmuch.html.

Index

A

academicians, 36, 175, 177
access to art galleries, 154
access to cultural capital, 185, 197
Accrington, 134
Addison, 12
admission charge, 19, 101, 162, 208
Affordable Art Fair, 11
Aitken, Charles, 78, 183
Albert, Prince, 1, 33, 46, 51–52, 55, 57–59, 61, 103, 120, 122, 182
Amalgamated Society of Engineers, 105
Angerstein, John, 41, 157
apprentices, 19, 132–33
aristocracy, 9–10, 18, 32–33, 43, 94, 102, 122–23, 125, 155
Arne, Thomas, 18
Arnold, Matthew, 74, 101, 125–26, 182
art
   despised Victorian, 181
   modern, 104, 159, 184, 207
   polite, 28, 57
art for the many not the few, 4, 200
Art for the People, 2–3, 154, 166–67, 189, 245
art galleries, 6–7, 37, 39, 72, 98–99, 121, 123, 127–29, 135–42, 160–61, 185, 194–95, 207, 211, 223–24, 245
art galleries and libraries, 39, 137, 225, 237
art galleries and museums, 72, 123, 185, 188, 207
Art Gallery Committee, 147–48, 161

Art museums in industrial Britain, 215, 230
Arts Council of Great Britain, 173, 213, 227, 229, 249–50
Arts Panel of CEMA, 175
Astors, 178
Attlee, Clement, 79–80

B

Baltic Centre for Contemporary Art, 210
Bank Holidays, 72–73
Banksy Exhibition, 211
Banksy *Toxic Beach*, 7, 210–11
Barnetts, 68–78, 80, 82, 96, 153, 183, 186, 214, 236–37
Barnstaple, 150–51
Bass, Michael, 133
Battersea, 81, 193
Bavarian royal collection, 32
BBC Great British Class Survey, 30
Beaumont, George, 43
Bell, Clive, 3, 153, 169
Belle Vue Gardens, 118
Bennett, Tony, 208, 214, 234, 254
Besant, 83–85, 153, 214, 237
Bethnal Green Museum, 55, 64
Betjeman, John, 179
Birmingham Corporation Art Gallery, 141
Birmingham Museum and Art Gallery, 129
Birmingham's art gallery, 122
Bishop of London, 71
Bloomsbury Group, 153–54, 169–70, 173, 180–81, 183, 205, 228, 248

Bloomsbury Group's country home, 171
Blue Boy, 107–9, 116
Board of Education, 166, 170
Bonython, 56, 215, 235–36
Booth, Charles, 78, 94
Borzello, 86, 215, 236–38
Boswell, James, 19
Botanical Society, 101
Bourdieu, Pierre, 6, 46, 141, 197–99, 215, 252
Boyle, Richard, 9
Bradford's National Science and Media Museum, 193
Bragg, Melvyn, 191, 209, 251
Bridgewater, Duke of, 10
Bridgewater Gallery, 104
Briggs, Joseph, 134
Brighton Public Art Gallery, 183
British Art, contemporary, 13, 18
British Institute of Adult Education (BIAE), 154, 166, 168
British Museum, 42, 45–46, 48, 71, 155, 159, 192
British Working Classes, 95, 226, 229, 239
Bullock, 35, 37, 39, 153
Burne-Jones, 71, 75, 81
Burton, 56, 66, 215, 235–36
businessmen, 57, 101–2, 120–23, 127, 130
Butler, R.A., 166, 170, 173, 175, 251
Byrd, William, 12

C

Camberwell Council, 82
Cambridge Arts Theatre, 168
Cameron, David, 201
Canaletto, 10, 12, 22, 34, 43
Canterbury Music Hall, 37
capital of culture, 99, 145–46
Caracci, Annibale, *The Three Maries*, 108
Carlisle, Earl of, 10
Carnegie United Kingdom Trust, 160, 224, 247, 251
Carr, Holwell, 43
Cartwright Hall, 121–22, 131, 138, 210
CEMA, 166–68, 170–72, 175, 177, 189
Central Museum, 63
Centre for Labour and Social studies, 219
Chamberlain, Joseph, 122–23
Charlotte, Queen, 16, 94
Chartists, 45–46, 59, 142
Chatterton, 107, 110, 116, 207
Children in Whitechapel Gallery, 76
Christie, John, 167, 169
Churchill, Winston, 74
Churchill family, 196
Church of England, 123
Church of England Liturgical Calendar, 80
City of London, 15
Clark, Kenneth, 128, 132, 165–66, 168–69, 171, 173, 176–77, 183, 228, 249
Class Ceiling, 219, 231
class inequality, 213, 252
closure of galleries and museums, 187
Coats, Peter, 132
Cobbett, William, 188
Cole, Henry, 55, 61, 64, 68, 107, 186, 192, 215, 235
Cole's career, 56, 59

collection, royal, 32–33, 74
Colonial Museums, 137, 221, 245
companies, railway, 105–7
Cook, Beryl, 210
Cook, Thomas, 1, 114, 116
Copley, John, 34
Coram, Thomas, 25, 73, 96
Cornwall, 43
Councillor Robert Crawford, 136
Courtauld, Samuel, 162
Courtauld Institute, 161, 166
Covent Garden, 23, 174, 178, 189–91
Covent Garden Opera Trust, 174
creation of regional galleries, 66
Cultural and Creative Industries, 205
Cultural Capital and Educational Attainment, 228
cultural capital of Europe, 32
Cultural Gifts Scheme & Acceptance, 213, 252
cultural icons, global, 192
Cultural Policy, 228, 247–49
Cultural Trends, 217, 253
culture
  emerging, 198–99
  high, 9, 46, 169, 175
  highbrow, 197–99
  working-class, 131, 186
Culture and Anarchy, 126, 213, 243
Culture and Class in English Public Museums, 221
Cunningham, 93, 217, 238–39

D

Dali, Salvador, 210
Dartington Hall Arts Enquiry, 163, 217, 228, 247
Dartington Report, 164, 166, 173, 177
David, Jacques-Louis, 16
Degener, Schmidt, Dr, 162
degradation, 24
Department of Culture, Media and Sport (DCMS), 200, 203, 253
Derby Museum in Liverpool, 141
Directory of museums in Great Britain, 137, 245
Disraeli, Benjamin, 45–46, 51, 112, 125, 130, 217, 222, 234, 244
Dorchester, 151
Dorset, 150–51
Dublin Exhibition, 104
Dulwich Picture Gallery, 38, 40, 64, 229, 237, 245
Dundee's art gallery, 133

E

East Lea Amateur Horticultural Society, 95
East London, 84
East London Aid Spain Committee, 79
East Tower Hamlets Society, 95
Edinburgh and Sheffield Universities, 206
Edinburgh Literary Journal, 2, 230–31
elite
  metropolitan, 6–7, 174
  new, 154, 175, 184
elite universities, 5, 198
Engels, 1, 100, 111, 125–26, 129–30, 144, 150, 218, 224, 239–40, 243

English cultural elite, 203, 220, 253
English National Opera, 191
English Provincial Art, 218
Entertainments National Service Association (ENSA), 166, 168, 186
Ephemeral Museum, 220, 240
Establishment of Museums in Large Towns Act, 123
Eton, 180, 202
Eugenics Society, 171, 179
European Capital of Culture, 204
Exhibition Commission, 59
Exhibition Road, 187
exhibitions
  major, 4, 12, 30, 42, 57
  temporary, 111, 149

F

Fairbairn, Thomas, 100, 104, 112, 114, 132
families, working-class, 94, 99, 185, 211
Ferens, Thomas, 123, 132
Ferens Gallery, 123, 132
Fielding, Henry, 13, 20
Fildes, *The Doctor*, 143
Fildes, Luke, 142, 146, 157, 182, 207, 209
Fine Art building, 127
Fine Arts, 36, 41, 127, 151
  redefined, 57
Fine Arts Commission, 54
Fine Art Section, 151–52
Fireworks Music, 9, 25
First World War, 2, 152–53
Fitzwilliam Museum, 172
Flanders, Judith, 218, 235, 238–39, 255

Forster, E.M., 169–70, 182, 218, 250
Foucault, Michael, 6, 142, 220–21
Foundling Hospital, 25–26, 28, 36, 96
Foundling Hospital Exhibition, 232
Foundling Museum, 25–26
foundlings, 24, 26
free admission to national galleries and museums, 191
Free Trade Hall in Manchester, 127
French Impressionists, 184, 210
French paintings, 183
French working-class crowd, 162
Friendly Societies, 94
Frieze Art Fair, 11
Frith, William, 37, 90, 143, 151, 165, 182, 207, 209
  The Railway Station, 144
Fry, Roger, 111, 169–71, 183, 230, 250

G

Gainsborough, Thomas, 13, 37, 107–8, 116, 122
  The Blue Boy, 109
galleries
  custom-built national, 43
  major London, 203
  new National, 44, 46, 158
  provincial, 134, 149, 160
galleries and museums, 162, 187, 192, 203, 208
gallery-goers, middle-class, 184
Gallery Wars, 51
Garrick, David, 16, 22
Gaskell, Mrs, 45, 111–12, 118, 144–45, 216,

219, 241, 246
Gateshead, 210–11
General Certificate of Secondary Education in England, 198
General Council, 103
Gentleman's Magazine, 18, 22
Geological Society, 101
George III, 16, 30
Georgian era, 20, 38
Gericault, Theodore, 35
Gin Lane, 23–24
Gladstone, William, 44, 46, 51–52, 64, 112
Glasgow, Mary, 167, 170, 172
Glasgow University, 130
Glastonbury, 199
Glyndebourne, 199
Glyndebourne Set, 167, 169
Goldsmiths University, 205
Gower, Earl of, 10
GPS Culture, 190, 247
Gramsci, Antonio, 6, 141
Grant, Duncan, 166–67, 169–71
Great Depression, 86, 134, 152–53, 159
Greater London, 46
Great Exhibition, 46, 57, 59, 102, 104, 106
Great Exhibition and museums, 57
Great Wessex Agricultural Show, 150
Green Lady, 209
Greenwood, Thomas, 136–41, 146–47, 220, 245–46
Guernica, 79–80
Guildhall Gallery, 85
Gulbenkian, Ulrich, 32

H

Hallé, Charles, 1
Handel, 9, 13, 18–20, 25, 154
Handel's music, 9, 12
Hayman, Francis, 12–18, 20, 22, 26, 213
Hemingway, Wayne, 209
Hewison, Robert, 3, 180, 221, 231, 249–52
Heywood, Abel, 218, 224, 242
Heywood, John, 215, 241–42
Historical Society of Lancashire and Cheshire, 102
history of Bradford's Germans, 124, 218, 224
History of Modern Leeds, 219, 243
history of patronage, 220, 237
History of Universities, 218, 235
history of Vauxhall Gardens, 17, 231
Hitler, 167
Hockney, David, 113
Hogarth, 12–14, 20, 22, 24–25, 30, 34, 228
Hogarth's paintings, 12
Hoggart, Richard, 5, 180, 221, 250
Horsfall's Art Museum, 136
Houghton Hall, 40
Howarth, Elijah, 137
Hull, 123, 132
Hume, David, 22
Hunt, Tristram, 124, 146, 191–92
Hunt, Holman, 71, 75, 112, 151
Hyde Park, 11, 53, 187

I

Illustrated London News, 108
impact of culture on regeneration, 146

xlix

Imperial War Museum, 203
importance of investment in arts and culture, 199, 219
Impressionist and Post-Impressionist artists, 164
inequity in museums and galleries, 206
International Journal of Cultural Policy, 228, 247–48

J

Jane Austen's London, 11
Januszczak, Waldemar, 11, 222, 231, 254
Jewish Arts and Antiquities, 79
Johnson, Samuel, 22, 30
Jones, Allen, 68
Jones, Tom, 167, 170, 172
Jude, 150

K

Keiller, John, 133
Kennedy, 83
Kensington, 51, 97
Keynes, John, 3, 154, 166, 168–80, 183, 189–90, 202–3, 249
Kingsley, Charles, 45, 54

L

Labour Governments, 3, 176, 199
labouring classes, 18–19, 30, 34, 38–39, 46, 50, 52, 92, 95, 119, 121, 136, 139
Lady Lever Gallery, 153
Laing Gallery in Newcastle, 133
Lambeth Council, 82
Lambeth Free Loan Exhibition, 82

Lancashire, 95, 101–2, 104, 117, 124, 134, 240
Lansdowne, Marquis of, 122, 156–57
Leeds Art Gallery Committee, 148
Leeds University, 148
Leicester Gallery, 184
Leighton, Lord, 71, 82, 154
Leisure and Class in Victorian England, 214, 238
Liberals, 123
Liberals of Manchester, 130
libraries, free, 81, 137, 139
Lister, Samuel, 131–32, 192
Liverpool, 90, 93, 98, 102, 104, 125, 128, 133, 141–42, 145–47, 157, 164
Lloyds, 60–61
London and Cambridge, 180
London and Leeds, 190
London Artists Association, 171
London Bridge, 9, 19
London elite, 100, 123
London museum mafia, 193
London School of Design, 59
London season, 9
London's Golden Age, 219, 232
London society, 25–26
London's parks, 11–12, 210
London's Vauxhall Pleasure Gardens, 2
Lopokova, Lydia, 169
Lord Rector of Glasgow University, 130
lottery funding, 191, 202
lottery tickets, 190, 195

M

Macmillan, Lord, 168, 170
Manchester, Art Treasures Exhibition, 100–101, 106, 109, 111, 114, 117, 120, 125–26, 216, 218, 222, 224, 242
Manchester Art Gallery, 222, 243
Manchester Art Gallery Committee, 147
Manchester Art Museum, 244
Manchester Art Treasures Exhibition, 1, 7, 99, 207, 225, 227, 240–41
Manchester Athenaeum, 111
Manchester City Art Gallery, 149
Manchester Corporation, 147
Manchester Cricket Club, 105
Manchester Exchange, 125
Manchester Guardian, 65, 110, 115, 123, 230
Manchester's Free Trade Hall, 130
Manchester's mill workers, 150
Manchester Town Hall, 145
Manchester University, 133
Manningham Mills, 131, 192–93
Maries, The Three, 107–9, 116
Markham, Henry, Sir, 160–61, 224, 247, 251
Martin, John, 1, 39, 47, 165, 209, 224, 231, 234
Marylebone Gardens, 14, 19
Massey, Edward, 133
Matisse Exhibition, 184
Mayfair Galleries, 209
Media Museum, 193
Medical Society, 101
Medusa, 35, 66
Metropolitan Museum, 17, 181, 204
Miers, 160–63, 224, 247
Mildmay, Audrey, 168

Millais, John, 71, 157
Millbank, 158–59
Millennium Gallery in Sheffield, 135
mills, woollen, 125, 192
Miss Joan Hunter Dunn, 179
mob, 49
Monamy, Peter, 12, 15, 20
Moore, Henry, 165, 171
Morgan, Morgan, 28
Morris, Thomas, 104, 117
Morris, William, 74, 125, 129, 223, 243
Morton, Charles, 37, 39, 216, 239
municipal galleries of Great Britain, 148
Murray, John, 214, 216, 221, 229, 236, 241, 248
museum in Bethnal Green, 64
Museum of Walkley, 134
Museums and Society, 213, 226, 235, 252
Museums Association, 137, 221, 223, 245

N

Napoleon, 35
Napoleon's Coach, 35–36
National Art Training School, 155
national collection, 41, 47, 49
National Council, 167
National Gallery London, 53
National Gallery of British Art, 157
National Lottery, 174, 215
National Media Museum, 193
National Monuments, 48, 225, 234
National Museums, 162, 226, 246
National Portrait Gallery, 64, 103, 122, 203–4

National Science and Media Museum (NSMM), 192–93
National Trust, 10, 68
Nation's Mantelpiece, 216, 234, 243
Natural History Society, 101
Newcastle, 1, 91, 94, 114, 133
New Chorlton Workhouse, 101
New Jersey, 228, 232–33
New Labour Social Exclusion Unit, 55
nineteenth-century society, 215, 224, 244
Norton, Charles, 112
Nottingham Castle Museum, 138

O

Obama, Barack, 75
Old Master paintings, 107, 220, 240
Orléans, Duke of, 10
Orwell, George, 189, 221, 224
Oxbridge, 176, 202–3
Oxford University, 198

P

Panic, 205–6
Parkes, 96–97, 225, 239
Parliamentary Select Committees, 46, 153
Peace Museum, 188
Peel, Robert, 43, 46, 102, 133
People's Galleries, 57, 120–21, 140, 229, 235, 238, 242
People's Palace, 83–87
Pepys, Samuel, 12
Philosophical Societies, 94, 101, 124, 145
Picasso, 68, 79, 164, 184
Pilgrim Trust, 168

Piper, John, 167, 220
Platnauer, Henry, 137–38, 221, 245
Pleasure Garden, 12, 14, 19, 216, 224, 232
Pontormo, 187–88
Porto Bello, 15–16
portraits of Victorian worthies, 136
Post-Impressionist artists, 164
Potter, Edward, 113
Poynter, Edward, 154–57, 165, 174, 225, 247
Pre-Raphaelite paintings, 145
Prescott, John, 5
Pride and Prejudice, 10
Prince's Pavilion, 16
prostitutes, 9, 13, 19, 37
public galleries, 32, 39, 47, 208
public houses, 60, 94, 133
Public Museums, 62, 224, 247
Putnam, Robert, 45

Q

Queen Victoria, 1, 33, 39, 55, 74, 83, 94, 143, 153, 187

R

Rabelais Society, 83
Raft, 35, 66
Ramsay, Gilbert, 183
Ranelagh, 14
Regent's Park, 11, 20
regional Schools of design, 65
Report on Public Museums, 224, 247
Reynolds, 23, 29–30, 36, 109, 122, 151, 210
Rijksmuseum, 162

Rosebery, Lord, 74, 76, 156
Rossiter William, 80–82, 153
Rothko, Mark, 68
Rousseau, 22, 128
Royal Academy of Arts in London, 227, 233
Royal Commission, 163, 247
Royal Commission on National Museums and Galleries, 162, 226, 246
Royal Council, 173
Royal Geographical Society, 137
Royal Horticultural Society planning, 97
Royal National Theatre, 191
Royal Opera House, 191
Royal Photographic Society, 193
Royal Picture Gallery, 50, 116
Royal Society, 27, 31, 149, 213, 221, 226, 233
Rule Britannia, 18
Ruskin, 50, 52, 109–12, 124–25, 127–30, 134–35, 143, 150, 153, 216, 220, 226, 243–44
Ruskin Societies, 128
Ruskin's St. George's Museum, 134
Rutter. Frank, 148, 161, 184, 226, 246

S

Salt, Titus, 1, 7, 112, 132, 215, 244
Saumarez Smith, Charles, 27, 53, 155, 157, 227, 233, 246
Savage, Mike, 197–200, 214, 220, 227, 231, 252–54
Scharf, George, 102–4, 106, 108–9, 111, 115, 119, 227, 240–42
School of Art, 124
School of Design, 57, 59, 62, 124
Science Museum, 192–93, 203
Science Museum Board, 193
Scotland, 16, 114, 218, 244
Scottish National Galleries, 209
Secondary Education in England, 198
Select Committee on Arts, 225, 234
Select Committee on National Monuments and Works, 48, 225, 234
Serpentine Gallery, 11
Shakespeare, 16, 20, 22, 74
Sheepshanks, 60–61
Sheffield, 56, 94, 128, 134–35, 164, 184
Sheffield Universities, 206
Shipley, William, 27–28, 213
Sir Henry Markham, 160, 188
Sir John Leicester, 40, 102
Sir John Millais, 157
Social Mobility Commission, 219, 226, 253
Society for the Encouragement of the Arts, Manufacture and Commerce, 27
Society of Artists, 23, 29–30, 32–33, 114
Society of Arts, 27–29, 31, 56–57, 129, 149, 185, 213, 221, 226, 233
South Asian art, 192
South Kensington Art Museum, 65
South Kensington Museum, 55, 57, 60, 62–63, 107, 151, 227, 236
South London Art Gallery, 82
South London Fine Art Gallery, 81
South Wales Coalfield Distress Committee, 167
Southwark and Lambeth Free Loan Exhibition, 82

Spain, 15, 79
Specialist exhibitions, 78
Spectator
  The, 12, 22, 158, 230, 247
  working-class, 90
Spring Gardens, 12, 29
state of regional museums, 160
Statistical Society, 101
Stepney, 83
St Jude, 68–69
Strong, Roy, 3, 154, 193
Sunday opening, 71–73
Sunday Opening of Museums, 225, 237
Sunday schools and Bible classes, 73
Sunday Society, 71–72
Sunday Times art critic, 11

T
Tate, 17, 30, 78, 122, 154, 157–59, 165, 183–84, 202–4
Tate, Henry, 142, 157–58
Tate Britain, 1, 54, 155
Tate Galleries, 67, 209, 238
  new, 65
Tate in London, 17
Tate Modern, 192, 226
Thackeray, 20, 51, 59, 89
Thomas Horsfall's Art Museum, 135
Titians, included, 41, 43
Tower Hamlets Society, 96
Toynbee Hall, 82, 135
Trades Unions and Trades Councils, 72
Trafalgar Square, 33, 40, 44, 46, 52
Treasures Exhibition, 100

Treasures of Art in Great Britain, 116
Treddlehoyle, Tom, 117
Tretchikoff, Vladimir, 209
Triumph of Britannia, 17
Trollope, Anthony, 43
trustees, aristocratic, 122, 157
Turner's painting, 54
Tyers, Jonathan, 12–16, 18–20, 25, 37, 114, 153, 185–86
Tyers' Vauxhall, 18

U
Unitarians, 102, 123
University College London, 155
University College London Bloomsbury in Bloom project, 239
University Grants Committee, 163, 202
University Settlement, 135, 244
Unwin, Thomas, 50–51

V
V&A, 64, 67, 187, 192–93, 203–4, 213, 252
Vauxhall Art Car Boot Sale, 20
Vauxhall Gardens, 9, 11–12, 17–20, 24–25, 28, 33, 114–15, 210, 216, 227, 231–32
  developing, 15
Vauxhall Gardens Pleasure Park, 9, 11
Veblen, Thorstein, 6, 228
Vettriano, Jack, 7, 209–10
  Toxic Beach, 8
Victorian art aristocracy, 155
Victorian art world, late, 154
Victorian councillors, 146

Victorian cultural history, 220
Victorian hardship, 142
Victorian industry, 136
Victorian London, 214
Victorian Philistinism, 111
Victorian powerhouses, 56
Victorians, working-class, 142
Victorian standards, 155
Victorian Values, 215, 224, 244
Victorian world of art museums, 66
Victoria's reign, 39
visitor numbers, 4, 62, 136, 138, 153, 163, 204
Vogue, 187

W

Waagen, Gustav, 50, 115–16, 229, 241
Wakefield Tulip Society, 95
Walker, Andrew, 133
Walker Gallery, 142, 145
Wallace Collection, 64, 122
Wallis
   Henry, 107, 110
     The Death of Chatterton, 110
   Whitworth, 141, 147
Warhol, Andy, 68
Warwick Commission, 205, 229, 254
Waterfield, Giles, 141, 145, 229, 235–39, 242–43, 245–46
Watts, 71, 74–75, 81
Watts's pictures, 74
Whitechapel, 68, 70–71, 77, 79, 82, 86, 183
Whitechapel Art Gallery, 220, 237
Whitechapel Gallery, 73, 76, 80, 183, 228

new, 153
Whitehall, 44, 172, 186, 202
White Working Class, 215
Whitworth, Joseph, 133
Whitworth Art Gallery, 133
Wilde, Oscar, 127
Wildsmith, John, 48
Wilkes, John, 26, 40
Wilkie, David, 38
Williams, Bill, 166–68, 171, 178, 180, 189
Williams, Raymond, 174, 176
Wilson, Harold, 190
Winkelman, John, 32
Woolf, Virginia, 169–70, 220
Woolf, Leonard, 169
Workers' Education Association, 141
Working Class in England, 125, 218, 240
World War II, 160, 173

Y

Yorkshire, 1, 95, 117, 124, 161
Young British Artists, 172

[Created with **TExtract** / www.TExtract.com]

www.ingramcontent.com/pod-product-compliance
Lightning Source LLC
Chambersburg PA
CBHW040520220526
45473CB00013B/2923